MASQUERADE AND POSTSOCIALISM

NEW ANTHROPOLOGIES OF EUROPE

DAPHNE BERDAHL, MATTI BUNZL, AND MICHAEL HERZFELD,
FOUNDING EDITORS

MASQUERADE AND POSTSOCIALISM

Ritual and Cultural Dispossession in Bulgaria

Gerald W. Creed

INDIANA UNIVERSITY PRESS
BLOOMINGTON & INDIANAPOLIS

This book is a publication of

Indiana University Press
601 North Morton Street
Bloomington, Indiana 47404-3797 USA

iupress.indiana.edu

Telephone orders	800-842-6796
Fax orders	812-855-7931
Orders by e-mail	iuporder@indiana.edu

♾The paper used in this publication meets the minimum requirements of the American
National Standard for Information Sciences—Permanence of Paper for Printed Library
Materials, ANSI Z39.48–1992.

Manufactured in the United States of America

Library of Congress Cataloging-in-Publication Data

Creed, Gerald W., [date]
   Masquerade and postsocialism : ritual and cultural dispossession in Bulgaria /
Gerald W. Creed.
      p. cm. — (New anthropologies of Europe)
   Includes bibliographical references and index.
   ISBN 978-0-253-35557-7 (cloth : alk. paper) — ISBN 978-0-253-22261-9 (pbk. : alk.
paper) 1. Rites and ceremonies—Bulgaria. 2. Mumming—Bulgaria. 3. Masquerades—
Bulgaria. 4. Postcommunism—Bulgaria. 5. National characteristics, Bulgarian. 6.
Bulgaria—Politics and government. 7. Bulgaria—Social life and customs. I. Title.
   GN585.B9C74 2010
   306.409499—dc22
                                                        2010020228

1 2 3 4 5   16 15 14 13 12 11

TO GENE OYLER,

who makes life a festival, and

THE MUMMERS OF BULGARIA,

who make festival their life

На ДЖИЙН ОЙЛЪР,

който превръща живота ми в празник,

и на КУКЕРИТЕ ОТ БЪЛГАРИЯ,

които превръщат празника в свой живот

CONTENTS

ACKNOWLEDGMENTS

Fieldwork for this project was funded by the George A. and Eliza Gardner Howard Foundation and grants from the City University of New York PSC-CUNY Research Awards Program. A fellowship at the Agrarian Studies Program of Yale University provided a year for library research and preliminary writing, as well as provocative discussions. Other stimulating intellectual environments also shaped the final product. The ideas on gender and sexuality in chapter 2 were first presented at a lecture for the Humanities Center at the University of Memphis in 2005 and developed further in a lecture for the Department of Anthropology at the University of Manchester in 2007. The arguments about civil society in chapter 3 were originally aired at the Annual Convention of the American Association for the Advancement of Slavic Studies in 2004, then elaborated fully at the National Science Foundation/University of Michigan Workshop, "Cultural Politics of Globalization and Community in East Central Europe," held at the Collegium Budapest in Hungary in 2005. They were also presented at the Russian, East European, and Eurasian Center of the University of Illinois in 2006, where I had previously presented a version of chapter 4 on atomization in 2002. I appreciate the thoughtful comments and criticisms I received at these venues which helped me develop my argument. My colleagues at the City University of New York (both Hunter College and the Graduate Center) have inspired me directly and indirectly, and often unknowingly; I am privileged to work in such a stimulating and collegial environment. Students contribute significantly to that atmosphere, and I have been especially inspired in this research by Mary Taylor, Larisa Honey, Martha Kebalo, Nathan Jones, and Stephen Amico. Maria Radeva provided helpful research and translation assistance.

Various individuals read drafts of the manuscript and improved the final product. Aisha Khan made important contributions to my arguments in chapter 5, Jane Schneider inspired ideas central to the conclusion, and Donna Buchanan provided important additions and corrections throughout the book. Rebecca Tolen approached me about publishing this project a few years back. I appreciate the catalytic inspiration of her original interest, and its long shelf life. She also helped me broaden the book's appeal. Rita Bernhard polished the prose and June Silay tended it through to the finish line. All remaining limitations and errors are my responsibility.

I must acknowledge Lyubomira Gribble who first introduced me to these masquerade rituals in Bulgarian language classes two and a half decades ago. As always, I owe tremendous debts to colleagues and informants in Bulgaria. First, I thank the many masquerade participants and promoters who generously shared their feelings and experiences, and sometimes even their homes, with me. They were my inspiration and my muse. It pains me to think that they may take offense at some of my arguments, as I suspect they will. For this reason I am not implicating them here, or in the rest of the book, where I avoid using personal names, and, when unavoidable, employ pseudonyms instead. Still I hope they will find most parts of my analysis compelling and appreciate the overall significance I attribute to their masquerade (a)vocation. I also thank the numerous Bulgarian scholars without whose assistance I could have done very little. These include especially Stanka Dobreva, Dimitur Dobrev, Veska Kozhuharova, Irena Bokova, Tsvetana Manova, Georg Kraev, Nataliya Raskova, Zhivka Stamenova, and Iglika Miskova. They not only shared their expert knowledge and advice, but many of them accompanied me on field expeditions. Many other individuals assisted me in too many ways to enumerate (or even recall after more than a decade of research); my gratitude is no less for my inability to specify it. I can only hope that they find this product a sufficient tribute.

Final and special thanks are reserved for two special people: my partner, Gene Oyler, for both encouraging me and then enduring the neglect that his encouragement produced, and my mother, Ruby Creed, who, I am sorry to say, did not endure it. She passed away in 2008 while I was in the thick of writing. The fact that I spent time on this book that I could have spent with her has so soured my reflection on it that I might have left it unfinished were it not for the fact that having nothing to show for my filial failings would be an even greater offense. I know she would be proud of the result, but I still wish I had spent the time I worked on it with her instead.

I took up the study of Bulgarian masquerade as an antidote to the depression that attended my prior research on the difficult and frustrating rural economy. That I also find losses to bemoan in these festive and joyous occasions probably says more about me than it does about postsocialist Bulgaria, but I believe it also exposes something about the difficult situation rural Bulgarians have endured over the past two decades. That they have continued these masquerades in the face of such adversity reveals more about their indelible spirit than all the analyses researchers could produce. Particular arguments withstanding, this book is a celebration of that spirit.

MASQUERADE AND POSTSOCIALISM

CULTURAL DISPOSSESSION

Each winter the seasonally quiescent countryside of Bulgaria is assailed by menacing masked figures. Sporting elaborate costumes that range from the animalistic to the fantastic, and bedecked with heavy bells that produce a deafening accompaniment, they invade the yards of villagers demanding food, drink, and money in exchange for invocations of fertility and abundance. Scholars date these rites to ancient, perhaps Thracian, origins (Fol 2004; Frazer 1920:335), and participants insist that they have been performed annually ever since, even during periods of state prohibition in the Ottoman and early communist eras. Such continuity may be impossible to confirm historically, but it is potently affirmed experientially, as to be present at these events is to feel an ancient communion.

Many Bulgarians expected such archaic practices to disappear when Bulgaria joined the contemporary Western world following the collapse of communism in 1989. My field research in the late 1990s seemed to confirm this prediction in some villages, but in many others I witnessed an increasing popularity of the rituals, and research in 2002 elicited renewed belief in their supernatural efficacy. How can we account for this expanding practice and belief? How could villagers who had accepted a secular scientific worldview acquire faith in what they previously deemed pagan "superstition"? Why would others, many of whom were so financially devastated by the transition that they could not afford the basic necessities of life, continue to hand over precious resources for ineffectual performances? Why were these rituals even available for expansion in 1989, that is, how did they survive the decades of socialist modernization that eviscerated most other folk practices? Indeed, why would villagers who were otherwise adverse to socialist resistance, and even acquiesced to the collectivization of their land around the same time, refuse the early communist state only on this front?

This book addresses these questions, but the main objective is to use the questions themselves as a provocation for a different type of analysis. That these questions exist confirms the importance and value of these rituals for Bulgarian villagers, and thus I suggest that we can get more from them than just their symbolic meanings and historical permutations. Put another way, the best single answer to all the questions posed above is that these rituals are intimate and integrative elements of people's lives, perhaps more so than other elements of life to which researchers have devoted more attention since 1989. So why not look to them for insight into the broader social, political, and economic forces impacting rural Bulgarians? Historians and literary critics have found the similar activities of carnival especially revelatory of an earlier European folk culture (Bakhtin 1984; Le Roy Ladurie 1979). Following their example, and the lead of Bulgarian participants, this book suggests that we can learn a lot about life in postsocialist Bulgaria by looking through the lens of this seemingly esoteric cultural practice.

Commonly referred to in Bulgarian as *kukeri*, or *survakari*, these rituals are all-consuming events. The visual attraction of the masks, the hypnotic sound of the bells, the intoxicating taste of wine or brandy, the bracing smell of animal-skin costumes, and the sheer feeling of physical exhilaration combine to monopolize the senses. To be present is to be absent from all else— little wonder participants and observers evince a stronger engagement with kukeri than with any other folk practice. The kukeri often work on their costumes far in advance of the event, and some of the village households they visit invest equal energy in preparing to receive them. As kukeri travel en masse from house to house, they generate a palpable anticipation that pervades the whole village for the duration of their rounds, the constant sound of their bells providing a reminder of their presence even when they are out of sight in distant neighborhoods. For individual villagers this perpetual excitement is punctuated by climatic episodes when the kukeri arrive at one's home to dance and jump around the yard, and when all villagers join the kukeri at the village square for a collective finale.

Though I witnessed this engagement personally throughout Bulgaria, the most poignant example came from California, and I did not really "see" it. I was observing survakari events in a small mountain village in the central western part of Bulgaria. Like most villages in 2002 this one offered few economic opportunities beyond subsistence farming, and many younger residents had left seeking better prospects. Such was the case for my hosts' daughter, who had moved to California with her husband a few years earlier. On the day of the event she called early in the morning (evening in California) to wish the family a happy holiday and to inquire about the preparations for the festivities. My host and I departed soon afterward to join the survakari group. When we got back to the house as part of the group's ritual rounds, I noticed that his wife was holding up a cell phone for much of the time we were there, passing it off to other household members when she had to congratulate and treat the mock wedding party that leads the survakari. I wondered if this new technology had acquired a symbolic role in the ritual, but when I returned to the house after the ritual I learned instead that her daughter had been participating telephonically, listening to all the commotion and sounds of the survakari visit. The mother said the daughter had stayed up most of the night in California, calling first every hour to see if the survakari were in the neighborhood, and then when they were nearby, every few minutes to make sure she didn't miss the visit. These calls had been on the house's land line so as not to cost anything on the Bulgarian end, but when the group arrived she had to call back on a cell phone so it could be taken outside among the fray, costing her family a significant number of expensive minutes (which they noted regretfully but shrugged off as justified). After listening to it all the daughter was in tears from a rather inconsolable homesickness. Her parents assured me that although she called on other holidays and special occasions, only survakari events elicited this response.

This is a signpost of cultural significance directing attention to these events. Following that direction I discovered a collection of insights into several topics of abiding concern to social theorists. Kukeri events reveal a notion of community in which conflict is constructive rather than disruptive. This model of collectivity easily incorporates and tolerates minority populations but without any pretense or promise to end ethnic prejudice. This combination underwrites a paradoxical variant of nationalism that is simultaneously foundational to social identity for Bulgarians yet rather benign in affect. Kukeri also reveal how a rigid gender system can facilitate greater flexibility for individuals than more flexible gender arrangements. When people understand gender as essentially fixed, highly transgressive performances, such as the transvestite brides who accompany the masked kukeri, are interpreted as just that—performances. An appreciation of gender flexibility recasts all relevant activities as potentially diagnostic of one's gender location, while the differential cultural value of these different locations constrains the desirability of choosing them. These and other lessons are extracted from kukeri activities in the chapters of this book. I raise them here to point to yet another provocative foundational question: Why have promising insights into such popular concerns gone unrecognized?

There are multiple nested answers, but two are primary. First, the location of these lessons is hardly well known. Whereas Bulgaria's musical traditions have established an important beachhead in world scholarship, thanks to renowned musicians and meticulous ethnomusicologists (Buchanan 2006; Rice 1994; Silverman 1983), the same cannot be said for much else in the country. Despite the best efforts of scholars across several disciplines (Cellarius 2004; Ganev 2007; Ghodsee 2005; Kaneff 2004; Meurs 2001; Todorova 2009), Bulgaria is hardly the first place that social theorists from outside the country think to look for inspiration. Located at the southeastern edge of Europe, it is a small country, about the size of Virginia, with fewer than eight million inhabitants speaking a difficult and unique language written in the Cyrillic alphabet. Prior to 1989 relatively few Bulgarians had migrated to Western countries, and for much of the communist era (1944–1989) access by Western researchers was limited and highly regulated. Although endowed with spectacular natural beauty, it is not well provisioned with valuable natural resources, and a significant proportion of the land mass is mountainous or otherwise ill suited for large-scale agriculture. Predominantly urban since the 1970s, thanks to massive modernization efforts by the communist government that also brought significant development to the countryside, rural-urban connections remained dense until they were broken up by the communist collapse, turning many villages into economic wastelands, certainly not obvious places to look for transition inspirations. Inattention was seemingly justified by popular choices after 1989 when the country repeatedly elected socialist governments, suggesting a collective reluctance to change. This peaceful paralysis could hardly compete for attention with the wars in neighboring Yugoslavia, reunification in Germany, the division of Czechoslovakia, and societal "shock therapy" in Poland.

Second, the cultural options/alternatives evident in kukeri are being eroded and reformed before they can be recognized, a process I characterize as cultural dispossession. This outcome was overdetermined by the cold war opposition that structured global perceptions for much of the twentieth century.

The story of Western democratic capitalism includes several moments that shifted how subsequent events were interpreted, and certainly one of the most formative in recent decades was the encounter with communism/socialism. To appreciate how much the cold war continues to shape politics and possibilities in the twenty-first century, one need only note that accusations of "socialism" continue to be quite effective in discrediting progressive policy initiatives in the United States. The division of the world into opposing camps of communism and capitalism for more than half a century means that no part of the world is untouched by the communist collapse. In this sense postsocialism is a global condition. As such, it not only includes events in Eastern Europe but also affects how those events are interpreted by others. The cold war opposition set up a global postsocialism that excludes recognition of the extant cultural resources in many former socialist countries.

The Perils of Postsocialism

Postsocialism is now twenty years old—an appropriate milestone to reflect on the phenomenon and what we know about it. During this period, copious research has analyzed numerous facets of the so-called transition process. Much of it has focused on what might be called core concepts of modern Western political economy: democracy, civil society, the market, privatization, rule of law, minority rights, and gender equality, often in concert with the supposed indigenous barriers to these goals: corruption, patriarchy, nationalism, and various socialist legacies. We have learned an enormous amount from these investigations, but when we look at this list collectively we should wonder about its cultural limitations. All analytical terms carry preconceived assumptions, but these are particularly freighted with Euro-American conceptions. To start our analysis with these foci is to establish an already and always ideal image against which the events in Eastern Europe are measured.

To the degree that populations and governments in these countries actually aspired to these ideals, this is a sensible approach, and there are many successes to report, including accession into the European Union (EU) by many of the formerly socialist countries of Europe. At the same time much is missed in this approach. Lost are the extant local alternatives and indigenous cultural resources or materials that could have been useful both practically and intellectually. Lack of recognition and use of these potential building materials made subsequent efforts to construct democratic or capitalist structures "from scratch" more alien and difficult, which produced a self-validating circularity in which the problems or failures could then be blamed on the lack of indigenous traditions, the planners having (dis)missed those that were extant because they did not match preconceived models. This dynamic validates the Western model itself as it remains unchallenged by the very difficulties it encounters, which are always displaced to the lack or failings of the society in transition. This also insulates dominant models from potential external influence—beginning with different practices or using different conceptual materials might produce a variation that, if successful or functional, could provide an alternative to existing ones. By disallowing distinctive inputs, innovative or alternative outcomes are precluded, and the seeming truism of "no alternative" is confirmed and reinforced.

This is part of a global dynamic, which Joseph Massad (2007:49–50) describes as follows:

> What is emerging in the Arab (and the rest of the third) world is not some universal schema of the march of history but rather the imposition of these Western modes by different forceful means and their adoption by third world elites, thus foreclosing and repressing myriad ways of movement and change and ensuring that only one way for transformation is made possible. . . . This ensures the success of the Western theorists' universal civilizational teleologies and unwittingly guarantees for them the production of a Western-defined outcome to the future of "humanity."

Nevertheless, ethnographically informed research in Asia, Africa, and Latin America has refused this outcome, insisting instead on the production of alternative forms of capitalism, democracy, and especially modernity (see, e.g., Blim 2000; Knauft 2002a; Paley 2008). These claims are much less evident in research on Eastern Europe, and when they do appear it is usually with critical rather than celebratory intent (for an exception, see Iankova 2002).

This underlines the link between culture, power, and geography. Being of the body, continentally speaking, has made the cultural diversity argument less compelling or essential for Eastern Europe (at least to non-anthropologists). How big of a problem can Eurocentrism be in a European country? If there are conflicts, are European standards not legitimate for places that aspire to be integral parts of that entity? These arguments, of course, deny the cultural diversity within Europe even as debates about "Europeanization" rage (Borneman and Fowler 1997). At the same time hybrid or alternative forms elsewhere in the world are less threatening because they can be associated with extreme alterity. Chinese models of capitalism are not likely to inspire Western innovations or critiques, as they are supposedly grounded in a radically different culture. Alternative models from Europe might be another thing entirely—less culturally alien and thus a potential inspiration. So while I do not suspect conspiracy or even ideological intent, the outcome of much research and investigation of the transitions from socialism has been to protect and reproduce a rather limited political and economic model for Eastern Europe.

It is too late to change this course. The die is cast, and as much as I would have liked to have seen more innovative and equitable outcomes, I now find myself hoping for a quicker and more complete replication of a standard European model in order to alleviate the pain and suffering still afflicting many individuals, notably the rural people who are the primary characters in this book. This change in attitude is reflected in scholarly debate about the continued utility of the term "postsocialism." Over the last few years scholars have begun to question whether "postsocialist" is still a useful analytical or descriptive category for the countries of Eastern Europe. This reflects, of course, the entrance of many of these countries into the EU and the integration of others into global networks of finance, commerce, and criminality. EU accession has been used by the U.S. government to justify curtailing designated research funds. Although I want to see a Bulgaria that can be discussed in the same category as Switzerland or Sweden, it is imperative to remember that we are not there yet, and until we are the postsocialist moniker, much like the postcolonial, reminds us that incorporation into European capitalism is not on an equal basis, even for European countries, and that this unequal incorporation may have long-term consequences. Moreover, and again in line with postcolonialism, postsocialism is not just the situation of former socialist countries, it is the condition of the world in the aftermath of a global cold war that derogated socialism and laid the groundwork for cultural dispossession.[1]

The prior condition as socialist satellite, however, can no longer bear all the blame for current difficulties; rather, the processes of the transition that followed and incorporated these places into an already established capitalist system in rigid and discriminatory ways are also culpable. This is not to excuse the horrors of socialism or to suggest that there are not still influential forces at work that can be traced to socialist practices; instead, it is a plea that we not allow those horrors to deflect attention from the processes that were set in motion by the transition itself (see Burawoy and Verdery 1999). Such sensitivity is subtly evident in the ways Bulgarians themselves refer to the period after 1989, commonly preferring a plural term "the changes" over the singular "transition" or, alternatively, simply marking the beginning of change with the term "after the 10th." The latter phrase refers to November 10, 1989, when longtime communist dictator Todor Zhivkov resigned, and it also apes the standard designation of the socialist period as "after the 9th" in reference to September 9, 1944, when the Soviet army liberated/invaded the country.

This book argues for the importance of postsocialism as an analytical category by critiquing its continuing and limiting orthodoxies. I look within rituals to which Bulgarians demonstrate and express strong devotion and commitment to reveal alternative understandings and interpretations of some of the central concerns of postsocialist studies. Anthropologists have been involved in related efforts continually since 1989, challenging assumptions about civil society, international aid, property, gender, and nationalism. I am not suggesting something completely novel in this sense but rather using ritual as a new nexus to bring together several critiques that have been pursued independently for a more concentrated assault on those models that continue to evaluate transition(s) in terms of objectives and criteria taken from a homogenized Euro-American exemplar. In so doing I also hope to capture more fully why this process was so disappointing for so long in one country. As Chris Hann's (2006) recent and related effort suggests, such endeavors are needed because individual interventions have failed to shake the ethnocentric foundation of transition studies generally.

It is essential to redouble this effort now for reasons already intimated: the accession of Bulgaria and Romania into the EU, two countries previously cast as among the most difficult cases for inclusion, is likely to be seen as the capstone of a successful transition for the region. This interpretation affirms the logic of transition assumptions and validates the model dictated by EU requirements as the only viable option, thereby erasing the alternative desires and opportunities that did exist. While failure sustains reflection on what could have been done differently, success seems to erode the very reasons for critically rethinking or reconsidering the process. Recent, if still partial, successes in the transition thus threaten to permanently erase alternatives. Success also encourages a retroactive evaluation of the difficulties and disasters of the 1990s as the inevitable pain of transition rather than the product of mistakes that were perhaps avoidable had extant cultural resources been recognized and responsive alternatives devised. This book, then, is something of a "salvage" ethnography of unrealized hopes and opportunities but one that is very important to the understanding and improvements of transition analyses in the future. In this effort, in a single country that is rarely given much attention, I recognized options and ideas that have not been documented by anthropologists working elsewhere in the region and, although these cultural options are already deformed and disappearing, their existence in the cultural repertoire at the time of transition is important. We will never appreciate what was lost in successful transition if we allow these alternatives to slip unnoticed into the global consensus. It is crucial to document what could have been.

As suggested above, this is especially evident in regard to ethnicity. Kukeri reveal models of ethnic/community interaction that are simultaneously conflictive and incorporative. These models are far from the multicultural utopia imagined by American liberalism, but they were equally far from the exclusionary and even violent fundamentalisms and nationalisms to which the Western ideal is supposedly opposed. The tense shift here is intended, as by 2006 this different notion of ethnic and community relations was already giving way to the idea of exclusion and even elimination. Instead of recognizing and improving local images of ethnic interaction, planners and advisers have replaced them with a standard model that is much more exclusionary and dangerous.

Ironically such outcomes can even generate impressions of progress. The more indigenous models come to conform to Western images, the more relevant, resonant, and appropriate are the Western mechanisms and institutions of redress offered to correct the problems. Missed in the resulting "improvements," however, is that the situation was not as bad to begin with and that perhaps community relations could have been improved without first making them worse. Similarly, as a result of changing gender expectations and relations introduced by the transition, the programs imported from the West to redress gender inequities become more appropriate and effective, which then becomes a sign of successful transition. Overlooked here, however, is the way forces reformulated gender relations at the start so as to make the solutions work.

These processes of cultural dispossession replicate the material trajectory of transition about which villagers complained the most (see Creed 1995, 1998). Looking at decimated ruins of agricultural installations, pilfered irrigation stations, and desiccated vineyards/orchards, villagers could not understand why these major investments of time, money, and labor had to be completely destroyed rather than reallocated, redistributed, or reformed. This new case of "creative destruction" was seen as making the transition more difficult and attenuated while facilitating capital accumulation by the privileged or, at best, the conniving—a folk version of David Harvey's (2003) analysis of the "new imperialism." The collateral damage of this strategy in the case of decollectivization is increasingly recognized across the political spectrum in Bulgaria, and I cannot resist saying I told you so, but the same dynamic in the sphere of sociocultural resources is less obvious and still unacknowledged. It was equally unfortunate and equally consequential in preventing the formation of hybrid or innovative forms of political economy and society.

Between 1997 and 2007 I also saw evidence of what could be called, adapting the language of Max Weber, "ritual re-enchantment"—the reinvestment of kukeri with supernatural possibilities that previously had been denied. This confounds the standard modernization paradigm that posits a universal stepwise progression of socioeconomic development. Weber and the modernization theorists he inspired suggest a unidirectional rationalization accompanying capitalism, replacing mystical beliefs in supernatural forces with secular understandings. While the same process was abetted via socialist modernization in Bulgaria, for some people the subsequent advent of capitalism provoked a re-enchantment of their economic circumstances as villagers tried both to make sense of, and counter, their continual devastation. This re-enchantment parallels a de-modernization, actually supporting the Weberian linkage but in a very different way, since this time the enchantment develops out of an already thoroughly disenchanted worldview and the justification of re-enchantment itself draws upon an enlightenment discourse that recognizes its own irrationality. This is a fascinating response in which people use irony and contradiction both to comfort themselves and challenge or criticize the system. For some, the embrace of an "absurd" belief was an effort to represent and mock the absurdity of the conditions they were living through, and, for others, the craziness of the situation made anything believable.

Taken together, these suggestions confirm that postsocialism occasioned a radical restructuring of village social relations in both practice and meaning. I am not speaking simply of people losing some relationships and having to develop new ones; rather, I am suggesting that the very nature of various relations was transformed. Relations between genders, between ethnic groups, and between fellow villagers were all redefined. Different understandings of these relations were characteristic of socialism; some of these were problematic for the transition, and others were completely disconnected. There was no design for these changes, as the differences were hardly appreciated or recognized by those drawing the transition blueprints. It was a fraught process, with villagers unsure who expected what from whom, who had changed their expectations and who had not, and to what degree. Hardly any of this was explicit, so people often misinterpreted one another's actions, further complicating the social relations of transition. This is one of the reasons why the transition did not proceed as smoothly as many anticipated, because it was not just about establishing institutions of representative democracy and private property. As most social scientists conceptually appreciate, but sometimes find hard to follow through in their analyses, even individual and property rights are, at their core, relationships between people, and what was involved in changing these laws and practices was nothing less than the complete renegotiation of the important relationships in villagers' lives (see Verdery 2003).

Social relationships are not easily abandoned, renegotiated, or replaced. The process transpired on many fronts as villagers tried to maintain particular relations, only to find them unviable or problematic. Massive migration, for example, ultimately removed a number of relations from the social field, which gradually simplified some village relations while complicating family relations that were now at a distance. Nationalist paradigms further challenged village- and placed-based identities that had been sustained under socialism. Civil society efforts denied the utility of extant sociopolitical integrations. With these grassroots mechanisms ignored and perhaps rendered ineffective, they withered away. The evolving nature of relations then eventually fit with the programs and institutions for redress copied from Europe and the United States, producing more apparent "successes." If we can document the prior alternatives, then these successes cannot be assumed as evidence of the superiority of the new system. Instead, they simply confirm the greater consonance of the new system with the renegotiated relationships produced by the denial or dismissal of preexisting alternatives. This dispossession parallels the material extractions of restitution. In both cases, what is lost is obscured by an apparent or rhetorical acquisition. Because they do not conform to Western models, alternative relations and arrangements are easily missed when those models, for example, civil society, social capital, or ethnic tolerance, define the research project. Looking instead at rituals helps us to deauthorize these expectations enough to see alternatives.

The Richness of Ritual

Once we recognize that the transition involved redefining and renegotiating social relations and expectations, the tool of ritual analysis becomes especially appealing. Ritual has been such an important focus of anthropological

research precisely because rituals are intricately linked to the quotidian social relations that are the stock-in-trade of ethnography. For Emile Durkheim
they help produce and reinforce the core social relations that make society
possible, and for subsequent functionalists they help confirm the ideal social
order or provide outlets for the problems and difficulties of real relations. For
interpretive anthropologists such as Clifford Geertz they simply reflect the
social relations that exist (stories people tell themselves about themselves).
Even the most symbolic analyses of ritual activity, such as those by Victor
Turner, draw upon social relations in their interpretation of ritual elements
and activities. More recent approaches influenced by performance studies
suggest that one's mastery in the performance of social and political roles
connects to their power. In other words, the nature of social relations is interactive including both culturally defined expectations and the skill of people
performing them, often in ritual. In the process of performance, rituals can
also change social relations. As Susan Harding (2000:129) nicely puts it, "rituals
are routinized public events that reproduce implicit cultural assumptions,
points of view, and social relations. Rituals also always alter cultural assumptions, points of view, and social relations, for no reiteration is ever an exact
replication." In short, if we are looking at social relations, the accumulated
wisdom of social science and the humanities would suggest that we pay attention to ritual.

The attention to ritual is also an important contribution to the anthropology of postsocialist Eastern Europe, which, as I have noted elsewhere (Creed
2002a), has not attended to ritual as extensively as other topics. This contrasts with significant prior interest in socialist ritual (Binns 1979/1980; Gal
1991; Humphrey 1983; Kideckel 1983; Kligman 1981; Lane 1981; Mach 1992;
Roth 1990), and a strong tradition of ritual analysis in the rest/west of Europe
(Argyrou 1996; Badone 1990; Boissevain 1992; Gilmore 1998). The difference
tends to reproduce the isolation of East European research from mainstream
Anglophone anthropology and perpetrates its detachment from indigenous
ethnography in the region where ritual figures prominently. Of course, there
are outstanding exceptions (e.g., Verdery 1999), but many of these concern
political ritual, which contributes to the common association of this part of
the world with politics. These efforts notwithstanding, compared to most
other topics, ritual has been neglected in postsocialist research.

There are justifications: many of our East European interlocutors curtailed rituals as the exigencies of economic transition left them with less time
and money. There is also the conceptual and practical linkage of ritual with

religion, which suffered under socialist atheism/secularism. The evolutionary penchant to view secularization as an irreversible achievement stalled attention to religion in parts of postsocialist Eastern European (except among missionaries who did not share this assumption and immediately flooded the region). The recent increase in attention to postsocialist religion is promising and will likely inspire more ritual analyses (e.g., Rogers 2005; Steinberg and Wanner 2009), but as I have already made clear, I believe there is more to learn from these rituals than insight into religious belief. Indeed, Bulgarians' skepticism about the supernatural efficacy of the rituals forces us to look elsewhere for understanding. Moreover, the distaste for, and distrust in, explicitly political avenues of expression that infected so many citizens during socialism makes it imperative to look in other forums to find politically relevant social expressions, and ritual is a fecund context.

This effort reflects a postsocialist extension of Gail Kligman's (1988) work on life-cycle rituals under socialism. Her attention to weddings and funerals highlighted village social relations, which I believe can be brought over productively to the study of rituals not defined by a family focus. Indeed, kukeri are especially revealing of the nature of diverse social relations precisely because they are not limited to kin, yet do not reach the level of an imagined national inclusion. They represent an important category of ritual between that of family and state, which has been especially vulnerable to the vicissitudes of modernity. While family-based rituals such as weddings and funerals may engage entire communities, and often invoke the nation, the focus remains on the family unit, and the ritual is usually perceived as essentially a family affair. At the other extreme, the state rituals and invented traditions that have captivated scholars of nationalism are more reflections of an established national image/power than windows into local social relations. As Pamela Ballinger (2003) illustrates with World War II memorials, these types of commemorations efface alternatives in an effort to generate/emphasize national uniformity—they eclipse local communities.

Kukeri do not celebrate a singular unit, nor do they strive to replace lower-order identities with higher-order ones. As such they provide a chance to see local expectations about social relations that may or may not conform to the national relations sanctioned by the state or global nation-state system. They are expressly about the articulation of the culturally significant groupings within which people live. They present a symbolic physiology of the social organism, rather than a descriptive anatomy. Though they are not family rituals, they often include family ritual symbolism, especially wedding imagery. In this regard these rituals can be considered "meta-rituals," since they consciously reference and manipulate other rituals. In so doing they underline the centrality of the referenced component at the same time that they provide a different message. This reuse of other ritual symbolism makes them particularly promising sources as commentaries about the nature of social relations, especially regarding how such units as the family fit into or operate with other types of social relations (a link pursued most extensively in chapter 4).

This analysis reflects a literal interpretation of kukeri, or what might be called an "anti-interpretation." Most investigations of similar rituals rely heavily on the notions of inversion and reversal (Bakhtin 1968; Gluckman 1963; Turner 1969), or what Don Handelman (1990:156) suggests is better described as "inversion—reversion." In this paradigm, spectacular but temporary violations of norms confirm and affirm everyday social parameters. Without denying these possibilities, following Abner Cohen's (1993) insights into the London carnival, I believe some meanings are more direct. The excessive violations of social norms in these events seem to demand extraordinary explanation, but such efforts deflect attention from the rituals' more straightforward statements. By emphasizing inversion and reversal we may miss spectacular statements about the quotidian.

This possibility suggests that we supplement Victor Turner's ideas of anti-structure and Mikhail Bakhtin's understanding of the carnivalesque with Clifford Geertz's notion of rituals as cultural texts and read elements of social structure from kukeri. It is notable that Geertz (1973) popularized his approach with a mundane event—a cockfight rather than a spectacle such as kukeri. Perhaps the type of event influences the choice of interpretive theory. When the activity maps easily onto social norms we accept a literal reading; when it *seems* to violate social norms we assume it cannot be a direct statement and opt for inversion. If so, our preconceptions of normalcy restrict our interpretive insights, revealing a persistent functionalist bias that has escaped the unrelenting attack on functionalism. Kukeri are full of wild and untempered activities that radically violate daily behavioral norms, but the violation may simply be exaggeration rather than reversal. Such exaggeration, then, can help us see the culturally particular resources easily missed in the muted expressions of everyday life.

Of course, ritual reversals can coexist with direct ritual reinforcement or validations. We need not assume that all elements of a ritual follow the same logic. These events are a product of obvious bricolage, bringing together various objectives, meanings, and functions. Some elements may be reversals, others straightforward statements. To further complicate matters, ritual participants may use and promote the popular interpretation of reversal to cloak direct motives that are socially proscribed. Moreover, the motives of ritual action can shift over time, and a straightforward ritual statement can be revalued and sustained as a reversal in response to new interpretive frames (see chapter 2). The same action or activity can take on different significance at different scales and even between different individuals. Anthropologists have rarely acknowledged such variety, opting instead for a singular approach to a particular ritual which forces us to choose the frame that resonates most. Combining multiple frames allows us to better appreciate how ritual revitalization articulates with cultural dispossession—kukeri provide evidence of cultural alternatives even as the rituals themselves change and those alternatives get redefined or disappear.

Parallels and Particulars

My aim in this ritual analysis is to provide insight into postsocialism as a process, but I do so with a single case that has many idiosyncratic elements. For many social scientists who study the transition from socialism this is an unlikely combination, as the value of insights is diminished in proportion to their particularity. But generalizations without detailed particularities are hollow and dangerous; they are like averages of highly bifurcated data in which the mean is so far from any of the included cases as to be meaningless. The experiences of socialism in Poland, Romania, and Bulgaria (just to mention a few with very divergent trajectories) were extremely different, as have been their paths through postsocialism, even if they all led to the EU. The obsession with generalization and quantification abets the dispossession I bemoan by, at worst, completely ignoring local variations and options, and, at best, treating them as mere particularities or exceptions. The novel or unique contributions that could have been bases of innovation or inspiration were precisely the detailed differences that are excluded by generalization.

This is not to deny similarities or the value of generalization, but privileging them and insisting on them is already an epistemic decision that may have helped divert attention from the options that existed across the towns and villages of Eastern Europe. This *is* a Bulgarian story, but similar dispossession has characterized much of the postsocialist world as existing practices and ideas have been dismissed, demolished, or discredited so that a singular political-economic model becomes the only perceivable option. I acknowledge that it is the only option, but it became so only through the processes documented here, and it is the job of anthropology to insure that these alternatives survive, if only in our knowledge of human possibilities. Certainly not every postsocialist country, or even most of them, shared the qualities or characteristics I find in Bulgarian masquerade, but they all likely had comparable cultural practices and arrangements that could have been productively integrated into the monolithic model that was impressed upon them. In this sense the story of dispossession is a general one.

The potential for useful comparison is not limited to postsocialist societies. As already intimated, kukeri share obvious parallels with well-researched carnival traditions throughout Europe and the Americas (see, e.g., Crowley 1996; Gilmore 1998; Supek 1982). Indeed, in Greece, events that closely mirror Bulgarian activities are called "carnival," and participants are known as "*karnavalia*" (Cowan 1992). An elegant photographic and documentary collection on comparative carnival customs includes these Bulgarian rituals as one of its eleven documented cases (Fol 2004), alongside the famous carnival traditions of New Orleans, Venice, and Port of Spain. I recognize that Bulgarian events share many elements and functions with carnival traditions, especially those in rural areas (e.g., Regalado 2004), and I appreciate why the comparison is appealing, especially for the many cases in Bulgaria where the rituals are tied to the beginning of Lent. But given common assumptions about carnival, I think the association distorts more than it reveals. In large measure the parallels are owing to the historical incorporation of these preexisting ritual elements into carnival practices as the latter became more popular and widespread following their origin in the Middle Ages (Mauldin 2004: 17 n.; Kinser 1990). To treat these prior and vital rituals as comparative carnival is to turn history on its head, especially in the absence of an equivalent countermovement of carnival practices into these Bulgarian rituals.

There are also clear parallels with Day of the Dead and Halloween activities in North America (Brandes 2006; Santino 1994), as well as masquerade festivals in Islamic north Africa (Hammoudi 1993; Silverstein n.d.), but the rituals are more similar to less well-known masquerade practices referred to as "mumming." Indeed, the term "kukeri" is translated as "mumming" in most Bulgarian-English dictionaries. Mumming is a generic term for masked rituals of apparent European provenance commonly performed at Christmas and New Year, but also around Shrovetide and All Saints Day (Glassie 1975; Sider 1986; Welch 1970). Examined comparatively, mumming practices run a gamut from ribald house visits by groups of crudely disguised villagers to large urban parades with elaborately costumed neighborhood units. A mummer's play is central to several traditions and is often associated with the ancient origins of theater. In one of the few efforts to characterize mumming rituals comparatively, Herbert Halpert (1969) devised a four-part typology of activities based on degree of formality and location of activity: the informal house visit, the visit with a formal performance or play, informal wandering around the village or town usually accompanied by boisterous behavior, and formal outdoor movements such as processions and parades. Examples of these mumming elements, separately and in concert, are documented throughout Europe, its border regions, and its former colonies. The Bulgarian versions include all these elements.

Despite significant similarities, the variety of practices included in the category and the evident proclivity of these activities to shed practices and adopt new elements limit the value of treating mumming comparatively as a singular phenomenon. What we can say, however, is that nearly all reports of mumming tell us something about the nature of collective social relations. Indeed, these enactments are usually explicit statements about the nature of local social relations. As Handelman (1990:15) notes about mumming and public events generally: "It is vital to the ongoing existence of any more-or-less dense network of persons that there exist media through which members communicate to themselves in concert about the characters of their collectivities." Dorothy Noyes (1995:468) goes further to suggest that "community is made real in performance." Mumming is the quintessential example. These are not only archetypal "community" rituals; they are usually symbolic commentaries on the very nature of community relations. As Henry Glassie (1975: 133) puts it, "mumming is a symbolic essay on the drama of social interchange."

By using the term "mumming" for the different rituals discussed here I am abetting a process of homogenization that has been under way in Bulgaria at least since the 1960s, when the socialist government reversed its earlier aversion and embraced the rituals somewhat generically as a component of national folklore. As will be clear in the chapters that follow, the rituals can be quite distinct in myriad ways, a diversity reflected in the plethora of terms used to refer to them. In addition to the popular terms "kukeri" and "survakari," they are also known as *mechkari, startsi, babugari, dzhamali, dervishi,* and many other names. Many participants insist that they should never be called by the same term, usually because this would mean the loss of a local term not widely used in favor of "kukeri" or "survakari." The same people, however, would sometimes slip and use one of these two common terms showing just how far the homogenization process has gone. The use of "mumming" is a decision of convenience when writing collectively about the various rituals examined in this book, and it is preferable to using either "carnival" or one of the dominant Bulgarian words for the above reasons.

Although Bulgarians insist on the unique nature of these rituals locally and nationally, similar traditions exist elsewhere in Eastern Europe. Macedonian variants are well known, and groups from Macedonia regularly attend Bulgarian mumming events. Of course, for many Bulgarians, Macedonia *is* Bulgarian and the ritual parallels are just further evidence of that fact. Mummers from Slovenia, known as *kurenti*, have also visited Bulgaria and are similar enough to Bulgarian models in dress and action as to obscure their foreign provenance. Figures that could also pass as Bulgarian mummers are represented prominently in the Ethnographic Museum in Budapest labeled *regölés* and described as pre-Hungarian New Year's fertility rites. In southern Hungary, the Croatians (or Šokci) in Mohács annually perform carnival customs evidently similar to Bulgarian models, known as *busójárás* in Hungarian, with groups joining the festivities from nearby Serbia. In Croatia itself villagers around Rijeka perform as *zvončari* (bellmen) dressed in sailor suits, animal skins, animalistic masks, and bells with the same objectives as Bulgarian mummers. In Slovakia, carnival traditions (*fašiangy*) replicate elements of Bulgarian mumming, as do Polish celebrations at Christmas and on various souls' days. A family resembalance is also evident in the Georgian Celebrations of *qeenoba* and *berikaoba*. What might distinguish Bulgaria then, at least within east/central Europe, is not the presence or history of such customs but rather their continued vitality and popularity across a large swath of the countryside.

Historical Context

Some Bulgarians explain the popularity of mumming by a unique national character, but then they use this association as a reason why the rituals must be maintained (i.e., to protect and maintain a Bulgarian essence), making it hard to distinguish the direction of causality. Others appeal to the usual explanation for Bulgarian exceptionalism: "500 years under the Turks." This might seem contradictory, but the impact of the Ottoman era is variable and less than clear (Todorova 1995, 1996). The common oral history of Ottoman prohibition of mumming rituals and the well-known examples of forced conversion to Islam likely curtailed the rituals to some degree (they are not generally evident today among the Muslim descendants of these converts, known as *Pomaks*). In general, however, Ottoman administration was not very in-

terested in local customs, as long as peasants handed over their tribute and
didn't cause problems. The overlords were not always around and if oral history is correct, it was not too difficult for villagers to find a place to enact the
rituals where they were not pursued. At the same time, Ottoman rule operated as a barrier to Western European cultural and interpretive models while
imperial domination gave the preservation of folk practice additional meaning as cultural resistance. The latter likely increased in the period of the national awakening from the middle of the nineteenth century.

Ottoman control also likely muted any aggressive efforts by the Orthodox Church against these "pagan" practices. The church was not proscribed,
but it was certainly circumscribed by its subjugated position. The church is
credited with maintaining Bulgarian language and culture during the Ottoman era, and in this role it might have found the preservation of such folk
practices defensible. Even if it did not, the church's weak political position
vis-à-vis the sultan and the Greek Patriarch under whose suzeranity it fell in
the Ottoman millet system contributed to a weakening of local ecclesiastical
power. Most rural Bulgarians I know are hardly devout, and many profess a
strong anti-clericism (graphically enacted in mumming rituals). This combination may help account for the continuation of rituals that diminished in
neighboring areas. We should also note the subsequent autonomy of the Bulgarian Orthodox Church compared to the hierarchical centralization of the
Catholic Church. Moreover, following the liberation from the Ottomans, this
Church had less than a century before it was again under the pressure of un-
sympathetic rulers, this time the Bulgarian Communist Party.

The later urbanization of Bulgaria compared to some other European
countries is also relevant. These are rural fertility rituals that likely seemed
irrelevant or unnecessary to urban populations. The subsequent diffusion of
a consolidated urban culture back to the villages as "high culture" or "civilization" could then redefine these events as "backward," "old fashioned," or
"rustic," even in the countryside. In Bulgaria, however, the primary urbanization of the country only began in the 1950s, and by the time a "superior"
urban culture held sway the Communists had recognized the political utility
of these rituals and authorized a festival system that regularly brought together ritual groups from all over the county to urban centers for competitive parades. This helped redefine the still vital rural practices as national
folklore and somewhat urbane. As the festivals expanded to include foreign
mumming and carnival groups they even acquired a quasi-cosmopolitan patina. So, in short, the contemporary vitality of Bulgarian mumming can be

traced to particular historical conjunctures. Since 1989 the festivals, which helped sustain village practice under socialism, have been maintained by municipalities often with the help of corporate sponsors. Village practice is also maintained by hopes of attracting tourists to the countryside or invitations to perform abroad.

The historical continuity of mumming both reflects and explains its contemporary significance and meaning to villagers. This significance, in turn, is why it is a promising place to look for alternative insights into important sociopolitical practices. Such significance is also reflected in an extensive indigenous literature documenting and analyzing the rituals. I draw upon some of these sources in my efforts, but for the most part my project is a very different one. Bulgarian ethnographers, historians, folklorists, and anthropologists have mined these practices for their symbolism and meaning, as well as their historical origins (for a sample in English, see Fol 2004). There is little I can contribute to these exhaustive efforts, which are thorough and sophisticated. Instead, I pursue a different agenda that uses mumming to challenge the way we think about events and practices usually considered distinct from the rituals. At the same time, the lessons extracted from mumming validate and support the different attention paid to them by Bulgarian scholars.

Mumming is not the only potential source for these lessons. Other traditional practices support similar conclusions. For example, rituals performed on St. Lazarus's Day (the day before Palm Sunday) and known as *Lazaruvane,* parallel mumming as rites of passage, but specifically for young girls who dress in folk costumes with noisy coin jewelry and floral headdresses to visit village houses, where they dance and sing invocations of abundance to the residents in exchange for eggs and tips. In some locations these rites also include elements of cross-dressing by one of the girls to represent a bridegroom (MacDermott 1998:203). They include numerous elements that support the lessons I extract from mumming and also seem to be undergoing a kind of revitalization (Donna Buchanan, personal communication). My choice to focus exclusively on mumming is justified by its greater popularity and my own need to delineate a manageable research context.

Research Context

The research for this book spans more than twenty years. It began in 1987 when I went to Bulgaria for dissertation research on the socialist village economy. I knew about the rituals from cultural vignettes presented in my Bulgarian language courses in the United States, but the area of the country where I ended up had no tradition of them nor were they directly relevant to my topic. More out of an anthropological attraction to the exotic than anything else, I made an effort through contacts from the Institutes of Sociology and Folklore to locate them, and was able, in 1988, to attend both a local enactment in the village of Kabile near the town of Yambol and two festivals: a small one in the neighboring town of Elhovo and a large one in the town of Breznik. The latter trip occasioned an invitation to observe a very different but equally intriguing masked ritual in the village of Gigan, tagged to the name day for Ivan. Later that year I encountered several village mumming groups performing at the Festival of Roses in Kazanluk. I was there to interview agrarian experts on rose cultivation and observe the rose harvest as part of my investigation of the country's agrarian export economy. I also used the occasion to observe and inquire about the rituals. I do not claim these experiences provide an adequate investigation of mumming under socialism, but they did inspire my hunch about its larger significance and my desire to pursue more focused research. They also provide a comparative supplement to the recollections of socialist practices I later collected through oral history.

Beginning in 1992 my research, nearly perforce, took up the dramatic unraveling of the socialist agrarian institutions and relations I had documented in 1987 and 1988. Since my visits to Bulgaria were usually timed to the agricultural season (spring and summer), there was limited opportunity to observe the events, even as an idle curiosity. My interest had to stay on the back burner, simmering. In 1997, as I was concluding this political-economic project, I extended my stay to include the winter and began what would be nearly ten years of intermittent field research on mumming.

The methods and techniques of this project could not be more distinct from my previous work. Rather than focus on a single village, I opted to investigate practices throughout the country. As my own appreciation of the significance of mumming had come from the experience of seeing it in context, I was convinced that observations would be crucial. This decision extended the time of the research because the rituals are only performed once a year and villages in a region often do so on the same day, making it difficult to catch multiple enactments during the same year. I was also unable to make trips every year although I did so in 1997, 1998, 2002, and 2005–2006, spending a total of nine months in the country devoted to this project. Beginning in January 1997 was somewhat unfortunate as it coincided with a dire economic crisis that provoked the fall of the government. In fact, in some villages the desperate situation made the thought of mumming seem absurd, and I saw evidence of ritual decline rather than revival (see Creed 2002a). In others, however, the commitment to the rituals under such adverse conditions drove home their significance and confirmed my decision to study them.

The first villages I observed were chosen in consultation with Bulgarian ethnographers and folklorists, but as I acquired more information about the rituals I began to select villages to represent different regions of the country and major variations in practices, with an eye to scheduling in order to observe as many events as possible. After selecting a village for study I would ask for permission to visit and observe the rituals from a village official or ritual organizer, which was nearly always forthcoming. My preference was to stay with a village family for a few days around the ritual in order to witness the preparations and subsequent events as well as follow-up assessments. In the few cases when this was not possible, I stayed in a nearby town (once in a nearby monastery) and traveled to the village. I was generally present to observe the full cycle of activities—from costume preparation, group planning meetings, and actual dressing to the day-long (sometimes two-day-long) ritual and post-ritual gatherings in homes and taverns. In all but a few cases I accompanied the main group of mummers throughout the ritual. During this time I talked informally with both ritual figures and the people they visited.

Before and after the rituals I sought out villagers described as enthusiasts or organizers as well as older/former village participants for their comments. I also spoke with people who seemed unengaged with the event as well as important village representatives: usually the mayor and the village librarian (technically the secretary of the village *chitalishte*—a presocialist Bulgarian cultural institution reformed along the lines of Soviet houses of culture "after the 9th"), whose job includes responsibility for village cultural affairs. Observations and conversations always included attention to more than ritual practice, particularly the economic situation in the village, which invariably occasioned political commentary as well. In all, I observed rituals in twenty villages and two towns.

When rituals were not being performed I traveled from village to village in those parts of the county where the rituals are common, asking people about local ritual practices. Usually accompanied by a Bulgarian colleague to ease suspicions, we arrived unannounced and began inquiring of villagers on the street or square about the events, commonly getting a referral to a local enthusiast or knowledgeable individual. Sometimes our presence and questions drew a group of informants on the spot at the village square or tavern.

The enthusiastic reception and response to our interest was a stark contrast to my prior experiences of fieldwork and was another indication to me of the extent of villagers' engagement with these rituals. In many villages we began instead with the village mayor or librarian, which would usually produce a similar referral. The subsequent conversations followed the same topics and questions that I pursued in the villages where I observed the rituals firsthand. When possible we spoke with more than one individual and tried to target both a younger and older participant as well as any interested or knowledgeable village officials. In most cases these investigations produced invitations to return for the ritual itself, and in several cases I did so, moving these cases into those counted above. Additionally, in this way, I visited and gathered information on twenty-four more villages and two towns, bringing the total number of locations visited for this study to forty-four villages and four towns. Information on many other locations is drawn from secondary sources by Bulgarian researchers (see, especially, Kraev 1996; Raichevski and Fol 1993; and Stamenova 1982). Indeed, the detailed documentation of the rituals from the southeast Strandzha region by Stoyan Raichevski and Valeria Fol (1993) convinced me that I did not need to visit the area.

These data are enriched by my attendance at five festivals in three different locations where I observed mumming groups from many other villages as they paraded in costume and enacted a vignette of village practice. The important relationship between this and village activity is discussed in chapter 1, but the point here is that even though it is a very different activity than that performed in the village, it provided another context to acquire information about the latter. I was able to observe costumes and elements of practice and then follow up by asking performers about the extent of local village practice and how it differed from the festival performance. These are very festive occasions and not ideal for extended discussions, but they did provide useful information. They also provided an occasion for me to reconnect with villagers I had met when visiting their villages and get their assessment of any changes since that time.

All this material, however, is not the foundation of the study. Rather, it is the knowledge from many years of prior research and observations in rural Bulgaria that allowed me to spot in these rituals the dynamics of social practice I suggest they reveal. In other words, what follows is not so much ritual interpretation (although I recognize all my observations are interpretations) as it is ritual recognition. My experience and knowledge of rural Bulgaria from different parts of the country allowed me to recognize the lessons of mumming I point to here. But it is also an interactive effort, as pursing those connections exposed possibilities about life in Bulgaria that I had not originally appreciated. Once I recognized enactments of broader social relations and conditions in these rituals, the effort to understand other ritual elements with the same logic led me to ask questions about social relations that I had not suspected or recognized previously. In this sense the ritual analysis goes beyond recognition to revelation. This approach adapts that popularized by Geertz (1973) in his analysis of the Balinese cock fight, which was also as much recognition as interpretation, despite his emphasis on the latter. I link that approach to a political and economic critique occasioned not so much by the content of the rituals or the means of analysis but rather by the dynamics of postsocialism that rendered many of the relations I am focusing on out of synch and exposed (cf. Kozhuharova-Zhirkova 2000). In mumming, then, we are able to spot some of the less obvious sociocultural casualties of the transition.

Roadmap

Chapter 1 provides a detailed description of mumming events. This is not as easy as it might appear, as the practices are nearly as diverse as the villages performing them. Furthermore, they are constantly changing as participants adopt practices from other villages or come up with their own innovations, so even a detailed description from one locale is limited temporally. This extensive diversity is reflected in the distinctive local terms previously sampled, although in some cases different terms are used for very similar enactments and similar terms are used by groups with much greater differences. I note some of these particularities along with the descriptions in chapter 1, but many more will be presented as evidence of my claims in subsequent chapters. I also provide a selective summary of how the rituals have changed, again focusing on those dimensions that are significant to the analysis but not discussed extensively in later chapters. One change crucial to all subsequent practice was the development of the festival system in the 1960s. Since that time the festivals have become increasingly integrated with local village practice, and this interaction must be kept in mind when discussing village activity. The festival connection is a major incentive for village mumming, but I also survey additional motives expressed by participants.

Chapters 2 through 5 take up several central themes in postsocialist studies, looking at how our understanding of these issues can be deepened by what we see in ritual and festival practices. The first is the study of gender and sexuality. This priority is appropriate given both the extensive attention devoted to the issue of gender in postsocialist studies and the central role that gender plays in these rituals. In addition to their fertility project, which is highly gendered, the rituals are also rites of passage to manhood. It is this role that partially accounts for their increasing popularity as a response to what others (Kideckel 2008; Ghodsee 2007) have seen as a gender crisis of postsocialism. In short, the difficulty men have in achieving the requirements of masculinity since 1989 have led to an increased embrace of these highly masculinizing rituals. This also helps explain the geography of ritual revitalization which is most evident where male economic roles have been most eroded. But there is more going on. Usually a central transvestite figure is present whose appearance and actions reveal complex gender expectations and relations. Many of these rituals are also homoerotic, and I believe that the ability to combine homoeroticism with masculinization points to a relationship between genders that is not as interdependent as assumed in most gender theory. I then note how forces of postsocialism and globalization are redefining this gender arrangement into one that is more in line with common Western assumptions.

Chapter 3 takes up two other dominant (and interrelated) themes in postsocialist studies: civil society and democracy. Here I rejoin a well-established anthropological critique of the notion of civil society and push it further to challenge notions of democracy generally. I suggest that we can see in the rituals (and festivals) elements that replicate the benighted generic qualities of Western civil society. Yet the civic dimension of these or similar activities are never acknowledged by political scientists and others who cite a lack of civil society as the cause for democratic difficulties in postsocialist contexts. I examine the ideological implications and consequences of this disjuncture exposing the neoliberal agenda of civil society efforts. I also find in the comments of participants a disturbing critique of democracy that denies the value of activism. I use this to suggest that although democratic institutions and practices are firmly in place, a particular understanding of democracy has coalesced that may actually diminish rather than encourage civic engagement.

There is a major irony in the anthropological reaction against the civil society concept. Though anthropologists have generally challenged the exclusive authority and presumptions of the model, many found a compatible argument in the late 1980s and early 1990s compelling. This variant, made famous by Istvan Rev (1987), focused on individual villagers and family relations rather than institutions and organizations, but presented a similar view of socialist society as bereft of social connections. Rev suggested that citizens of Eastern Europe had been atomized into isolated families by socialist policies that made them dependent upon the state and distrustful of one another. In chapter 4 I suggest that this conclusion misses the different ways that interaction and interdependence could be organized and experienced under socialism, as revealed in mumming. This implies nothing less than a different understanding of the nature of community. The way the atomization argument is reproduced in postsocialist models is especially revealing, as the dense family relations of socialism, supposedly freed of their political and structural limitations, are challenged as unhelpful and even troublesome. In short, East Europeans are seen as needing social relations because the intense ones they do have are redefined as invalid or at least problematic. The obvious devaluation of a potentially indigenous alternative could not be more evident.

The particular nature of social relations revealed in mumming is not limited to connections between Bulgarians but can also be read in relations between different categories of villagers. This brings up, in chapter 5, the central concern of postsocialism with ethnic minorities and nationalism. Mumming events are full of ethnic/racial imagery and symbolism, especially in reference to the Roma. The nature of these activities suggests a notion of ethnic relations that is not greatly different from that between ethnic Bulgarian families, that is, one that is simultaneously conflictive and collective. This allows us to posit a mumming model of ethnic interaction in which opposition is expected and partly incorporative. Linking this with Benedict Anderson's (1991 [1983]) definition of nations as "imagined communities," I suggest that this specific notion of community may have inspired a different understanding of nation, allowing us to posit a contributing factor to Bulgarian exceptionalism (sometimes characterized as "weak nationalism") in relation to Balkan nationalisms. This alternative model explains why ethnic relations were not immediately improved by Western ideas of tolerance and multiculturalism.

The conclusion turns to the notion of modernity to integrate the themes of the analysis. It suggests that the failure to see the messages of Bulgarian mumming has much to do with assumptions about modernity and that taken together the rituals indeed suggest an effort to define what researchers working outside Europe have called an alternative modernity—albeit an alternative that never got a chance to coalesce or even be recognized. The failure to read these messages provides a rather graphic illustration of how the neoliberal project redefines or dismisses alternatives as a way of establishing its own inevitability. Although vital and even revitalized, the rituals were already moving at the time of my research from an alternative to an adjunct in this process as devotees sought ways to commodify the rituals for a tourist market. This is not simply a case of capitalism's well-known co-optation of critical practices into marketable goods but is equally the grassroots product of ritual afficionados trying to insure the perpetuation of the practices in a radically changing context, and in so doing sacrificing some of the meanings and components they were devoted to. Their continuing commitment to the rituals, now changed in meaning to fit with the new political and economic context, helps establish devotees' attachment to the new situation through their ritual devotion. Such ritual dynamics are thus clearly elemental to the apparent "successes" of the last years. In many cases these successes simply replace old problems with new ones, which are sometimes more threatening but not necessarily recognized as new by outsiders because they replicate standard Western experience and expectations. In this way mumming illustrates how culture shapes political and economic outcomes but how alternative modernities can lose their alterity in the process.

CHAPTER ONE

A MUMMING SEASON

Two periods of concentrated mumming activity bookend winter in Bulgaria, with a large number of villages performing the rites in early January and others in late February to mid-March. Commonly the former are linked to New Year's celebrations and the latter to the beginning of Lent. Prominent festivals are scheduled purposefully between these periods of intense activity, or soon after the last events in March, so as not to conflict with local practice. Together the extended preparations, ritual enactments, follow-up banquets for participants, and the festivals make winter in Bulgaria a mumming season.

New Year

Nineteen miles southwest of the capital city of Sofia, well within commuting distance and connected by regular train service, sits the industrial mining town of Pernik. This city of more than eighty thousand hosts the largest and most famous mumming festival in the country, held every other year in late January. As a relatively new city that grew up with the expansion of coal mining in the twentieth century, Pernik has no tradition of these rituals being performed in town, but the villages west of town, which supplied much of its population, provide ardent exemplars of the custom. As a result, the town and its surrounding area are recognized as a center of Bulgarian mumming (see Bokova 2000). Not only do most villages in this area have vital mumming traditions, they are similar enough in practice to justify a composite description.

Every year, on the evening of January 13, large bonfires inaugurating the ritual dot the hills around Pernik, and the noxious fumes of burning rubber from discarded car tires, which have increasingly replaced valuable and depleted firewood for this purpose, waft across the area. If you venture into one of these villages you'll likely encounter a small crowd of villagers gathered around the fire, close enough to be slightly illuminated but too far away to benefit fully from the fire's warmth, suggesting a prohibited or reserved proscenium. You may hear the music of a small band playing Bulgarian folk themes off to the side and then the sound of bells in the distance, not a tinkle or a jingle but the deeper, sonorous reverberation of large heavy bells, growing louder as they approach. As they get closer you may also recognize a different sound, more like the hollow and tinny sound of a cowbell but far too loud and deep to be the ordinary variant. These combined sounds advance in unison with a regular rhythm—two slow peals, followed by a quicker three. This sound gradually overwhelms the music of the instruments, except for the drum which takes up the beat of the bells.

The atmosphere among observers is anticipatory, and one might even say festive, but to the uninitiated outsider it is also a bit ominous. Nervous children clinging to their parents with unusual fortitude add to a gnawing sense of unease. As the ringing gets louder and its source becomes visible uncertainty matures into anxiety. Advancing slowly toward the fire is what could only be called a monster. Nearly eight feet tall, covered in animal skins, carrying a large staff topped with boxwood greens, the creature advances with steps in the previously described rhythm: a measured right and left, then a quicker right, left, right, now again a slower left and right, followed by a quicker left, right, left. Each step is more like a small leap which jostles a collection of enormous brass bells tied around its waist, producing the previously described soundscape.

As it comes into clearer view, the creature's head, itself nearly three feet high, is mesmerizing. The face appears to be made of wood carved with exaggerated human features and a threatening grimace, the rest of the head is a combination of animal skins and horns put together in a way that is simultaneously artistic and terrifying. One's gaze is shaken from the figure only by the recognition that there is another behind it, and another behind that, until you realize it's a troop of forty or more in all, explaining the increasing decibel level. Just to the side near the front of the line is the group leader, dressed in what might either be an antique military dress uniform or a contemporary drum major outfit. The whistle he blows constantly to mark the beat of the steps suggests the latter, but the large sword he brandishes flamboyantly confirms the former. The creatures he is leading all resemble one another but with individual differences. Some wear heavy elongated brass bells with heavy clappers, and others have darker, thinner bells made of a lighter metal, shaped in a sphere that provides its own echo chamber, deepening and weighting the sound from the simple thin clapper. The masks are the most varied. Some have more wood carving and less animal skin, others are all animal skin with no wood, and still others incorporate whole animal heads and even a whole dead fox, teeth bared for effect. A few use these materials to create multiple heads on a single figure, perhaps with menacing teeth in mouths that flap open and close as the figure jumps.

The group slowly circles the fire, making a few revolutions before stopping and facing the flames. The figures then begin to jump in place, continuing the same rhythm but gradually increasing the tempo until the rhythm is completely lost and the action devolves into a frenzy of constant random jumping and twisting that produces a deafening noise. By this point the first-time observer is expecting something severe, perhaps an animal sacrifice, or maybe worse. Instead, the figures stop, take off their masks and set them on the ground behind them, revealing a group of young men from about sixteen years old to their early thirties, hardly threatening or dangerous. Closer inspection reveals that two of the figures are girls in their late teens. The awe produced by their masks is lost, but it is replaced by a reverence for the emotion evident in their faces as they now repeat the same dance without the masks. There are varied levels of engagement, from the somewhat bored to the ardently engaged, but most tend toward the latter. The combination of concentration and exertion over several repetitions of the dance cycle produce an exhilaration that is both physical and emotional.

Here the figures, and the ritual in general, are called "survakari," reflecting their association with the New Year.[1] January 13 of the current calendar corresponds to New Year's Eve (December 31) on the older Julian calendar, which was followed in Bulgaria until the second decade of the twentieth century when the state adopted the Gregorian one. So January 14 is, as Bulgarians describe it, "New Year by the old style" and survakari are New Year rituals. Given the association with New Year, it is not surprising that some villages shifted these activities to follow the new calendar. Indeed, most of the villages in the regions south and east of Pernik celebrate on December 31/January 1, although, ironically, in most of these places the figures are not usually called "survakari" but rather "babugari"—a term that has no other known meaning and no reference to New Year. The villages around Pernik all continue their survakari traditions on the 13th and 14th. One participant reported that his village had once tried to stage the rituals on the 1st, but found it was too hard to pack in other New Year celebrations with survakari rituals. Besides, he added with a wink, "this way we have two holidays."

To understand why survakari events might be difficult to combine with other activities, we can return to the group by the fire. Some new figures have appeared in the crowd of onlookers and the atmosphere is getting more festive. A couple of men dressed as overly buxom, "loose" women are parading around provocatively. Another transvestite, seemingly puritanical in contrast, is dressed in traditional peasant folk costume and accompanied by a young man, also smartly dressed in traditional male folk attire. A disheveled priest with a tattered Bible and metal pail is blessing them on their marriage, along with anyone else he meets, with a cold spray of holy water dispersed with a small bunch of leafy boxwood branches. Some of the audience take out small bottles of homemade brandy from their coat pockets and share it with their friends. Villagers move from group to group exchanging New Year's greetings and village news. There is much to talk about because some of the observers no longer live in the village but are back to see the ritual.

Everyone comments on the survakari—how many there are, how they look, and how well they are performing. The consensus is that it's a good showing. The small band is playing folk tunes and the survakari are quieter, some pausing to have a smoke or a swig of someone's brandy, the sound of bells returns intermittently as subgroups of survakari spontaneously erupt in synchronized jumping, and others take off after young girls who run away to avoid being pinched or embraced with smelly animal skins. The survakari periodically reconvene for a group dance. "Dance" is a term of convenience for this element of the survakari ritual. Being more like a patterned march with jumping, it is certainly not what the English word usually implies. It does, however, follow Bulgarian usage which often refers to this activity as the *survakarski horo,* horo being the typical folk dance form in which dancers hold hands and dance in a line.[2]

In between periods of survakari activity some villagers join a horo around the fire. After an hour or so, when it seems that the event might be morphing into the generic village folk dance common to other occasions, the regimented echo of disciplined bells and a whistle is heard again in the distance. "They're arriving" passes from person to person. There's a renewed cacophony of ringing as the survakari scurry to get into a line. The earlier sense of anticipation returns to the crowd. Once again we hear the beat of a drum and bells approaching, but we don't have to wait as long to see what's coming because these figures are carrying torches that cast a glow on their faces, making them visible at a distance. Most are not wearing masks and the illumination doesn't reach their lower body, so for a short while it looks like a line of disembodied heads floating toward the village square.

These figures are from a neighboring village and, having completed the same opening ceremony at their own square, they have come to join their neighbors in a meeting that is both sociable and competitive. For all practical purposes the visiting figures are indistinguishable from the hosts. Despite the apparent similarities, they insist that they are not survakari but rather *mechkari*. Mechkari comes from the Bulgarian word for bear (*mechka*), which clearly resonates with their dress. Participants from villages who refer to the figures with this term (the minority in the area, most using the term survakari) take it as a point of local pride that they have a distinctive term. When pressed to explain the difference, however, they readily admit that there is none. Like survakari in some other villages they don't wear masks on the opening-night ceremony, but they do during the next day's activities. Their masks are similar to those previously described. Some villages in this area are noted for distinctive mask styles. Leskovets, for example, emphasizes animal horns in intriguing interesting formations (see figure 1), and Noevtsi includes very tall masks with a large number of whole animals. In some cases these dominant styles are associated with one or two master craftsmen in the village who make the masks for others. Other individuals may follow standard village motifs.

When the mechkari reach the village square their leader is met by the leader of the survakari, the two generals cross swords and exchange greetings, and their respective groups parade past each other in two lines going in opposite directions. The new group then circles the fire while the hosts remain quite off to the side. The mechkari repeat much of the activity previously enacted by the local group, circling the fire in step to rhythms whistled out by the leader, always concluding with a period of constant unstructured jumping that produces overwhelming sound. After several of these dances, the survakari group returns to the bonfire making a larger circle around the outside of the visitors. They begin going in the opposite direction, jumping to the same rhythm but not in synch. The impact is a bit disorienting as figures pass in different directions to contrary beats, but the different beats make it possible to distinguish the sound of each group and this in turn makes it possible for one group to try to overwhelm the other. This amounts to a contest to see which group is loudest and can overwhelm the other, perhaps by sheer volume drawing members of the other group into its own tempo. The group with the most figures might seem to have an obvious advantage, but not if the other group has more and bigger bells or is more skilled at maximizing the sound with its jumping technique. The mechkari manage to hold their own beat, but they are weaker and their beat harder to hear. The effort ends in a wall of sound as both groups increase the tempo toward a collective jumping that is now twice as loud as either group alone.

No winner is declared or expected, leaving participants and observers free to comment and discuss the relative strengths of the two groups not only in terms of volume but also regarding costumes, the size of the group, and the general enthusiasm of the performers. Villagers champion their own group's performance when it is comparable, but they will also criticize it and say it is weak, especially if it has far fewer participants than the visiting group or than in previous years. Some villages have reputations as being weak, meaning they have very few performers.

The mechkari finish by throwing their torches into the fire and dispersing. Friends and acquaintances from the two groups seek each other out and perform a sort of *pas de deux,* jumping in unison to the standard beat for a few repetitions and then ending with freestyle jumping together. During the informal socializing, the leader of either group might collect his charges and have them start jumping again, which will provoke the other leader to do the same in another competition in sound. Then, without any clear provocation, the mechkari leader rounds up his troops, and they all casually head back to their village.

The survakari also head off but not for their homes. They have hired a bus to take them to another village that is too far away to reach on foot. Survakari from this village had come as guests the previous year, so this year they are "returning the favor." They all board the bus, including the transvestite figures. The largest masks are left behind, but the more manageable ones are taken along. There is not enough room and a couple of men volunteer to drive their cars. Some of the villagers decide to drive over as well and invite others to fill up their cars. The destination is described as having a weak tradition, primarily because the village has been so depopulated over the last several years. Still, when the bus arrives there are more than twenty people in costume on the square, although they are noticeably older. There is a drummer but no other musicians. They call themselves survakari but their costumes are completely different. Rather than animal skins or furs, they're covered in torn strips of red and white cloth. More than just a substitute for expensive skins and furs, the red and white cloth conjure another pre-spring custom known as *martenitsi*—red and white tassels worn on March 1 to ward off evil and insure fertility and luck. I assumed the cloth was an innovation of convenience, but a mummer from the visiting village told me they had also worn cloth until a few years back when a village sponsor donated the money for the village to buy the more "authentic" looking animal skins. So, for at least one village, the skins were a more recent innovation adopted because they looked older or more traditional. It is certainly logical that animal skins or furs predominated prior to cheap industrially produced cloth, but some of the earliest photographs of mummers in the early twentieth century show cloth/rag costumes as well as fur. The masks on display around the village square are also notably different: covered in feathers rather than fur and horns. They have wooden frames made of tree branches, often bent to produce rounded forms. Fabric is stretched over the frame, and feathers or whole parts of fowl, such as wings, cover the entire form. Perhaps because the materials are lighter, the masks are extremely tall, some measuring over six feet. The impact is less menacing but equally impressive, given the larger size and the elaborate patterns that can be rendered in the feathered mosaics. One has the abbreviation for Happy New Year written in feathers on the mask; another has the name of the village.

The meeting here is a bit less choreographed. The visiting survakari exit the bus and immediately begin moving around a fire that is only smoldering by this point. They repeat the steps they performed at home and while they're performing the local survakari put on their masks and form a circle behind them. These large constructions constrain the wearers' mobility so their steps are a bit more measured, but they still manage to parade around the fire and produce an impressive amount of noise. They keep their masks on for much of the time the visitors are present, as if the size of their masks compensates for their smaller number. Overall, the interaction here had less of a competitive feel, perhaps because the numbers were so disproportionate, the styles of each group less comparable, and, most important, the villages were not close neighbors, as in Bulgaria proximity often breeds village rivalries. After this joint activity, the two groups remain rather segregated at the square. There is some visiting and socializing between groups, but not everybody knows someone from the other place, so many people remain in their own group and periodically break into a survakari dance at the instigation of the leader.

After half an hour the visiting survakari get back on their bus and head home. When they get there, the musicians are still playing at the square and a crowd of villagers are dancing. Some of the survakari join them, others head to a village bar to drink and socialize, and still others head home to rest up for the next day's activities.

The following day is the core of the event and it is exhausting by any measure. The survakari begin gathering in the morning at the village square and perhaps also a village location where ritual materials are stored. In one village I was told that I should be at a deserted hut where masks were stored by 6:00 AM to be part of the preparations. After an hour of waiting in the dark and bitter cold an older man finally showed up to unlock the door and gratefully light a fire in the small stove. It was another half-hour before others started showing up. When an unofficial quorum was constituted around 8:00 they began complaining about the tardiness of others—saying they weren't "serious" and attributing it to excess drinking the previous night. Most survakari arrive dressed, except for the mask and bells they carry. Survakari help one another get the heavy collection of bells securely belted around their waists with individual bells positioned so that they ring to maximum effect. They test them by jumping and then have someone help reposition them until they are comfortable and sound right.

Different preparations are under way in a couple of village houses where, with the help of parents, following instructions from grandparents, young men are being dressed in the traditional folk costumes of wedding members: a bride, groom, and wedding sponsor (*kum*), and perhaps additional figures such as the father and mother of the groom (*svekŭr* and *svekŭrva*). Following standard wedding protocol, the groom and his sponsor, carrying a wedding flag and accompanied by a drummer, go to collect the bride at his house. The whole wedding party then heads to the village square. Ten or so adolescent boys and girls dressed in rags are already there smearing their faces with the ashes from last night's bonfire. The rubber ash from the tires makes the result quite dark and they refer to each other as Gypsies. For the outside observer, whose attitude has gone from uncertain anxiety to festive enjoyment over the course of events so far, a new cause for unease inserts itself. Some survakari with masks are already at the square as well. They are soon joined by the rest of the masked figures and, led by the general, they gather around the ashes of the bonfire for an abbreviated and less enthusiastic replay of the previous night's dance (see figure 2). Another couple arrives: a man dressed as a bear led on a chain by an apparent trainer carrying a broken fiddle. The trainer doesn't have a blackened face, but he is obviously marked as a Gypsy by an occupation that is exclusively Romani. Soon the imitation priest and the wedding party arrive and the entire group sets off to canvass the village.

The group visits each house in turn. The general leads the group followed by the wedding party, including the priest and drummer, then the Gypsies. The masked figures follow behind. Simply walking with their bells makes a major commotion and alerts villagers to their arrival, but they also periodically march in their characteristic rhythmic steps, which is much louder and arresting. When they reach the gate of a village house, the general, the wedding party, and the Gypsies proceed into the yard in that order. If it is a large one the masked survakari might join them, but more often they remain outside where they might dance in the road in front of the house, or rest with sporadic eruptions of jumping and noise making by individuals. If one starts, another is likely to join in, and it might spread to a few others or even the whole group. As the day goes on, they begin to use this time to sit and rest a bit.

If the proprietors have not been drawn outside by all the commotion, the wedding party knocks on the door and calls out their names. When the owners emerge, they are greeted by the bridal couple and the priest, who proceeds to bless the owners: "for many years" he says, as he slings holy water. The proprietors shake the hands of the couple and perhaps kiss their cheeks as they congratulate them on both their marriage and the New Year. They then give the bride some cash. The woman of the house also gives the couple some dried beans and dried sausage, which the bride hands over to a Gypsy figure lugging a large burlap satchel for this purpose. The owners then offer the bridal guests some pork headcheese and produce a bottle of homemade brandy for a toast to the newlyweds' health and fertility: "for many years and many children." After the bottle has passed around the wedding party and everyone has taken a gulp, the last person offers it back to the proprietor, who tells him to keep it. It is handed to an older Gypsy figure carrying a five-gallon plastic canister, into which he empties the brandy before returning the bottle. The priest blesses them again, and the proprietor drops some coins into his pail of holy water. The bride and groom thank their hosts, perhaps kissing their hands, and turn to go.

As the group departs the drummer goes up to the owners and says, "for the music, for the music," getting a *lev* or two (the Bulgarian currency) pushed under the cords on the side of his drum. The Gypsies then descend on the owners and are each given small change until the owners deplete their purse and pockets. As the party takes its leave, everyone hands over the money they received to the general who collects it all in a sealed box he carries. Waiting at the gate is the bear trainer and his bear; both enter the yard as the rest of the survakari move on to the next house (see figure 3). The bear trainer gets the bear to perform for the owners, basically rolling over on the ground or patio. The bear then embraces the man of the house in a bear hug, rocking back and forth to suggest wrestling. The bear relaxes his hold as the man makes a move to his pocket to extract another lev or two which he puts in the trainer's fiddle.

By now, the survakari group are on to their next house, where the owners are outside waiting in anticipation with a spread of food on a picnic table, including the usual pork headcheese as well as a warm pot of sauerkraut and pork, a collection of cakes and cookies, and a warm plate of what might be called the Bulgarian national dish, *banitsa,* a baked strudel-like concoction of egg and feta cheese layered between thin sheets of pastry dough. After the priest greets the owner couple, the man of the house complains that the priest isn't playing his role well, that he should be offering more blessings, "to have sheep the size of cows, and cows the size of elephants." After giving detailed instructions he insists that the masked survakari come into the yard. The survakari oblige and dance in a circle around the yard; they are rewarded with offers of food and drink by the woman of the house who takes a plate of banitsa and a bottle of brandy out to the yard. The survakari comment on the high quality of the bandy and keep the bottle to share among themselves rather than pouring it into the collective container. When the bear trainer arrives, the man of the house greets him with a wrestling stance and proceeds to wrestle the bear to the ground. It is a short match with no apparent winner as the trainer breaks it up while everybody laughs and the man's wife shakes her head at his youthful enthusiasm. The trainer is well tipped for his service.

Variations of these scenarios occur across the village as the survakari move from house to house. Sometimes the meetings are brief—a short blessing for a single owner, a small cash gift in return, and perhaps a departing offer of candy for the wedding party. At other houses a veritable feast is offered, and the whole family is there to greet them. One man brings out an antique shotgun and fires it into the air in imitation of the extinct ritual practice of firing a gun to confirm a bride's virginity after a marriage consummation; another villager opts for more contemporary wedding symbolism, popping the cork from a bottle of champaign and offering it to the participants. Generally the more extravagant the greeting, the longer the group stays. In some cases the masked figures don't accompany the wedding party to the house at all, staying instead at the nearby intersection as the wedding party visits all the houses on a cul-de-sac. Being on the road is handy, because the figures can stop any cars that go by and demand a toll to let them pass, which they usually get. The survakari group is joined by a couple of transvestite burlesque figures in lewd, provocative costumes. One wears a "price list" offering kisses for 10 lev and sex for 30. Another has exaggerated breasts ending with the tops of a baby bottle, suggesting grotesque nipples.

The route through the village has been planned so that the group arrives at the home of the bride or groom in the early afternoon, where the wedding party is invited inside to sit down for a scaled-down wedding meal. Since the group has eaten and drank at half the houses in the village by this point, the meal is appreciated more for the respite than the food. The Gypsies and masked figures wait outside but also appreciate the time to rest. The stash of goods the Gypsies have been lugging, now including beans, flour, eggs, nuts, apples, and cured meat, is unloaded here and the collected brandy transferred to another container for temporary storage along with the produce. The bear trainer catches up with the group and empties his fiddle of money into the general's box when the party comes out of the house. They are all now ready for the second half of the village. Despite the rest, some of the survakari show signs of fatigue and rarely break into spontaneous jumping. Others, in contrast, are feeling no pain, having indulged more in the proffered spirits. They seem even more animated, if less stable.

The second half of the day continues much like the first, albeit with increasing urgency as the group is significantly behind the pace required to cover the village before nightfall. They are reprimanded by one man who says he's been waiting for hours and asks why they are so late. Another man meets the group on the street several houses below his own and says he can't wait any longer because he has promised to do some work for a friend, but he still gives the general some money before he heads off. When the group gets to his house, the general leads the survakari into the yard for a short dance even in his absence. As the group crosses the village square again en route to the last neighborhood, they stop by the two stores on the square; the wedding party goes in with a couple of masked figures who jump around the store as the proprietors give the bride money. This group also stops by the mayor's office, and

the mayor does the same but only after insisting that the priest enact the wedding ceremony appropriately. The survakari then visit the last houses, one of
which is the home of one of the mummers, and the produce and brandy collected on the second half of the day are left there. Reenergized by the completion of their rounds, the mummers return to the village square with a degree
of enthusiasm similar to that with which they began nearly ten hours earlier.
The masked figures, without masks, form a circle and perform their steps one
last time. They then disperse—several head for the village tavern to continue
drinking, the general and the wedding party head to the village library to
count the money, and the rest of the group disperses to their homes for a special family meal.

Among the four locations around Pernik where I observed all these
events (Yardzhilovtsi in 1997, Cherna Gora in 1998, Gigintsi in 2002, and
Batanovtsi in 2006) there were evident variations. Some of these differences
have been covered in the above composite description. Gigintsi figures wear
the red and white cloth costume and have extravagant feather "faces." Although these masks seem more extravagant, they are actually more afford-
able, as chicken, rooster, duck, and goose feathers are more available than
animal skins and have fewer alternative uses. Villagers report saving feathers all year for this purpose. A master mask maker in Gigintsi said that villagers used to use parts of the fowl intact, such as the whole wing, which could
be spread out on the mask for a more interesting display, but that nobody was
willing any longer to give up edible parts, so they just use the plucked feathers. Masks with feathers pasted to cheap fabric using homemade glue are
cheaper than animal skin variants, but they are also less durable. They often
do not survive a year in storage and, if they do, they require significant repair work. Mummers working in a feather medium can thus expend a lot of
time on masks each year. The time is much greater in the years of the Pernik
festival, when they want new designs previously unseen by the audience or
judges.

There is also noticeable variation in house visits. The Cherna Gora priest
said and did very little at each house, whereas his counterpart in Yardzhilovtsi
replicated various elements of the wedding ritual at most houses and imitated
priestly recitations with an impressive, if exaggerated, authenticity. The latter
wedding party sometimes concluded the interaction by dancing a short horo.
Batanovtsi included equal proportions of both extremes, with the minimalist
variant increasingly dominating as the day wore on and it was clear the group

was way behind schedule. When I asked if the Cherna Gora priest ever made invocations for fertility, one of the mechkari said he was young and didn't really know how to fulfill his role yet.

The Gigintsi group was much smaller than the other three, perhaps only a dozen participants compared to over fifty at both Cherna Gora and Batanovtsi, and more than a hundred at Yardzhilovtsi. The smaller number of survakari might also account for why the would-be masked figures were more integrated with the wedding party and usually treated along with the latter as opposed to waiting outside to be invited in or offered treats independently. The size of these different groups corresponds directly to the different size of the villages, but weather may also have been a contributing factor, as it was especially bitter the January that I was in Gigintsi. The entire village had been covered in several inches of snow for weeks, which had turned into a thick ice pack. Although survakari repeatedly told me snow and ice were preferable to mud, this was an extreme situation. Few paths were cleared of ice and the village is extremely hilly, so getting to many houses required ascending or descending steep icy slopes. I fell more times than I can remember, much to the amusement of the survakari. They were far more sure-footed despite their bulky costumes and alcohol consumption, except for the general who began to fall repeatedly as the day wore on and the alcohol accumulated. A few households were deemed inaccessible, but I was amazed (and distressed) at the extreme situations the survakari insisted we could tackle—many of which deserved ice picks and shoe spikes in my opinion. It was so cold the batteries in my video camera would not function, and the low temperature may have also accounted for why many more villagers invited the group into their house rather than treat us outside the door or in the yard. The survakari maintained that they still enjoyed doing this, but they also complained about the extreme conditions and they were clearly enduring significant discomfort. This is definitely not carnival. Their commitment to the ritual in the face of such adversity testifies to the depth of their connection, which is why we might want to pay close attention.

The Gigintsi wedding group only included a drummer, a general, a bride and groom, and a priest. There were also two somewhat ambiguous figures referred to by some as Gypsies but not specifically marked as such: one had his face colorfully painted rather than blackened and carried a bugle which is not a typical instrument for Romani musicians, the other carried a satchel for collecting produce but otherwise wore no costume. This might be considered the minimal core group of the ritual; the greater the number of participants, the greater the variety of ritual figures. There is almost always a bear and bear trainer as previously described. The survakari in Gigintsi explained that they didn't have one because they had worn out the bear's costume and needed to get another, which they assured me they would have by the time of the Pernik festival, still a couple of weeks off. Supplementary roles, if there are enough participants, generally include additional wedding figures (for example, marriage sponsors or parents of the newlyweds), a greater number and variety of carnivalesque figures (such as doctors with transvestite nurses in addition to the ubiquitous lewd transvestites), and a plethora of Gypsy figures—again referred to categorically by that term but not all clearly marked as such. Yardzhilovtsi had several groups of diversely arrayed figures roaming around on their own, demanding tips or taxes from anybody they met on the street. Two groups set up literal roadblocks at the two main entrances to the village, so that there was no getting in or out without paying a toll. I was warned that one needs lots of change and small bills to be out and about on the 14th and I was prepared, but I still ran out as the demands were rather unrelenting. The village also had additional musicians accompanying two different groups of mechkari, and, as in Cherna Gora, there were multiple generals—one leading the wedding party and another leading the masked mechkari.

In Gigintsi, Cherna Gora, and Batanovtsi, the conclusion of the ritual was not as elaborately or formally marked as was the beginning, but in Yardzihlovtsi it was the reverse. The various groups came together at the village schoolyard with full-scale wedding enactments, nearly full orchestras playing folk music, masked figures donning much more extravagant masks than had been worn during the day, and folk dancing and constant noisemaking by the mechkari. In the village of Noevtsi the elaborate, animal-adorned masks are parked on the square and the figures wait on opposite sides of the square until dark when the survakari enter the village square with torches, meet, join together and, after the usual dancing/jumping, extinguish their torches to conclude the ritual.

Most survakari groups in this area canvass their villages during the day on the 14th, but a few do it during the previous night, waking villagers not lucky enough to be at the end or beginning of their circuit. A nighttime canvass is more common in the areas where the ritual has been moved to January 1, especially south and southeast of Pernik in areas surrounding the Pirin and Rhodope Mountains. In many of these cases the ritual gets under way much later, as the various characters only come out to the square after welcoming in the New Year with their families. In these regions we also find a distinctive term and costume style. The figures are commonly referred to as "babu-gari" and are dressed in costumes made of angora-like goat skin, instead of the sheepskin common around Pernik. They usually wear tall cylindrical or conical masks made of the same. Covered completely in this uniform way, these figures are both simpler and more bizarre than those previously de-scribed.

The markers of human involvement and manipulation are less evident here, sometimes even the bells are concealed by the thick long stands of hair, so the figures strike the observer as somehow more natural, perhaps compa-rable to a Sasquatch. Their characteristic movement is also distinctive; rather than the leaping and jumping of survakari, they move with an exaggerated torso twist that makes the bells around their waist ring but also sets the long hair of their costumes flowing back and forth in an impressive, nearly hyp-notic display. For this the English term "dance" seems more appropriate. They usually accompany a wedding party, but the subsidiary figures are not primarily Gypsies but rather old folk—young people wearing masks with ac-centuated age characteristics and enacting the infirmities of old age, espe-cially stooped posture and ambulatory deficiencies. This has led to specula-tion that the term "babugari" is perhaps derived from the word "*baba*," which means granny, an idea perhaps supported by the fact that in some other vil-lages the word for the masked figures is "startsi," which means old men, and the central transvestite figure is call a "baba" rather than a bride.

Late Winter/Pre-Spring

"Startsi" is also a common term for the masked figures that appear later in regions to the east and north of New Year's mumming traditions, although the more common term for these figures is "kukeri." In these areas the rituals are tagged to the beginning of Lent in February or March depending on the date of Orthodox Easter.[3] Orthodox Lent begins in stages with a prohibi-tion on meat beginning a week before a ban on cheese. In some locations the rituals occur on the Sunday before the meat fast begins; in others they mark the beginning of the cheese fast. In actuality many villages have loosened the Lenten tie and choose a date around this time according to new priorities dis-cussed later in the chapter.

Late winter/pre-spring rituals share many elements with New Year events. In some villages, such as Lesichevo and Kalugerovo, the ritual figures wear long goat-hair costumes much like the babugari, although without the tall conical masks. More often the costumes and masks in late-winter events in-

clude fewer animal skins/motifs and more elements of traditional folk costumes, such as decoratively woven and embroidered aprons or vests, combined with extensive use of fabrics, braid, sequins, mirrors, and beads. There
is usually a central female transvestite figure, variously referred to as a bride,
a virgin, an engaged girl, or in a few cases a grandmother with a child (represented by a doll). There may or may not be a priest, and, if not, the leader may
be the bride's male escort, often called her fiancé, or a special masked kuker
carrying a phallus. In cases where there is no bride figure, the group leader is
the central character, sometimes called an "Arap"—a darkly blackened figure
of rather indeterminate origin.[4] The plural form "Arapi" is also used in a few
places for the collection of auxiliary figures elsewhere glossed as Gypsies, although usually with the addition of explicit Middle Eastern markings. In
some villages the auxiliary figures lack any clear cultural or ethnic referent
and are referred to simply as *plashilki* from the verb "to scare."

In general, late winter practices vary somewhat more from village to village than the rituals in Pernik villages. Consequently a composite description
is less valid, while an effort to include all the variation would be totally disorienting. So here I describe the particular events I observed in 2002 in Mogila, a
village of about five hundred residents seven kilometers east of the city of Yambol in southeastern Bulgaria, an area commonly acknowledged as the center
of kukeri customs. I'll mention some of the variations I witnessed in two
nearby villages with similar practices: Pobeda (2002) and Kabile (1987), but
reserve many other variations to illustrate points in subsequent chapters.

Kukeri celebrations began in Mogila on Saturday morning, February 23.
There was no ceremonial commencement; rather, the kukeri began gathering
at the square and when the bride and "enough" other figures had arrived
(in this case, about twelve) the drummer struck up a song, the others gathered around him, and they all set off on the canvass. The transvestite bride
wore a striped red and white skirt covered by an elaborately embroidered
white dress apron, white blouse, and a red wool vest. His head was covered
by a white scarf with flowers appended—a rather simple imitation of a traditional folk bridal headdress. He carried a purse over his shoulder rather than
the traditional distaff carried by the bride in Kabile. The masked kukeri wear
very similar dress: skirts, dress aprons, blouses, and vests. Unlike the bride
they wear a traditional male leg covering—white wool wrapped around the
calves with black crisscrossing bindings, finished off with primitive shoes
made from pigskin (*tsurvuli*). They also wear a leather harness, often adorned
with beads, that supports the extensive collection of small bells around their

waist—the number varied from ten to well over fifty. Their masks are shaped like a bishop's miter that also covers the face, with holes for mouth and eyes and a protruding red nose, all covered with different colored sequins in elaborate patterns. Many have one or more mirrors at the top, often explained as another tool to deflect evil. They are edged in ribbon, with a collection of long ribbons flowing down the back of the mask. They make a brilliant impact, especially if the sun is shining on the sequins.

When the group set out to visit houses there was no fiancé or priest among them. The former joined the group before they had hit many houses, but the priest didn't arrive until the early afternoon. Prior to the future groom's arrival the bride was escorted by a masked kuker (much as he was the entire day in the village of Kabile) and then the betrothed couple led the group until the priest arrived whereupon he took the lead with the couple close behind. The Pobeda group was always led by a bride and groom and there was no priest. As the day wore on in Mogila more participants joined the group including additional masked kukeri, a couple of teenage girls among them, as well as a collection of comic figures: a bear trainer with a bear, Gypsy figures wielding lipstick, a couple in pajamas with overstuffed buttocks carrying a set of bellows full of ash, and a shoe-shine team. The new figures provided an infusion of energy just as the kukeri, who had been at it all morning, began to slow down a bit. When the group reached the field at one end of the village they all lay down on the ground for half an hour or so, which also revitalized them.

Whoever was leading the group would test the gate of the village house as the group approached. A locked gate meant no one was home or they were not receiving the kukeri (there were instances of both). If the gate was open they would enter the yard and proceed to knock on the door. The entire group entered if there was room in the yard. The betrothed couple would greet the people as they came out of the door with a few dance steps, which quickly gave way to a sort of free-for-all. The kukeri messed up the hair of the householders, pushing off hats and scarves in the process. The priest anointed everyone and occasionally dumped his whole pail of water on select residents while masked kukeri descended on them hitting them on the back, poking them with the shepherds' crocks they carried, pinching their thighs and generally roughhousing and wrestling, eventually throwing them to the ground.

A common tactic was for the kukeri to approach a man, attempt to pinch him on the inner thigh, and then put an arm around the man's thigh and lift him up. If successful this one-legged lift tips over the victim or at least leaves him grabbing onto the kuker to stay upright, subjecting him to more pinches and preventing escape. Other times a pair of kukeri worked together, each taking a leg and lifting the man up together, perhaps jostling him in the air before setting him back down. The shoe shiners insisted on shining the host's shoes but actually smeared polish up his entire leg while beating the foot painfully with the wooden side of the shoe brush. The worst abuse was reserved for men, but girls and women were also hit lightly and marked with lipstick by the Gypsies or covered in ash by the bellows carriers. In several houses women and young girls locked themselves in the house and watched from the safety of windows or balconies. Kukeri tried to enter these houses to get to them but desisted if the doors were locked.

At some point in this melee a household representative offered his or her hand to the bride, sometimes an older grandparent, sometimes the working-age parent, and, less commonly, a younger family member. This person had money in hand, which the bride took as he kissed the proffered hand. The money was put in his purse, and the kukeri jumped ecstatically by way of acknowledgment. Eggs were also given to one of the children collecting them in a basket, a few of which ended up being thrown by kukeri at young male bystanders. Homemade wine was offered to all the guests by the hosts, and most houses also offered food: fatback and bread was common, and perhaps sandwiches, cakes, and cookies. Some households offered wine for the kukeri to take with them, but the group only had one container, which restricted them to collecting only one type of wine (this day it was white). They had nothing to put red wine in, and when the container was filled with white wine they made no effort to secure another or find a place to store it but just turned down the offers. They might take a bottle if the host offered one with a secure lid and if someone was willing to carry it, but generally they declined. That is not to say that they were not interested in drinking, which they did with abandon at each house. By early afternoon the priest, the bear, and the trainer were quite drunk, making them objects of ridicule and rendering their ritual roles rather moot as they were too drunk to fulfill them correctly. The entire group sometimes ended up together in a single yard when the greeting was especially protracted, but more often the bear trainer and shoe shiners followed individually and later, extending the mumming experience significantly for each household.

In mid-afternoon, while the group was making its way around the village, a bus arrived with about twenty individuals from the village of Turiya, approximately seventy miles northwest of Mogila. I had observed rituals there in March 1997, so I was familiar with what I saw and actually recognized some of the participants, who also remembered me. These figures call themselves "startsi" and are most noted for what they don't wear. They go shirtless with small feminine vests accentuating their otherwise naked torsos. They wear traditional mid-length peasant wool pants and wool leg wrappings, completed with traditional pigskin shoes adorned by a red and white yarn tassel ball. They generally wear about ten large bells of the round spherical type around their waist. Their masks all have nearly identical faces consisting of an oval piece of black felt, with eye, nose, and mouth holes outlined in white felt. Overlapping strips of red and white felt cut into a sawtooth pattern outline the perimeter of the face, and small pieces of animal fur provide mustaches and goatees. This is attached to a piece of goat skin that provides the back of the mask, supported by a thin wooden stick that ascends to a peak about two feet above the face. The peak is topped by a doll in bridal attire, and variously colored ribbons dangle down from the doll to the top of the mask face. The startsi typically wear pieces of these ribbons tied around their arms, neck, or wrists, and a ribbon is also tied around the handle of the wooden swords they all carry. They do not have a bridal couple but instead a transvestite baba carrying a baby (which is a doll), although some participants refer to him as a bride. He leads the group.

In Turiya itself, the leader was accompanied by a collection of ash-covered Arapi dressed in Middle Eastern attire, albeit a ragged variant. They were followed by a camel driver leading a man in a camel costume.[5] At each house the camel died or got sick and was revived, often by some action on the part of the proprietor under the camel driver's direction. This might include offering some homemade brandy, well known for its medicinal properties in Bulgarian folk medicine, but definitely providing money to the camel driver for additional treatment. Neither the camel driver and his camel nor the Arapi, all of whom were central figures in Turiya itself, performed on this day in Mogila. The visitors consisted of only the transvestite granny and the masked startsi. This group, many of whom were staying overnight at the same house where I was staying, came to "help" and "fill out" the experience, and the Mogila group planned to reciprocate with a trip to Turiya on its mumming days a couple of weeks later. The Turiya startsi followed the Mogila kukeri around the village but hung back at bit, out of the way, either outside the gate or on the margins of the group inside the yard until invited to engage more centrally by the homeowner. Most owners included them and treated them to wine and whatever food had been prepared. Some also treated the transvestite with money and were rewarded by a startsi dance resembling a slow-motion

Figure 1. Survakari from the village of Leskovets, near Pernik, in town for the 2006 festival.

Figure 2. Mechkari in Cherna Gora dance around the remains of the previous night's bonfire before embarking on the village canvass in 1998.

Figure 3. Bear figure in the village of Yardzhilovtsi in 1997.

Figure 4. The groom and transvestite bride lead a folk dance in front of a Lesnovo home in 2006, joined by two members of the household in a camel costume.

Figure 5. Kukeri in Mogila enjoy refreshments, sanctified with holy water by the mock priest, at the village bar after the completion of their rounds in 2002.

Figure 6. The Kabile transvestite bride, perched atop a wooden plow, offers collective blessings for the village at its kukeri finale in 1988.

version of the twist—much more standardized and choreographed than the running and jumping of Mogila mummers.

As the group continued around the village some houses were passed by—a death in the family during the preceding year was the common explanation—and a few residents turned the mummers away. Many met the group at their gate with wine, money, and eggs rather than having them come into the yard. This seemed to reduce the extent of harassment but would still elicit a dance from the couple and the requisite jumping of the kukeri. Conversely, at other houses the group was requested to perform more than the usual activities. One host asked the entire group to dance around several fruit trees planted in the yard. Several times the bride was given a broom with which she swept the area in front of the door. This replicated the standard activity of the kukeri in Pobeda, where the bride enters each yard with a small broom and sweeps all around, especially in front of the door. With the assistance of kukeri the Pobeda bride also hurls anything sitting around the entryway out into the yard, such as the ubiquitous work shoes left by the door. In Mogila such mischief was reserved for a couple of kukeri who, unlike the others, never removed their masks and followed the group at a distance behaving more maliciously, one swinging a rather large branch at onlookers and pushing over garbage cans or anything else found along the street in front of the house. In cases where the kukeri had been locked out, one of these two often climbed over the wall or fence and threw items around the yard. There was clearly a menacing aura to their presence evident in both their actions and onlookers' anxious expressions as they passed.

After visiting about two-thirds of the houses in the village, the Mogila group returned single-file to the village square, formed a circle, and then disbanded. Many went home to change clothes, but they soon returned to join the others who went directly to the tavern on the square. Much merrymaking ensued, beginning with beer and grilled ground meat (*kebabcheta* and *kufteta*) at tables outside the tavern (see figure 5), followed by dancing to *chalga*[6] music inside the bar (where the aggressive horseplay of the day periodically erupted again), and concluding at the homes of kukeri where small banquets and drinking continued late into the night.

All this took a toll on the second day of the two-day event, as many kukeri were too hung over to carry on with the same gusto. Most of the kukeri who managed to get to the square at the appointed hour Sunday morning were teenagers too young to have been drinking the night before; their older compatriots were still knocked out. As the latter began to arrive, their slow gait and the grimaces produced by the clang of their bells confirmed the cause of their tardiness. Eventually a critical mass of kukeri accumulated, as well as the bride- and groom-to-be, and they picked up the canvass where they had left off the previous afternoon. The late start put the smaller group behind schedule so the house visits were a bit abbreviated, and the group literally ran between houses. On this day, then, they more closely resembled the Pobeda kukeri who always ran quickly from house to house, providing a visual explanation for the Bulgarian idiom "to run around like a kukeri bride." The Pobeda event was also not as jocular, with less roughhousing, limited drunkenness, and even some admonishments from the bride to the masked kukeri about weaknesses in their performance. Seemingly symbolic of this stricter regime, the Pobeda groom-to-be carried an old shotgun. The quicker pace, however, was hard on the hung-over Mogila kukeri. A few visiting startsi with their transvestite joined the group after an hour or so, as did some additional local kukeri who had managed to pull themselves together. Despite the late start and physical disabilities, they insisted that they had to visit all the houses, which they did by early afternoon, only an hour behind their ideal schedule.

By the end many participants had recovered their vigor, perhaps from the hair of the dog that bit them. Others who had slept off the worst of their hangovers joined them as well, reanimating the group. Some of the missing Turiya startsi now emerged, dressed not in their masks but in the black-face makeup and costumes of the Arapi described previously. Various other figures came out as everyone prepared for the finale on the square, considered the central event of the pre-spring ritual cycle.

By early afternoon the Mogila village square was abuzz with people and activities. Cars were parked on the side of the road leading into the square, confirming the presence of visitors from the town of Yambol and neighboring villages. There were a couple of Romani merchants selling cotton candy and inflated cartoon figures tied to strings. There was a table with chairs for VIPs set up in a prime viewing location, supplied with wine and food. These guests included the mayor and some donors who had given significant funds to underwrite festival travel expenses for the Mogila kukeri group. Everybody else stood around the perimeter of the large square, two or three deep in some places.

Continuing a socialist-era formula, the activities got under way with a performance by a traditional folk dance troupe from the city of Yambol, accompanied by bagpipe (*gaida*) music. After this, the startsi from Turiya enacted an abridged version of their own ritual finale, which I had witnessed in situ in 1997. A grass hut was set up in the square and the entire entourage, led by the transvestite granny and his escort, circled the hut several times, dancing and strutting in the usual startsi form. There was taunting between the Arapi and the masked startsi, which eventually devolved into a mock battle between the two groups, with the startsi getting the better of the Arapi who rolled about on the ground rather than standing to fight. At some point in the scrimmage, the transvestite granny got into the hut with an Arap other than his escort, followed by several other Arapi piling in as well. His jealous escort then set the hut on fire and the molesters ran away, allowing the startsi to save the baba and child. The hut burnt down as the startsi escorted the redeemed baba and child around the square and the group departed.

The Turiya performance was followed by a Mogila camel group, which had not been out for the village canvass. The group included a man in a camel costume led by two handlers who performed the previously described scenario of camel death and recovery in front of a young symbolic village couple dressed in traditional folk costume. After this, the kukeri group that had been assembling down one of the roads leading to the square entered to the accompaniment of bagpipe and drum music. There were many more participants than for the village canvass. In addition to more masked kukeri, including a group of about twenty children, there was a bear led by a Gypsy couple (the woman leading the bear and the man providing a mock accompaniment on a fiddle), a man with a donkey figure attached at his waist (as if he were riding a donkey), and two young men dressed as comic women (not obvious prostitutes but very buxom with a bit too much makeup), wearing scarves around their head and dresses that had to be continually adjusted for the sake of modesty. The couple that previously received the camel drivers joined the bride and his fiancé pulling an old threshing board with a bag of straw and a wooden container (much like a cheese hoop) used to hold seed while sowing. The bride figure carried a cradle with a doll.

The first masked kukeri pulled a large wooden plow as if they were draft animals. These two and the next six kukeri that entered the square were no longer wearing their sequined masks but rather large animalistic masks, imitative of some rather large animal heads with pronounced snouts and threatening mouths. These masks were made by a village craftsman who keeps the masks at his house and lends them out to kukeri to wear for the annual mumming finale. Several kukeri carried an animal skin (usually rabbit) on a rope attached to a handle. The same instrument had been carried by a couple of the

Kabile kukeri (and kukeri in other villages I visited as well), and they would regularly slap the pavement with the animal skin as they moved through the village, making a loud whip-like popping sound. The kukeri also seem to be wearing more bells than they wore on Saturday and Sunday morning. The entire group circled the square with the masked kukeri remaining around the perimeter of three sides of the square and the other figures moving to the center where the threshing board and cradle were left. The bear trainers enacted a visit to the symbolic family with the bear walking on their backs (a form of folk massage with curative potential). All the while the donkey frolicked around using the donkey's head to lift the skirts of various female characters, only to be chased away by the bride.

As with most kukeri events, the major activity of this finale was a pantomime enactment of the agricultural cycle. It began with the groom measuring off his plot, first using his shepherd's staff and then stepping it off to confirm the measurement before marking the corners. Then with the bride leading two masked kukeri pulling the plow, and the groom behind the plow, they enacted the plowing of the plot, followed by the man sowing the field from the wooden seed holder. He then rolled the emptied container on the ground to divine the outcome of the coming agricultural season—if it lands open side up, it will be a bountiful year, but if it lands upside down, the year will be disappointing. The bride ran after the container as it rolled and tipped it with his foot so it fell right side up, thus insuring a good year for the village. This was followed by a pantomime harvest for which the bride enlisted several of the masked kukeri to assist as they walked across the imaginary plot bending to imitate the cutting of sheaves. The bag of straw was then spread on the square, and the donkey was corralled by the bride, with some comic difficulty, to pull the threshing board over the "wheat." While these characters were distracted by their work, a villager emerged from the crowd and grabbed the doll from the cradle. He was immediately apprehended by masked kukeri who quickly broke from their ranks to nab him. The bride retrieved the doll, and the kukeri beat him rather forcefully. In Pobeda and Kabile the bride himself was the object of larceny attempts, both during the canvass and at the finale.

With the harvest completed and the baby secured, the groom was lifted up on the shoulders of two kukeri and in a loud voice called for a bountiful harvest and general abundance. In Pobeda and Kabile this capstone invocation was offered by the bride from atop the upended wooden plow, which he climbed upon with the support of the masked kukeri (see figure 6). The masked kukeri, who have marked each important event in this performance with excited jumping, then joined hands with the other performers and began a horo around the square, which the public gradually joined.

This finale was similar in form to the one I observed in Kabile and Pobeda, but it was decidedly more comic. The Kabile performance was the most somber. The Pobeda event included comic elements, but they were somewhat segregated from the serious ritual. The children's group, for example, came to the village square first and then exited rather than being part of the major group. In Mogila and Pobeda the plowing was made difficult by recalcitrant kukeri forced into service as draft animals; in both cases the offending kukeri had to be disciplined or exchanged for more cooperative ones, but the episode in Mogila was comically elaborated, whereas even this element had a serious overtone in Pobeda. It was hard to be serious in Mogila with the bear and its trainers roaming around the square jesting with the public, while the energetic and mischievous donkey constantly pestered the performers no matter what serious effort engaged them.

From Ritual to Festival

In addition to the annual village enactments described above, and the occasional reciprocal invitations to visit other villages, mumming groups from across Bulgaria also mobilize for a circuit of annual and biennial competitions held in several towns and cities across the country. These events consist of large processions along the main street of town leading to the central square where individual village groups perform in turn before a large audience and a panel of judges. Each group is preceded by a sign with the name of the village or town, usually carried by a villager in folk costume, and accompanied by musicians. Upon reaching the square the masked figures typically fan out to form a circle, the size depending on the number of participants in the group, and then move around in a circle demonstrating the steps and rhythms typical of village practice while also showing off their costumes and masks. Inside the circle the other figures set up props and carry on in character. The masked figures stop in place and the action shifts to the group in the center, which then reenacts some element of the village events.

The most common performance is an idealized house visit. Idealized because, as noted in the previous discussion, house visits vary significantly within a village. Traditional practice is also stressed, so the couple being visited is likely to be represented as traditional peasants in folk costume rather than contemporary villagers. There is also a bias toward more traditional ritual figures such as the bear and bear trainer over the comic, burlesque, or political figures that animate village practice. The latter, however, may also be present, especially in groups with large numbers of participants. Rather than a house visit, some villages perform an abridged version of their village finale, including, for example, the enactment of the agricultural cycle.

I use the term "festival" to distinguish this activity from the previously described "rituals" because these are common terms used by Bulgarians for the two different venues. I also believe they make sense analytically, but I recognize that the festivals are actually more stereotyped and perhaps ritualistic than local activities and also clearly operate as national ritual, whereas many village rituals display a freedom of expression that is nothing if not festive.

Given the focus on the performance at the square, and the fact that the line of groups awaiting their turn moves slowly and haltingly, the festivals cannot accurately be called parades. But the groups are lined up in a rather long procession, and that, too, becomes part of the festivities, as the groups perform or "practice" while they wait their turn. When they do advance along the line, they are likely to put on their masks and strut to their traditional rhythms in parade fashion. Here the experience is closer to that of the village ritual. Indeed, the street will likely be lined with an audience that prefers this close-up experience with the groups to the more distant observation of rehearsed performance at the crowded square. The public here might have their picture taken with a striking costumed figure or even ask one to dance with their young child as a means of insuring health and warding off evil. Each group will also have some co-villagers present for support—they will follow along beside the group rather than watch their competitors at the square. After a group completes their performance at the square they often continue informal activities at an area removed from the major festivities. Again, they might be joined there by villagers who have come to support them, as well as relatives or friends from the town. After all the villages have performed at the square the judges award modest monetary prizes and medals to the best groups.

In any year there are several such festivals across the country. As previously mentioned, the most famous by far is held in Pernik every other year. It is so large that it requires two full days to accommodate all the groups that attend. Tourists come from all over Europe, as well as Asia and the United States, to see the event, and the organizers also invite carnival groups from other European countries to participate. The town is now a member of the European Federation of Carnival Cities, which includes members from non-

European countries as well. Despite this international flavor, also evident in the socialist era but to a lesser degree, the vast majority of groups and the dominant impact are still Bulgarian. The success of the festival has garnered Pernik and its surrounding villages a central role in the national(ized) image of these rituals. More modest festivals occur in towns like Yambol and Razlog, and even in some villages such as Kamen and Kalipetrovo. These events are smaller than the Pernik event with fewer groups attending, usually from a more circumscribed area of the country. In 2002 I was personally aware of seven such festivals that took place between late January and late March, and there were probably others I did not hear about.

The festival experience seems a world away from the village ritual previously described. The latter is a classic communal rite with supernatural overtones but is also rich in innovation and spontaneity, whereas the festival is more reminiscent of a staged performance by an amateur folklore ensemble. The group that performs at the festival is usually much larger than the group carrying out the ritual in the village. Still, it would be a mistake to draw too stark a contrast between these events which are interactive and reinforcing. For many mummers, participation in festivals is the main attraction, but village activity is considered an obligatory prerequisite. This is their own interpretation, since extant village activity is not required by any festival organizers. Indeed the festivals were first devised in the 1960s precisely to displace what Communist Party officials considered backward village practices. With the festivals, leaders hoped to redefine and relocate village rituals that were ideologically objectionable (superstitious), and perhaps even politically threatening (think large organized groups of masked men), into highly regulated urban folkloric performances. By gathering together the disparate practices of different villages into joint festivals, the diverse rituals were recast as a single custom that could then exemplify a pan-Bulgarian folk culture in support of nationalistic objectives. The subsequent spread of the term "kukeri" for many of these rites not previously known by that term is evidence of this outcome. Designation as "folklore" also intended to downplay the existing vitality of the rituals, since folklore was already and always something that was old and needed to be preserved or protected. Preservation "as folklore" implied an academic or performative re-creation. Of course, as Donna Buchanan's (2006:pt. 2) analysis of professional ensembles shows in detail, these re-creations also recast the history and meaning of these traditions.[7]

Unlike some other folk practices, however, mumming was a thriving tradition at the time of attempted co-optation, and was still closely associated and identified with particular villages. From the start, their staged performance referenced a village activity and a village group. Ironically the associated emphasis on authenticity in folklore and folk performance helped reproduce this link to actual village practice. For many mummers, to perform in festivals without a village reference would be inauthentic or a misrepresentation. In these festivals, groups were never "fulfilling the ritual" in the same way that an amateur group might perform the semi-forgotten or neglected rituals associated with rainmaking but rather were always re-performing the village performance, and this required the latter to make the former authentic. As we will see in chapter 5, this association with local/village identity becomes important in understanding the ethnic and national imagery of the rituals. Festival participation has also helped sustain village practice by insuring that villagers have the necessary ritual paraphernalia which can be expensive and time-consuming. Animal skins and bells are costly and the masks can be so elaborate that they require weeks to construct. If villagers have these materials for festival activity, then they are available for village use as well (and vice versa).

The festivals are particularly valued by performers for the travel they occasion. Usually the group rents a bus and travels together. There is plenty of alcohol shared en route, and the journey itself becomes an enjoyable and festive occasion. Longer trips can be expensive, but some village groups use the money they collect in the village to help cover travel costs; they admit that they could not afford to go to the festivals without the village collection, and this is yet another connection that sustains the rituals in the village. Once at the festival the participants are usually provided free lodging if needed and perhaps some food. There is also the hope of winning a prize which could be used to cover some of the travel expenses. So these trips are subsidized in various ways and provide villagers a chance to see and visit other parts of the country that they might otherwise rarely see. The most impressive groups might garner invitations to other countries where the subsidy is more significant. In several of the villages I visited, the ritual group had performed in folk festivals and parades abroad, usually in Western Europe. These opportunities not only provided a rare chance to sightsee but also offered an external (Western) validation to the local activity. They are also major sources of conflict and jealousy. Groups might be approached directly by a foreign organizer who has seen them at the Pernik festival, but sometimes invitations are issued to county cultural workers who then decide which village group in their county should get the offer. Accusations of favoritism and nepotism abound.

The popularity of these festivals nationally and internationally has validated the rituals in the eyes of villagers, which translates into efforts to sustain and support them locally. This popularity also includes the attention of folklorists and ethnographers like myself. In Bulgaria there is significant scholarly attention to these rituals, and the Pernik festival is always preceded by an academic conference. Researchers go to villages and towns to observe local practices, but they are also likely to appear on the panel of judges at various festivals. Having a judge on the panel who has studied your village is certainly considered an advantage by villagers hoping to win a festival prize. It indicates recognition of the village's significance and establishes a social relationship. Many of the scholars who study these rituals are well known to village practitioners, and on the numerous occasions when I have traveled with these scholars to villages, they are almost always asked for advice to improve the village's festival performance. The specialists then debate among themselves the impact and desirability of their "involvement." Some argue aggressively against such involvement, whereas others counter that by having and participating in the festivals they are already involved.

Although the dominant support flows from festival to village ritual, these two contexts are mutually reinforcing. The commitment to village activities makes the festival meaningful, and it is hard to imagine that the festivals could generate such enthusiasm and support were the participants not attached to the rituals at home. For many enthusiasts, the village activity trumps the festival in importance, and some villages with ritual activity do not even participate in the festivals; the most common explanations are that the group is too small, ineffectively organized, or insufficiently provisioned with impressive costumes and masks. Still, the festivals are renowned nationally and are often covered by national and local media, so the attention to the rituals generated by the festivals supports their local continuity even in villages that do not attend them.

Motivations

Mumming is fueled by many motivations other than festival participation. The most obvious are the purported supernatural objectives. In addition to driving away evil and danger, the rituals explicitly aim to promote fertility, abundance, health, and longevity, goals collectively reconceptualized by some as inviting generic good luck. I spoke with Bulgarians around the country who expressed a straightforward belief in such ritual efficacy, and who believed the failure to carry out the rituals would result in material losses or bad luck. I noted an increase in this belief over the years of my research, concomitant with an increase in ritual and festival activity in many parts of the country. It is not too much of a stretch to see this as a budding revitalization movement, as it coincided with deteriorating socioeconomic conditions and increasing political frustration. As one mummer observed, "These customs have survived thousands of years, now that I think about it, many more than the countless messed-up systems that have come and gone in this country. Tell me, would they have lasted all this time if there was no effect." Such believers were joined by others who I do not think believed in the ritual's material efficacy but liked the political message implied by embracing it—a lack of faith in the country's or the world's rationality (see chapter 3 and the conclusion). Even at the end of my research, however, individuals espousing belief in any sort of supernatural link remained a minority. One villager actually reversed the logic of the mummer quoted above and opined that the country would not be in such a mess if mumming was effective.

Much more common was what I call the "agnostic retort," which did not advance any supernatural role but stopped short of denying the possibility. The agnostic often attributed the idea of the supernatural role to the past or to others: "they say it drives off evil" or "people used to say it scared off bad spirits." If pressed about their own beliefs, they were noncommittal, offering shoulder shrugs and concluding "who knows." For many Bulgarians the supernatural dimension of the rituals is much like superstition in the United States. People do not have to believe in supernatural powers in order to avoid walking under a ladder or diverting from a path crossed unexpectedly by a black cat. Many Bulgarians express a similar sentiment toward mumming, disavowing belief in its supernatural promise but not wanting to miss the blessings just in case. If all these individuals are counted, the potential role of supernatural belief in these rituals is significant. Some find a more practical explanation for the same positive benefits. In an emic ecological analysis that Marvin Harris would celebrate, villagers in the Rhodope Mountains told Barbara Cellarius (2004:204) that the loud and boisterous activity of the kukeri actually drive away snakes and other vermin from around the house and garden, clearly protecting the household economy.

Apart from the material impact of the rituals, participants express a collection of motivations that one might lump together as identity-based, in that they suggest a connection between the ritual practice and senses of self. These include national, village, and family affiliations. As previously noted, a common explanation for participation by ritual enthusiasts was the importance of such customs for defining Bulgarians as a people (*narod*): "If we lose our customs and traditions we lose ourselves; without these traditions we don't have any way of knowing ourselves. We'll no longer be Bulgarian." Interestingly, this notion works with either an essentialist or a constructivist understanding of nationalism, and is certainly not surprising or unexpected. That mumming traditions are so vital compared to many of the other folk customs that might fill this bill makes their role as ethno-national boundary markers especially important. These rituals are also thought by many to be uniquely Bulgarian. I was constantly assured by mummers that I could only find these activities in Bulgaria. As noted in the introduction, there *are* similar rituals throughout Europe and its former colonies, although, with the exception of carnival, which is distinctive enough to justify exclusion, Bulgaria appears somewhat unique in the extent of current practice.

With some caveats and noted reversals, we can plot a shift in mumming motivations parallel to the transformation of *căluș* rituals in Romania described by Gail Kligman (1981), from supernatural enactment to nationalistic folk performance. What becomes quickly clear in longer discussions with participants, however, is that it is not only their national identity they preserve in these rituals but their village pride as well. They maintain and reproduce village rituals to avoid embarrassment from mummers in other villages. Not to stage them is to suggest that the village lacks the strong character and self-respect that the rituals reflect. It would imply that there are not enough standup guys to see that the rituals are fulfilled, which diminishes the reputation of everyone who hails from the village—past, present, and future. The importance of village identity is thus a central motivation behind the rituals and figures centrally in subsequent discussions here. It also explains why many mummers return to their village of origin, or even go to an ancestral village where they have never lived, to participate in the rituals.

Mumming also enriches these local identities with the aura of resistance. Mumming is not so much a vehicle of resistance as it is a practice that allows villages to don the mantle of past resistance, first against Ottoman overlords and then against communist administrators, both of whom tried to curtail mumming at different times. Stories of both efforts were recounted to me by villagers. In the former case it was part of village oral history passed down through many generations. Ottoman authorities apparently found the unruly performance destabilizing, not unlike the British colonial response to some Indian rituals as described by Nicholas Dirks (1997). Many older villagers then drew a parallel between such Ottoman efforts and those they experienced directly during the Stalinist era of the 1950s, when the Communist Party tried again to prevent the practices.

In both periods villagers insist that the rituals were performed, although sometimes clandestinely. In these cases the participants retreated to the woods and mountains, often under the cover of darkness, where they performed reduced enactments, sometimes consisting of only a few men in token costumes with a few bells. Given that noise and spectacle were elemental to the ritual's supernatural effectiveness, it is nearly impossible to perform these rituals effectively *and* surreptitiously, so these efforts suggest that the politics of the event had eclipsed some of its supernatural objectives. The main outcome was to show the practitioners' tenacity and cunning. This history granted the rituals new value after 1989, when any prior resistance to the Communist Party became cultural capital that could be converted into political and financial benefits. In a country with few examples of outright resistance to the communist regime the survival of the ritual became potential evidence of noncompliance. The continuity of practice bespoke a resistance on the part of the village that could position it above those that caved in to all Communist Party demands.[8]

Still, all villagers do not participate in the rituals, so insuring village honor and abundance falls to a minority. Their willingness to shoulder the responsibility for all is often linked to family traditions and an unexplainable internal volition. The greatest consensus I obtained across all discussions with participants and nonparticipants was the insistence that one had to have a personal motivation and attachment to the rituals in order to participate. This was most commonly expressed by the Bulgarian word *merak,* translated variously as "longing," "desire," or "yearning." Merak springs from inside oneself and cannot be explained. "It's inside of you and you cannot not do it," as if the ritual were, in fact, not the product of the performers but rather a part of the performer's "soul," an internal force that moved them to don the costume and move.[9] Merak cannot be effectively produced by someone else's encouragement, nor can it be suppressed if it is present, although it can die out inexplicably.

One's probability of having ritual merak is greatly increased if other members of one's family have it, especially fathers or uncles. This means that you grow up surrounded by intense ritual activity and will likely be directly involved from an early age. Children are commonly dressed in ritual costumes and paraded around the margins long before they are able to actually participate in any organized mumming activity. In this sense, ritual participation is recognized as a family tradition and is said to be passed on by inheritance, although it is understood more as an element of "soul" than "blood," since brothers from the same family were commonly distinguished by the presence and absence of merak. Because this desire comes from inside oneself, it is indeed an important element of one's sense of self, and having villagers with merak is a reasonable measure of the character of the village as a whole.

Although merak is hard to describe, it is easy to recognize. As I tried to relate in the preceding descriptions, ritual enthusiasm and engagement seem to overwhelm many of the participants. This commonly includes a complete personality change as quiet or reserved men become outgoing and boisterous. There are also apparent physical effects. Merak makes it possible for men to withstand temperatures below ordinary endurance with no complaint and carry out strenuous activities beyond their ordinary abilities without expected fatigue. I would be tempted to suggest adrenalin rush as an explanation were it not for the fact that it lasts far too long. In Mogila after the full day of canvassing, the participants were equally animated when they returned to the village tavern after having been home for dinner and having changed into street clothes. A woman there assured me that "they are not like this the rest of the year. Only for these days," and indeed it was a very different impression of the villagers than I had gotten on a previous visit. Alcohol may be a contributing factor but certainly not the determinant one—many of these men are heavy drinkers the rest of the year as well, and others do not drink excessively during the ritual.

Mummers are also not in the type of altered state associated with ecstatic ritual (cf. Lewis 1971). Indeed, although merak reaches its fullest expression in ritual events, it can be seen outside the ritual context, and I often saw it in conversations with participants at other times of the year. My methodology of visiting villages and seeking out knowledgeable informants insured that I was often directed to the most involved activists with the most merak. For some, I could see the transformation immediately upon identifying my research interest. The mere mention of my interest in mumming produced a transformation in the individual and an outpouring of information. My trip to Gorna Vasilitsa was perhaps the most exemplary. After speaking with villagers on the square and getting the same referral from a couple of sources, we headed off to the upper hamlet of this divided village (more on this in chapter 3) to find the man. When we got to his house there was no one in sight, and the gate was locked. Several calls got no response, although a neighbor came out of a nearby house and assured us he was home. We were actually debating about what to do next when a man in his late thirties with a full beard and in work clothes emerged. After a hesitant and perhaps suspicious greeting, we explained why we had come. There was a physical change in the man—his expression became animated and his body grew more erect—and he quickly invited us into his yard.

His joy and enthusiasm increased with each question, and after about ten minutes he seemed unable to stand still. He then went into the barn and began pulling out all sorts of ritual paraphernalia, hurling it out the door into the yard in front of us. Eventually he emerged with what was the largest bell I had ever seen; it was wider than the man himself and reached from his waist nearly to the ground. It was made expressly for the ritual and was his pride and joy. As we continued to admire the bell, he took off into the house telling us to wait where we were. He soon emerged from the second-story window and began climbing up to the attic opening, employing what resembled rock-climbing techniques on whatever outcrops the simple architecture of the house provided. Hanging from one arm on a pulley beam extended from the top of the attic window, with one foot braced on the small ledge below and the other leg dangling precariously in the air, he used his free hand to reach in and pull out more masks, which he hurled down to us. I was mortified by the damage he was doing to the elaborate masks as they dropped a couple of stories and more terrified that he was going to fall. The horror of being responsible for an injury had me begging him to stop. He only did so after he had thrown down several masks for us to see. Most of them were significantly deteriorated, so I felt better about the fall they endured, but they still revealed significant artistry and workmanship.

He subsequently invited us inside to continue the discussion over coffee. When I commented on his evident enthusiasm for the ritual, he replied: "all year I'm a kuker, but only two days am I human." The implication is that only during the two days of kukeri celebrations does he express his true self—the rest of the year he is in disguise. The Bulgarian word for human, *chovek*, also means person, so he is perhaps also suggesting that since mumming is always a part of him, it is only during these two days that he attains maximal personal dignity through self-expression. If so, this achievement is likely linked to expectations of masculinity, since chovek is also sometimes used in Bulgarian for "man." I pursue the latter connection in the next chapter but here simply want to note the visceral connection and commitment that many ritual participants have to these customs. I had similar if less extreme experiences across the country. In more than a few cases the individuals insisted that they don their ritual costumes for me, which can be an elaborate and difficult process. As I noted in the introduction, the contrast with my previous experiences of interviewing rural Bulgarians on political and economic topics could not have been more extreme. I only needed to identity my interest in mumming to be embraced and provided with an outpouring of information. Some of this information was politically sensitive and revealed problematic relations in the village that would certainly have been censored or minimized were I asking directly about local politics, yet they came out easily in the context of ritual discussions. This difference convinced me of the value of these rituals as a window into Bulgarian life and postsocialism generally.

The commitment to these rituals was also evident materially. Many costume elements are expensive, and I heard numerous stories from participants about the large amounts of money they had invested in the rituals. More often these reports came from members of their families complaining to me about the sacrifices forced on the family by a husband, father, or son's ritual merak: savings for major purchases such as appliances and even automobiles "squandered" on expensive bells and rare animal skins, as well as time taken off work with no pay, not only for the rituals but to travel across the country to locate desirable or rare costume materials. In one of my favorite such tales a woman from Razlog reported that her husband had used the substantial state payment they received for the birth of their third child (equivalent to four or five months salary at the time in 1973) to buy a new set of bells before she and the child even left the hospital. As a result they were left without cash for various infant needs. She later learned that he had actually borrowed additional money in order to make the purchase, which took some time and sacrifice to repay. Thereafter she always referred to them sarcastically as "the golden bells," because "for all they cost us they should have been gold." Improvements to costumes with such purchases sometimes allow the owners to lend their older or inferior models to someone else, so the costs of extensive village participation can be subsidized in part by one or more enthusiasts.

A woman in Gigintsi told me she sold a prize hen to a ritual fanatic because he loved the feathers and insisted he had to have them for his mask. Seeing that hen had inspired him to design a whole new mask. She refused at first because the hen was a good layer, but he insisted and threatened that if she didn't sell it to him he'd steal it. "So I sold it to him. What was I going to do? I know he'd have taken it, just like he said. They are serious! Better to get a good price, and he paid me a good price, I made sure of that." Mind-boggling tales of sacrificing money or time and crazy stories of risking injury or arrest, all for the sake of the ritual, were a basic trope in the accounts of the rituals I solicited from participants and their relatives.

Of course, a large part of this commitment comes from sheer enjoyment of the events. Indeed, they are often referred to as games or play rather than rituals or customs (although see note 2 in this chapter). This factor was brought home to me at a conference I attended in Trent, Italy, on comparative European masked rituals. A presenter at the final session of the conference began his discussion of Irish mumming by accusing the assembled scholars of taking all the fun out of these events. In truth, this is part of my objective here—to take the fun and games out of mumming so that we can see the serious cultural resources the rituals exhibit and the important work they do. However, the fun is essential to their effectiveness in these serious roles, so it is important to keep the sheer joy of these events front and center. They are great fun and, having been involved in so many, it is easy to appreciate why villagers would want to participate and to insure their survival.

Changes

Just as the motives for participation have shifted over time, so have the particulars of practice. Contemporary events contain figures and characters that can be traced to different historical periods from Ottoman soldiers to communist-era civil-defense agents. The festival system added a major motor to the pace of change. Most notable is what one might call costume inflation. All the older villagers I asked confirmed that the large extravagant masks, which literally overwhelm the rituals today, developed in an effort to make an impression with the festival judges and audience. Masks have gotten progressively larger, sometimes reaching twelve to fifteen feet. They may require two or three men to even carry them, and even more hands to get them on and off a man's shoulders. Balancing such constructions is a challenge and may even require counterweights to keep the wearer from tipping forward or backward. The large masks are also adorned with more arresting elements, including the aforementioned animals such as foxes and wild fowl, perhaps with the latter in the mouth of the former. A similar inflation is evident in bells with bigger and more numerous collections needed to make greater impressions. The gigantic bell owned by the mummer in Gorna Vasilitsa was used primarily in the festivals and perhaps at the village finale. As he explained its value, the village group always gets more attention at festivals, including media coverage, when he wears that bell.

Ironically the increasing centrality of masks in festivals has diminished their importance in village practice. Participants could never carry these unwieldy constructions all day or maneuver them through the village gates and yards, nor could they make the requisite noise that comes from vigorous jumping. Some of the largest masks are worn only for the ritual inauguration or finale. More moderate ones might be carried and worn intermittently. In the village of Yardzhilovtsi the mechkari deposit their masks at a central point in a neighborhood until they have visited the surrounding houses, they then put them on again for the trip to the next neighborhood whereupon they remove them once more. And these are not their largest masks—the massive masks they don for the finale are too big even for this limited use. This means that for most of the household visits the majority of participants do not wear their masks. Some older villagers complained about this change, noting that in the past complete anonymity was mandatory and not knowing identities made the event more interesting. In other villages such as Mogila mummers still wear the manageable sequins-covered masks for house visits, and then switch to the larger animalistic festival masks for the village finale on the square.

In some villages the house visits have ceased altogether, and the village activity is reduced to a performance at the village square, much like the festival performance. Indeed, the activity on the square has sometimes grown into a mini-festival complete with judges and prizes for the best mask or costume. This socialist innovation added a material incentive which threatened the perpetuation of the rituals after 1989, when village administrators could no longer afford the expected monetary awards. Lack of awards became a common excuse for anemic turnout. These linked outcomes cannot be blamed solely on mask inflation, however, since it is not necessarily the villages with the largest masks that have reduced house visits. The kukeri of Vasil Levski, for example, wear the same conical hoods they have worn for decades, and yet participants no longer visit individual houses. In Kalugerovo the masks are even easier to manage, and yet the house visit is supplemental at best to the central event on the square.

The festivals have also inspired groups to change costume materials. As suggested above, animal skins and animal elements have increasingly replaced synthetic material and fabric. There is also a shift from short-hair sheep skins to long-hair goat skins, which has significant gender implications pursued in the next chapter. Participants describe these innovations as more appealing, and, like the masks, they are thought to make a stronger impression with the judges. They are also justified as being more "authentic," but this is a mythic authenticity since some of the oldest pictures I saw from ritual groups dating to the interwar period showed just the opposite: simple, makeshift costumes with normal-sized cow/sheep bells.

The assumed "authenticity" of animal materials reflects the belief in an ancient origin of mumming prior to the availability of cloth or sequins. This notion also runs counter to a rough correlation between location, costume, and timing of the rituals, which, although not definitive, is evident enough to suggest that the animal fascination was not original everywhere. In gross outlines the animalistic costumes and themes are more pronounced in New Year's customs, which are more common in mountainous and semi-mountainous regions, whereas the use of fabric and other materials is more evident in the late-winter/pre-spring events, which are more common in the plains. The costumes and timing thus reflect different economies. The centrality of pastoral activity in the hills and mountains makes the animal imagery more resonate and the materials more available, whereas the focus on agrarian activity in the plains economy makes material from crops like cotton or flax more available and meaningful (although wool remains very central here as well). The latter costumes also incorporate more reflective materials (first mirrors and now sequins) which are commonly linked by researches to veneration of the sun, an obvious focus for an agricultural cult.

The different timing also fits with this correlation. Given that the rituals are intended to drive away evil and bring luck, it is interesting that one can associate the different periods of ritual practice with the especially dangerous times in the two different economies. The winter ritual falls just at the time when flock and herd animals are birthing, and the pre-spring rituals mark the transition to the growing season which can also be dangerous if early warmth sparks growth that is destroyed by late frosts. The historical documentation necessary to confirm this proposition does not exist, but the logic of the model and its rough fit with current ritual activity certainly justify consideration.[10] The economic link is yet another possible factor explaining the commitment to the rituals and their value as cultural repositories.

Another change evident in the memories of current practitioners is the loosening of the age and sex criteria for participation. An earlier requirement that mummers be bachelors is only rarely enforced, and ritual participants now include retirees as well as young children, including some girls and young women. Time compression is also a commonly cited change, as village rituals have been squeezed into shorter and shorter time frames. Within the memory of older villagers the rituals actually continued for weeks. The participants would dress in their costumes and go around the village during the evening every night for a week, or even once or twice a week for a number of weeks, leading up to the major village activity, which itself might require a few days. On these earlier excursions they might visit the houses of friends or co-participants to socialize, eat, and drink. The rituals today are commonly reduced to one day, two at the most. This reflects the extensive involvement in wage labor in the socialist period which made it difficult to juggle longer celebrations.

Winter rituals usually fall on either the 1st or 14th of January. The former is a holiday, of course, but those who celebrate on the latter brag about not allowing work discipline to affect their practice and insist that many employers in the area fully expect the workers to be out on that day. Ritual enthusiasts around Pernik claim that the practice is so pervasive that employers cannot afford to take action or they would lose a large part of the workforce. This was indeed a limitation in the socialist period with its perpetual shortage of workers, but much less so since 1989. By the late 1990s I was regularly told that particular ritual participants (such as someone good at the role of priest or a man particularly suited for the bride or the man with a more attractive bear costume) were missing from the ritual because of work demands.

Pre-spring rituals are tagged to Lenten fasts which begin on Monday. In some cases villages shifted the main event from Monday or Sunday/Monday to Sunday or Saturday/Sunday to avoid work conflicts, but in most villages the major events have "always" been held on the weekend. However, there has been a loosening of which weekend. In the past the rituals were performed the weekend before either meat or cheese Lent. Now villagers increasingly choose a weekend around the time of Lent based on a number of other factors, including the desire not to have too many villages celebrating on the same day. The latter could limit the audience at the finale, preclude borrowing ritual paraphernalia across villages (which might reduce the number of participants), and prohibit mutual agreements between villages to join each other on their ritual dates. Some villages have even established a set calendar time (e.g., first weekend in March) as their ritual date, so that it no longer changes from year to year according to the date of Easter. So there has been a reduction in the time span of village rituals but an increase in the opportunities to continue the activity in other venues, including visiting other villages and attending festivals.

Of course the link to Lent is itself an earlier innovation, as the rituals are pre-Christian in origin and perhaps even anti-Christian in practice (the common priest figure is a comic anticlerical one and otherwise the rites have few Christian elements). Ironically the connection to Lent was stronger during the socialist period than it has been since, and no villagers expressed a robust allegiance to the ritual link with Lent. This has happened as expressed belief in the rituals' supernatural possibilities has increased a bit. Clearly the meanings of various elements of the ritual have shifted dramatically over the years, and I do not intend to pursue that type of symbolic analysis here. But one shift that seems so obvious and yet is rarely recognized merits discussion. The masked figures are universally said to drive away evil and bring good fortune, but one way they do that is to embody evil. They are the personification of multiple dangers and are placated by villagers with material offerings to secure their departure. Not to treat them and get them on their way is to invite their return all year long. They become the evil that can then be driven or, more accurately, bribed away by the villagers. Villagers and participants alike, however, insist that they are simply good forces that drive away the bad, despite the monstrous imagery and their often threatening actions. I believe there has been a shift from the former to the latter interpretation in line with the general historical move in Europe away from relations of reciprocity with the supernatural as mapped out convincingly by Jane Schneider (1990). This also partially explains the declining importance of masked anonymity: as evil incarnate, the individuals should not be recognized as human much less as neighbors; however, as benevolent co-villagers simply trying to be more threatening than the evil they seek to dispel, they need not be inhuman or unknown. This switch in rationale also supports my claim that these activities are not primarily reversals. Let us now see where a more direct reading can take us.

CHAPTER TWO

GENDER AND SEXUALITY

Driving to the village of Brezhani in southwest Bulgaria is a fitting prelude to a mumming encounter. Located at the northern edge of the Pirin Mountains, at an elevation of nearly six hundred meters, the first-time visitor has the feeling of leaving the known world behind. This impression is hardly unique to foreigners; I was traveling there in 2002 with two Bulgarian sociologists from Sofia who expressed similar sentiments. The narrow road, which doesn't go much beyond the village, twists and turns as it ascends allowing only circumscribed views of the surroundings. Not that there is much to see beyond the forests and hills in this sparsely inhabited area. Unexpectedly, around another sharp curve, the village spreads out in front of you across a small valley below. At first picturesque in this quasi-Alpine setting, the charm diminishes as you approach and the signs of neglect so characteristic of rural Bulgaria in the 1990s become evident.

I had been given the name of a village mumming enthusiast here by an accidental informant in another village. Inquiries at the village square revealed that he lived at the far edge of the village. When we arrived he was not at home, a common problem with this particular research protocol, so we began talking to a middle-aged man sitting on a pile of wood on the street across from the house. He was also a mummer, here called babugari. As we talked, a couple of young men joined us, then another, and another, until there were eight or nine, all participants in mumming and happy to tell us about it. They celebrate on New Year's and I noted to myself, with some disappointment, that direct observation might be difficult since I doubted the village was predictably accessible in the winter. This was confirmed when one of the young men told us that mumming was so popular because villagers were usually stranded in the village by snow with nothing else to do.

Well into this discussion, the man we had originally been looking for returned and invited us into his house, actually his basement *mehana*, a sort of tavern-like social room with low tables, stools, and folk decor where men clearly gathered regularly. Some of the men we had been talking with joined us, a few others took off, only to return later with friends. Word had spread quickly around the village that a foreign ethnographer was interested in mumming, and it produced a spontaneous gathering of mumming devotees. Before long the large room was full with twenty to thirty men of various ages, listening to the "interview" and contributing to what became a group discussion. Their effusive enthusiasm revealed more than the actual comments, which were often hard to follow or document because of the cacophony of excited voices. Luckily they had paid a videographer to tape the entire mumming ritual this year, and they played it on the conveniently located television while we talked.

In this casual men's-club atmosphere it was impossible to miss the link between their investment in mumming and masculinity. One young man arrived to see the video playing and complained, "We've watched this twenty times already since New Year's!" and then quickly began watching again and commenting energetically. Another entered and approached a friend sitting near me and tried to convince him to come outside for a game of volleyball, to which his friend replied, "be quiet, we're talking about babugarie here," suggesting with his tone that this was patently more important than volleyball. In a context where collective socializing is itself a masculine attribute (cf. Loizos and Papataxiarchis 1991), the fascination with mumming as a topic for regular sociability, even displacing sport for many young men, powerfully demonstrates its link to masculinity, which in turn reveals much about its continuity and increasing fortunes in places like Brezhani.

The lessons learned in Brezhani were primarily experiential. The link between mumming and masculinity was no surprise, given that the rituals were traditionally all-male affairs, commonly restricted to bachelors as part of their passage to manhood.[1] Still, the emotional and deep engagement with mumming in a collective male context outside the ritual activity itself convinced me that it is linked to male subjectivity (that is, an individual's sense of himself as a man) in more than a ritualistic way. In this chapter I suggest

that this link helps explain the continuity of mumming, both during socialism and afterward, as a redress to what others have labeled "gender crises"—
men's inability to fulfill expected gender norms as a result of changing socioeconomic conditions. But this explanation runs up against contrary changes
in ritual practice during the postsocialist period, especially increasing female participation in several villages. The paradox is resolved by looking at
the nexus of globalization, sexuality, and shifting notions of modernity. The
way this resolution works out suggests a potentially different understanding
of gender relations than that assumed in most analyses of gender, notably one
in which masculinity and femininity are less interactive.

In what follows I first point to some of the clearly masculinizing elements
of mumming events and then discuss various political and economic changes
since World War II that challenged masculine identities, making the masculine dimensions of mumming resonate. Next I discuss the contrary change of
increasing female involvement and look to newly arrived global frameworks
for interpreting mumming symbolism to account for how these seemingly
feminist and masculinizing impulses work together. This, in turn, reveals another change in mumming from a channel for suppressed homoerotic desire
to a vehicle for homophobia. In sum, changes in mumming over the past ten
years show alternative understandings of gender and sexuality in Bulgaria, as
well as their increasing reformulation in line with Western models.

Mumming and Masculinity

The most explicit evidence of mumming as essentially a ritual of masculinity
is its traditional role as a rite of passage to manhood. The associated restrictions on age and marital status are no longer commonly enforced, but they
are remembered by participants as part of the traditional rationale for mumming and thus continue to confirm the rituals' masculinizing effect. In short,
the history of mumming as a means to manhood produces its contemporary
value for demonstrating and enhancing masculinity. Moreover, mumming
as a rite of passage still exists in at least one location, the village of Lesnovo,
which is nearly a suburb of Sofia. Villagers there celebrate mumming, known
as *devidzhi*, on the weekend around the name day for Ivan (*Ivanovden*), which
falls between the more common mumming dates of January 1 and 14. The
central wedding party must all be members of the age group that will be leaving during the coming year for compulsory military service.

During the socialist period the beginning of compulsory military service (typically after graduation) was ritually elaborated with banquets, some-

times held jointly for the whole age group in the village but increasingly sponsored individually by each family with a son going into the army. There was also a smaller banquet following the swearing-in ceremony at the completion of boot camp. Military service was a commonly acknowledged symbol of adult status (even though it only seemed to intensify the doting of mothers over their sons). Much like mumming traditionally, the military was both a symbol of manhood and a formative force in producing masculinity. As mumming's supernatural efficacy in promoting manhood lost credulity, the rite-of-passage meaning was retained in Lesnovo by attaching the ritual to another socially significant (modern) and practical ma(r)ker of manhood—military service. The Lesnovo mummers are thus different every year, unlike most other villages where there is significant continuity, and participants constitute something of a fraternity. Even in Lesnovo, however, the masked figures and supplementary characters are not restricted to the same age group and include both older and younger individuals who participate annually, broadening the significance of the ritual beyond a rite of passage (although this role remains primary).

Certainly part of the ritual's utility as a rite of manhood is tied to the strength and endurance that the rites require. The large masks might seem to be the most physically demanding, and this is definitely behind the desire to have ever bigger models, but, as noted in the previous chapter, the masks have gotten so overgrown that some mummers no longer wear them for the village canvass. This might seem contrary to the suggested masculinizing role of the rituals, but the declining use of masks can actually enhance the value of the ritual for individual men wishing to demonstrate masculinity, as now their activities and talents can be associated with them individually. The more rigid masking discipline of the past would limit the ability of individual men to benefit from the masculine displays of the ritual, as their identity might not be evident. So, in regard to masculinity, as the rituals' performative dimension has eclipsed its constitutive functions, it has become more important to know who is who. Now men can wear large masks in part of the ritual and then remove them to make sure everyone sees who commands this large asset and who has managed the demanding maneuvers.

Similarly, without masks, it is also clear who has the most or largest bells. The ubiquitous bells are perhaps the most explicit testimony to manly strength and endurance. Depending on the type of bells, their number, and their size, the collection can be extremely heavy. I lifted complexes that weighed more than seventy-five pounds, and fifty pounds was common. This burden is carried on a day-long trek around the village with constant running, danc-ing, and jumping to produce the deafening noise that signals the mummers' approach and helps drive away evil. The bells also demonstrate mummers' ability to endure and withstand pain, as some of the large models can be quite hard on the body. Mummers wear padding around their waists under the top of these bells to hold them away from the body and reduce bodily contact, but they still get hit. Many bragged to me about how bruised they had been at some point, and one young man dropped his pants to show me the black and blue evidence on his thighs from the previous day's mumming.

Masculinity is also confirmed by one's endurance to the cold, as the rituals usually occur during very cold periods and the mummers are out-side most of the day. This element is most explicit among mummers in and around the town of Pavel Banya in central Bulgaria, including those from the village of Turiya described in the previous chapter. Their skimpy vests leave most of the upper body exposed to the frigid winter air. In Turiya it-self the ritual culminates with the scantily clad mummers jumping into the village stream, which is even colder than the air. In the village of Dunavtsi a large village fountain serves the same role. Mumming there is so important that when they refurbished the village square they paid careful attention to the construction of the fountain so that mummers could easily jump into it without danger of injury. The cold is less problematic for the mummers cov-ered in animal skins. In fact, if the weather is not terribly cold, they often brag about their ability to endure the heat that builds up under their fur costumes as a result of the physical exertion. This endurance and strength articulates well with another explicitly masculine element: the warrior or fighter motif. Mummers are clearly fighters; many carry symbolic weapons such as wooden swords, and others carry staffs, shepherd's crooks, and the whip-like contrap-tions with an animal skin tied to the end that they wield both offensively and defensively.

Many of these weapons are obviously phallic symbols. To carry or wear them is to assert and display an essential element of one's manhood other-wise not given public exposure. The loom beams carried in several mum-ming traditions, which are four to five feet long and carved with a rounded joint on one end to fit into the loom, are the most apparent phallic symbols, but in some villages the lead mummer carries or wears an explicitly carved wooden phallus. In Kabile the phallus is about three feet long and covered in red fabric to further confirm its meaning. A similar meaning for bells was confirmed for me by a young teenage participant in the village of Mogila. He

wore no costume but simply had three bells hanging in front of his groin—
two rounded bells on each side at the base of a long bell. The phallic and scro-
tal symbolism was both explicit and intentional, and validates a more general
interpretation of mumming bells as exaggerated public demonstrations of
private/personal manhood. A big bell suggests a big penis, and having many
bells is the equivalent of "having balls." In short, when it comes to bells, size
matters, and more is better.

In several mumming traditions, imitative sex with the transvestite bride
or burlesque figures is a common element that allows men to publically demonstrate their sexual prowess, another common expectation of manhood otherwise publicly censured. It suggests an uncontrollable sexual appetite that can
be provoked by any female image, and a man can show others how he would
perform *if* the transvestite were indeed a woman. This usually takes place between the man of the house and the transvestite bride when the mumming
group visits a household, but it can also occur spontaneously on the streets as
the mumming group is canvassing the village. This is especially valuable, as
it allows male observers a chance to assert their masculinity as well. In so doing, however, they provide yet another occasion for the mummers to do the
same by stopping the sexual assault and defending the bride as demanded by
honor and shame ideologies. In the context of male sexuality, transvestitism
itself is an important masculine statement, as it testifies to a degree of virility
among village men collectively that makes it dangerous to have real women
around. This is also the lesson of the traditional prohibition against women
leaving their houses during mumming. Females encountered by a mumming
group could supposedly be raped with impunity. Of course, the danger of
men losing control over their vigorous libido is increased by alcohol consumption, also a masculine demonstration. Being able to drink heartily all
day and continue with the discipline of mumming, as well as mock sexuality,
highlights multiple elements of the masculine persona in rural Bulgaria.

Given all these opportunities for asserting and enhancing elements common to many masculine images, it is no surprise that one of my informants,
without any prodding other than a question about why he participated, offered
that "mumming is the most manly of Bulgarian customs." In Michael Herzfeld's terms, the ritual is a wonderful opportunity for "performative excellence," which includes "the ability to foreground manhood by means of deeds
that strikingly 'speak for themselves'" (Herzfeld 1985:16). This robust masculinity is surely at the heart of mumming's continuing vitality, as men have increasingly withdrawn from other folk practices, producing what might other-

wise seem like a feminization of (disappearing) folklore. This is part of the general feminization of tradition described nicely by Kligman for Romania (1988:257). When one thinks about folklore generically in Bulgaria the dominant images are of women, from the proverbial collection of village grannies who are called out to perform at village holidays and local festivals to the world-renown female choirs marketed under the moniker of "The Mystery of the Bulgarian Voice." Buchanan (1997, 2006:359–371) has documented the multiple associations and stereotypes that combined to make female vocalists, rather than male instrumentalists, the focus of international marketers and consumers of Bulgarian folk music. As she notes, some of these Western cultural assumptions, such as the association of women with the rural, authentic past, are also evident *within* Bulgaria, and these global affirmations came back home to reinforce the image of folklore as a female specialty. The continuing engagement of village men with this particular folk practice cannot be divorced from its overwhelming masculine gestalt. Indeed, a similar correlation is evident to a lesser degree in enduring celebrations of *Trifon Zarezan*, the vintners' holiday of first pruning in early February. This double exceptionalism—a vitality in the face of otherwise diminishing folk practice and a predominantly masculine ethos in the face of feminized folk imagery—reinforce each other and work together to secure space for mummings "performative excellence."

Socialist and Postsocialist Emasculations

Enactments and enhancements of masculinity were particularly resonant to men under conditions of both socialist and postsocialist attacks on male authority and power. Socialism challenged male authority politically, whereas postsocialism added an economic assault. As noted, the socialist state's early attack on mumming lent it an aura of political resistance—a quality historically associated with ideal masculinity in Bulgaria and the Balkans more generally, well known in the veneration of the *haiduk* (bandit) tradition in song and folklore, as well as in images of the *bairak* (standard bearer) and *yunak* (brave one). When mumming was subsequently embraced as a paragon of national folklore, this political valence was transferred to the idea of national protector/hero, which resonates especially for Bulgarian men, as the example of Vasil Levski clearly shows (Todorova 2009). Levski as a potent symbol of manhood and national defender exemplifies the mutually parasitic nature of these two qualities.

Of course, this evolution also transpired in the context of an explicit ideological effort to promote gender equality, if not uniformity (Schrand 2002). This was mainly felt politically outside the household, as the household head lost political clout in village administration, now handed over to Communist Party leaders and administrators, many of whom were eventually women. As a result, at least in the Soviet case according to Ivan Kon (cited in Amico 2007:138), "from early childhood to death the Soviet man felt socially and sexually dependent and constrained." The clout of some women in the Party, and the loss of political power for many men, was ramified in household relations. One approach to socialism would suggest that the impact was perhaps less than expected given the degree to which the household itself became a fortress against the impact of these socialist innovations. I interrogate this claim in chapter 4, but, regardless, there was certainly some reorganization of the gender hierarchy as women gained significant political influence in the Party and the government. Many have noted the glass ceiling in communist polities verifying a continuing inequality, as well as the double and triple burdens that accompanied women's wage labor, especially in the countryside. The point is that what may not have been a loss of male privilege generally was still experienced as a loss of local political power, and this diluted the nature of masculinity for village men without necessarily empowering or advantaging women in a significant way. Other validations of manhood gained attraction as local political power declined.

This helps explain the spread of mumming practice across a broader age span of village men during the socialist period, continuing beyond the years of bachelorhood well into middle age. Notably this spread did not continue among the elderly. In one instance, in Turyia, I saw a much older man dressed as a masked mummer, but his wife eventually showed up to drag him home chastising him for coming out and telling him it was embarrassing for someone his age to carry on in this way. This corresponds to the cultural acceptance of declining masculinity with advanced age, so that there is no need for older men to resort to mumming. Mummers in their fifties sometimes talked remorsefully about having to quit mumming soon, as it was not "comfortable" or "appropriate" "after a certain age." They also explained that the strenuous exertion was too taxing on them physically (although, in the cases of some rather strapping older men, this was obviously a rationalization). The participation of men whose masculinity is culturally recognized as naturally diminished by age challenges the masculine quality of the rituals for other men and is thus less acceptable.

Another force that expanded in the socialist period was sexual repres-

sion. The rather repressive culture regarding public sexuality and the moral-
istic strain to the new socialist man gave these sexualized rituals a new value
as venues of sexual expression. Of course, this value was itself curtailed by the
very environment that made it attractive, as there were concerted efforts to
purge more graphic sexual elements from performances (notably the carrying
of explicit phalluses), and as these kinds of practices took on shameful con-
notations, practitioners became somewhat embarrassed by them. The impact
was more evident in festivals than local practice where the sexual element had
greater reign. Ritual was itself a sexual surrogate and in typical carnival fashion
also defined a context where sexual expression was freer, if still constrained.

Postsocialist democratization increased freedoms and restored possibilities for local political power through the ballot box. Many researchers have
also noted the return of stricter presocialist gender roles for women. This
was perhaps somewhat less evident in Bulgaria than elsewhere because of the
continuing legitimacy of socialism, in which case the emblematic rhetoric
of gender equality was not universally or automatically rejected. More consequential, however, was the economic devastation visited on villages by the
economic policies of the 1990s. In the countryside any desire to re-traditionalize
gender ran up against hard material impossibilities, since the economic options were limited. In short, men were unable to fulfill the mutual support for
the family expected of them under socialism, much less take on more. Contrary to early expectations that women would be the big losers of the changes,
in many places men have suffered equally, if not more. In short, most elements of the village economy were completely liquidated, leaving few economic options other than subsistence farming, which had been feminized to
a large degree under socialism (constituting the "third burden" commonly attributed to women in addition to their roles as wage laborers and homemak-
ers). Efforts at commercial farming, more compatible with a masculine image because of men's continued dominance in mechanized agriculture under
socialism, rarely succeeded (cf. Shreeves 2004). As the economy began to re-
bound a bit, usually through foreign investment, the economic areas that
were most prominent—tourism, textiles, and footwear—were highly feminized professions under socialism and rebounded to female workers.

Researchers working in Armenia (Platz 2000), Romania (Kideckel 2008),
Kazakhstan (Shreeves 2004:224), and Bulgaria (Ghodsee 2007) have all reported that men experienced their economic difficulties and the differential economic fortunes of women as (d)emasculating. Ghodsee (2007:23) says
that "demasculinization" in parts of Bulgaria provoked a "gender cataclysm"

which she defines as "a sudden and violent upheaval in an existing system of gender relations that is both unexpected and seemingly irreversible. Similarly Rozita Dimova (2006) has reported that the increasing access of Albanian women to higher education in Macedonia is experienced by Albanian men as a threat to their masculine identity contributing to a "gender crisis."

In Bulgaria, this "crisis" is compounded by the cultural expectation of men to protect their wives, daughters, sisters, and mothers from harm, as the poor working conditions of sweatshops have gained national attention. While women's employment in the tourist industry, mostly along the Black Sea coast and in mountain ski resorts, offered decent prospects (Ghodsee 2005), the more geographically dispersed textile and footwear factories, largely units of Italian, Greek, and Turkish outsourcing, became notorious for exploita- tive labor relations and dangerous working conditions. This issue gained na- tional prominence while I was in the field in January 2006 when two sisters, age thirty-seven and forty-nine, with no known health problems, died within eleven days of each other at the same place of employment—an Italian-owned shoe factory in the town of Dupnitza, south of Sofia. Although the causes of death could not be linked to working conditions, the factory was in viola- tion of various labor regulations, and the weird coincidence struck a national nerve precisely because it resonated with the experiences of so many families involved in textile enterprises.

According to a countrywide survey of large factories carried out by the Bulgarian Confederation of Independent Trade Unions in 2006, more than three hundred thousand Bulgarians were working in conditions that pre- sented an imminent personal threat, primarily in textile and footwear facto- ries where women constitute 90 percent of employees (Terzieff 2006). During my research I was privy to numerous complaints about the horrible con- ditions under which women labored in garment factories and workshops. Men's unemployment, itself economically emasculating, made it difficult for them to insist that their wives withdraw from such situations, eroding yet an- other masculine expectation—defense of female family members. Some men thus ended up not only depending economically on their wives but depend- ing on the exploitation and abuse of their wives. Parallels to the manifest prostitution problem and related concerns about the traffic in women were not missed by villagers who talked about the economic and sexual abuse of women collectively.

A similar anxiety was evident regarding the migration of women out of Bulgarian villages to work temporarily (and often illegally) abroad, which removed them further from their husband's protection. The postsocialist economic crises provoked massive emigration from Bulgaria (Vassilev 2005) and extensive temporary labor migration, especially to Germany, Italy, Spain, and Greece (Markova and Reilly 2007). My experience in villages since 1989 suggests that whereas early labor migrants were predominantly men going to work in construction and agricultural jobs, by the end of the 1990s these opportunities were constricting and women could more easily find work abroad as domestics and caretakers of children or the elderly. I noticed an increasing number of households where the wife/mother was working abroad. Whereas the jobs of male labor migrants were highly seasonal, allowing them to return home for part of the year, the jobs of Bulgarian women were not. Many relatives reported to me that their wives or daughters working abroad even hesitated to insist on vacation time, either for fear of losing an otherwise desirable job or concern about their ability to get back into a country where they were living and working illegally. This left increasing numbers of husbands and children without a wife and mother for extended periods. In most cases these absences were filled by older women (the migrants' mothers or mothers-in-law), but it still pressured husbands and fathers to take up some of the slack, adding another threat to established gender profiles.

My conversations confirm that Bulgarian mummers (and non-mummers for that matter) perceive all these various difficulties as challenging their manhood—often expressed as shame at their inability to fulfill their economic role as a husband. In Bulgarian the words for husband and man are the same, *muzh*, and similarly for woman and wife, *zhena*, highlighting the link between gender identity and family obligations. Thus the common question put to me by several men following descriptions of their rather dire situations—*"Kakuv muzh sum?"*—could be translated both as "What kind of husband am I?" and "What kind of man am I?"

But this is only part of the story. The problem is compounded by the fact that the loss of their occupations has rendered their masculinity more central to their identity. I have argued elsewhere that occupation became central to identity during the socialist era (Creed 1995, 1998), and without it, men become more invested in other aspects of self. The associated economic problems have simultaneously rendered consumer-based identities unavailable (Creed 2002b). Thus gender has been made more important in villagers' identity profile by the loss of occupations and the inability to access the new consumer identities vaunted by capitalism. For this reason we must take care that useful shorthand phrases like "gender crisis" and "gender cataclysm" not be taken out of the context in which they have been coined: a complex interrelationship between diverse forces and multifaceted subjectivities (see Gal and Kligman 2000a).

These same forces have made it impossible to redefine masculinity in alternative terms. This predicament is captured well by Kideckel's reworking of Sherry Ortner's (1996) idea of "gender damage" into what he calls the "frustration of gender." "Workers' postsocialist experience strips away the predictable contents and practices of their sexual identities, provides few tools for creating new practices, and leaves people with troubling insecurities about themselves" (Kideckel 2008:156). Perhaps this is why postsocialist gender realignments provoked more of a sense of "crisis" than the socialist gender challenges that preceded them. That earlier transition surely contained the elements outlined in Ghodsee's (2007) definition of a gender cataclysm, but the system also offered viable alternatives.

Scholars of masculinity have acknowledged that any society is likely to have various acceptable profiles of masculinity, usually aligned with different socioeconomic groups (Connell 2000). These alternatives, however, are hierarchically organized with the dominant variant often referred to as hegemonic masculinity. Many of the political and economic erosions discussed above threaten elements of this hegemonic/dominant masculinity in Bulgaria, which was generally shared, supported, and confirmed by most rural Bulgarian men. These men also lack any resources with which to construct and promote an alternative vision. They are stuck with a hegemonic masculinity they can no longer achieve. I suggest, further, that even under more favorable conditions, all groups of men are not equally endowed with the cultural and social capital needed for their categorical variations to acquire validation *as an alternative*. To create an alternative one must possess some significance, or cultural capital, which rural Bulgarians are increasingly denied (cf. Creed and Ching 1997). This collection of factors has made both the threats to masculinity more consequential and the excellent performances of masculinity such as mumming more meaningful.

In the village of Karavelovo in central Bulgaria, the rituals were described to me as having rebounded after several years of anemic activity. This was attributed in large part to the efforts of a few activists who recruited others and helped them acquire the costumes. When I spoke with one of these activists he reported enthusiasm on the part of recruits and said they required little convincing, apart from assurances that he would help them secure the required elements of the costume (which, notably, entailed a lot of work for his

wife). The discussion of his mumming efforts, however, was constantly interrupted (as if by way of explanation or justification) by the fact that he had un-
officially lost his job in a nearby machine factory at the age of fifty-two. He
was still technically employed there, but they rarely had any work for him.
His wife was also unemployed, as was his son-in-law who lived with them.
His daughter was the only employed family member, and she worked as a
seamstress in one of the aforementioned sweatshops. The way he moved repeatedly and effortlessly between these factors and his mumming activism
left no question about their linkage. Part of the connection was the free time
he had for organizing now that he was no longer working, but mumming also
provided a retort to these erosions of his manhood. I must note, however, that
we found him at the village pub and, when he took us to his house to talk further, his wife was chopping wood, a chore usually done by men. Apparently
domestic chores, even masculine ones, are less effective for demonstrating
masculinity than mumming.

The utility of mumming for this purpose is a historical product of its continued practice and meaning under socialism, based in turn on its traditional
link to manhood and its flexibility in expanding and accentuating those elements. It is hard to imagine that it could have been revitalized for this masculinizing effect were it not still thriving to some degree in 1989. Indeed, in most
places where mumming was not popular it has not been revitalized, and we
find alternative responses. Among Muslim Bulgarians and Turks a rise in Islamic belief and practice of a more conservative ilk, funded by foreign Islamic
organizations advocating more traditional gender roles, provides opportunities for performing masculinity (Ghodsee 2010). In urban Bulgaria where the
rustic associations of mumming make it unattractive, new manly options include the muscular mafia boss and bodyguard, as well as the more accessible
sports fanatic (Buchanan 2002).

In other parts of Eastern Europe with less vital mumming traditions,
the rituals have not been revitalized or reenergized (at least not to a degree to
merit much comment). Instead we see a variety of other responses. Rosemond
Shreeves (2002:224–25) suggests that private farming was embraced by some
men in rural Kazakhstan as a way to reestablish their male role as providers,
but that its combined commercial and subsistence status made the new identity ambiguous. In Hungary Mary Taylor's (2008) fascinating history and
contemporary study of the dance house movement, a folk dance revival that
began in the 1970s and continues today, lends itself to a similar interpretation, as many of the dances and the etiquette of the dance house convey a tra-

ditional masculinity. Kideckel (2008) documents some of the negative demonstrations, notably increasing domestic violence which, he suggests, is an eruption of masculinity under siege for Romanian men. In the former Yugoslavia a collection of recent studies suggest militarism serves the same purpose. Warfare may be the ultimate in performative excellence, and these studies demonstrate that, for soldiers in different parts of the former Yugoslavia, the opportunity to redeem an eroded masculinity was an incentive to fight (Milićević 2006; Munn 2006; Zhivkovic 2006).

The case of nationalist conflict brings up the important link between masculinity and nationalism generally. Various feminist scholars have noted the masculine essence at the core of nationalist projects (Enloe 2000; Nagel 1998; Williams 1996), suggesting that the appeal of nationalism can also be traced partially to an effort to salvage threatened masculinity, explaining to some degree the attraction of nationalist politics in many parts of the postsocialist world (Gal and Kligman 2000a). This is not so evident in Bulgaria, which was rather late to evince rabid nationalist ferment (see chapter 5). Still, the value of mumming as masculine reinforcement is related to the link between folklore and nationalist imaginaries (Herzfeld 1982), allowing mummers to perceive themselves as (masculine) defenders of the nation through their maintenance of core folk practices particular to Bulgaria. As mentioned in the previous chapter, mummers often explain their participation explicitly via the centrality of the rituals to Bulgarian national identity. This also redresses the accusation of one Lesnovo resident, who joked that the declining birth rate, which was threatening the Bulgarian nation, was because "boys don't want to fuck anymore." While offered in jest, this explanation certainly reveals the link between emasculation and nationalist angst, which mumming redresses.

Nationality is partially a place-based identity (even for the diaspora), but other, narrower place associations also acquire increased importance with the decline of occupation. Place had been an important dimension of identity for Bulgarians during the socialist period, as one's place of residence (or origin) vied with occupation in how people categorized one another. Stef Jansen (2008) has pointed out this link among Bosnian refugees for whom place, or rather what he calls their location in a time-place context that had been wiped out, became increasingly significant for men deprived of customary assertions of masculinity. Mumming is at once a national *and* a local ritual as local particularities are often highlighted and competition between villages is evident in both village and festival activities. Mumming thus combines masculine, national, and local village identifications and is especially effective at simultaneously reasserting endangered masculine gender qualities while emphasizing alternative identity vectors to compensate for any remaining deficit.

One might expect these dynamics to be most evident in places where men made comparatively greater economic contributions to their families prior to 1989, such as mining regions. In these places notions of masculinity were less affected by socialism's efforts at gender equality and the economic forces of postsocialism were more likely to be experienced as emasculating. Miners were paid relatively well under socialism and enjoyed special perquisites such as earlier retirement and better pensions (if they actually lived long enough to collect), as well as special permissions to migrate to urban locations. These advantages created a greater differential between the economic contributions of men and women in miner families. This combined with the rather macho nature of the work to accentuate the quality and importance of masculinity.

Not surprisingly, then, two major examples of the emasculation argument in Eastern Europe draw on data from mining regions (Kideckel 2008; Ghodsee 2007). Both cases describe how mining zones were uniquely affected with regard to gender by the changes after 1989. According to Ghodsee, the Pomak miners she studied in the towns of Madan and Rudozem in the central Rhodope Mountains were the "most 'manly' men in the entire country" under socialism. After the changes, the "miners went from being the ultimate embodiment of communist masculinity and the wealthiest workers in their communities to a group of relatively unskilled men lacking the appropriate education to compete in the new national and international labor markets" (Ghodsee 2007:3). Kideckel (2008) found gender frustration in different parts of Romania, including the deindustrialized Făgăraş region of Romania, but it was especially profound among the miners of the Jiu Valley. Brezhani, the Bulgarian village I described at the beginning of this chapter, where I first appreciated the intimate link between mumming and masculinity, was a coal mining village. Enthusiasm there for the rituals was so elevated in 2002 that for the first time one neighborhood group of mummers celebrated twice: once as usual on January 1 and again on the 14th, old-style New Year, in a nearby hamlet from which many neighborhood families had relocated. Brezhani mummers also reported actually visiting the mines to insure their productivity and safety. Officials in the village of Eleshnitsa, not far from Brezhani and also a mining village, reported expanding interest in mumming after 1989, as well as a major increase in participation beginning in the late 1990s, following the closing of the mines in 1994.[2] Mining was also important in many of the villages around Pernik, which, as noted, maintain one of the strongest commitments to mumming. Like Kideckel, I suggest that men's grip on masculinity was slipping generally under postsocialism, but it was clearly more tenuous in some places for a combination of reasons: a more robust masculine ideal, a greater economic drop from a somewhat advantaged position under socialism, and the complete lack of options in these often remote regions. That mumming is also more vital in many of the same places supports the link between mumming and masculinity.

The link is confirmed by the fact that many of the changes in the ritual over the last half-century (including some noted in chapter 1) expand precisely those elements that convey a manly aura: larger, more menacing masks, worn less often; bigger, heavier bells, carried in greater numbers; and an increasing preference for animal-skin costumes rather than fabric. While the latter is sometimes defended as a return to earlier tradition, the rags worn in villages like Gigintsi have a deep history, and villagers have no recollection or knowledge of mummers ever wearing skins. Moreover, a few villages that previously used short-hair animal skins have switched to the more dramatic (and more expensive) long-hair variant. This is clearly what happened in the village of Kalugerovo, where everyone readily admits that their costumes were copied from the neighboring village of Lesichevo and that there is no history or tradition of long-hair costumes. Most mummers who noted these changes simply said that the animal skins (or the longer-hair skins in those cases) "looked nicer," were "more attractive," or made "a bigger"/"stronger impression." One man in Gigintsi, however, defended his village's persistence with red and white rags by saying they were authentic, whereas other villages had changed just because they considered skins "more manly." A mummer in Kalugerovo implied the same with his explanation of the shift to long-hair costumes. "The boys can really show off in these costumes," he said, while mimicking the shifting shoulder swagger that sets the hair flowing, and which, without the costume on, bears a striking resemblance to the cool gait of male hipsters in New York City. "They feel like a *man* in these costumes." Not coincidentally, the long hair needed for these costumes is only found on male goats, raised primarily for stud. So while mummers in Brezhani have varied and striking costume options, including unique ones covered in vegetation commonly worn at festivals (see figure 7), one Brezhani mummer insisted that "the merak is for long-haired costumes."

Figure 7. Brezhani babugari at the Pernik festival in 2006.

Figure 8. A mixed group of male and female mummers from the Sushitsa district of Karlovo in 2006.

Figure 9. Devidzhi in Lesnovo, in 2006, sexually tease a bystander.

Figure 10. The transvestite bride and other kukeri attack the thighs of a villager in Mogila in 2002.

Figure 11. One of the kukeri troupe members in Pobeda, in 2002, performs comic sex play for the camera.

Perhaps the best proof of manhood, however, is the recent removal of costumes. The near naked torsos of mummers around Pavel Banya began to show up in the socialist period. Before that the mummers wore white shirts under their vests. What better way, within the limits of existing propriety, to present one's manhood than baring your chest; and what better way to make the masculine message front and center than having a large group of bare-chested men?

The conclusion seems straightforward and in line with much current research: these masculine and masculinizing rituals retain and gain resonance from a context that makes gender more central to men's identities and simultaneously undercuts other demonstrations of masculinity. This motivation reshapes the rituals themselves in ways that make them more expressly and expressively masculine, creating a positive feedback loop. Although this seems somewhat clear-cut, it is complicated by a glaring paradox that demands explanation: one of the contributions to the continuing and growing popularity of the rituals is an increasing participation of women (see Botusharov 2000). Girls are common among the Gypsy or plashilki figures, but young women have also become increasingly evident among the masked mummers (see figure 8), as well as other roles.

Feminist Incursions for Masculine Reinforcement

Early in the morning of January 14, 1998, I was at the square in the village of Cherna Gora, near Pernik, talking to mechkari as they gathered for their canvass, when I spotted the bridal couple approaching. The couple had not participated in the previous night's opening ceremony, so I was anxious to see these central figures. From a distance I was struck by the bride's femininity. By this point in my research I had seen many transvestite figures; only one had approached credibility as a female, and many missed the mark by a significant degree, so this level of realism made an impact. I watched closely to see if my impression held up under closer scrutiny. It did not, because as the bride approached it became clear that she was not a transvestite at all. Convinced of this, but remembering the emphasis placed on transvestism in these rituals by folklorists and informants alike, I sought verification from the participants around me. They confirmed that she was indeed a young woman and explained that the man who usually played the bride could not get off work and no other man was capable.

The surprise must have registered on my face, as I was immediately engulfed in a defensive disquisition that had obviously been rehearsed. "Why can't a woman play the role? Why does it have to be man? If the man is playing a woman, why can't it be a woman to start with? Isn't it better to have the real thing?" These were partly rhetorical questions, but the speakers also pushed me for a response, clearly seeking "expert" validation from an ethnographer. After I assured them that I was there to learn how *they* performed the rituals and had no investment in transvestism or any other element, they calmed down and assured me, ironically, that a man would perform the role of the bride at the Pernik festival, which was a week or so away. In 2006 a young woman also fulfilled the role of the bride in the town of Batanovtsi, near Cherna Gora. In 2002 a woman performed the role of bear trainer in Mogila and is one of the major boosters of the village ritual.

Why do men seeking masculine validation in mumming advocate and defend women's increasing involvement? The most obvious answer is that they have to. The previously described economic decimation has exacerbated a demographic crisis in the countryside. The actual rural-urban population ratios do not reflect the extent of the problem, with the percentage of urban dwellers increasing only about 5 percent since the changes, but that number must be put into a larger context of general population decline. According to Rossen Vassilev (2005), a total of nine hundred thousand people, mostly young, emigrated from Bulgaria between 1990 and 2004. In addition, the birthrate has been below replacement levels, combining to reduce the overall population from nearly 9 million in 1988 to slightly more than 7.5 million in 2006. Villages are at the end of a collection of negative demographic impacts, losing population to both migration abroad and urban migration, while also suffering disproportionately from the low birthrate owing to the older age profile of village residents. Often having small populations to start with, the experiential impact of these processes is amplified.

This demographic outcome is uneven according to geographical location and village resources, with more advantaged villages able to grow at the expense of smaller, more geographically inconvenient or economically disadvantaged locations that are nearly "deserted" or "disappearing," as Bulgarians often describe them. For example, to return to mining areas, the presence of mineral deposits kept many men from leaving these places, either because the mines continued to operate with a declining labor force that sustained hope of a possible return to work for others, or because the unemployed expected the value of the deposits to attract investors to buy the mines and start private extraction. In most cases they were disappointed, but the situation helped keep a significant number of mumming-age men around in a situation of gender frustration.[3] In these places there was no shortage of male participants and few female inclusions, but in many more village locations the very survival of mumming required incorporating all available participants.

These economic and demographic consequences are part of, to use a hackneyed gloss, globalization (indeed, one can say that socialism's collapse was the capstone to globalization), and this process has other notable impacts on mumming. Simply put, mummers are increasingly aware that mumming, certainly apart from its more carnivalesque variant in urban festivals, is perceived by some as an old-fashioned relic of the past that was only sustained in Bulgaria by the artificial insularity and support of the socialist system. This association of folklore, even when it serves contemporary political roles, with a backward rusticity is noted by ethnographers working in Serbia (Simic 2007) and Croatia (Schäuble 2007). In Bulgaria, apart from ethnographers and folklorists, I was regularly met with surprise and even embarrassment when I told urbanites about my research: that I was interested in such frivolous activities surprised them and that their country might be closely identified with these activities embarrassed them. Some expressed astonishment that the rituals were still practiced, and a few insisted that they were certainly extinct, my own observations notwithstanding: they wagered that villagers had staged performances for my benefit that would not have transpired were I not there asking about them![4] While many mummers brag about the unique nature of Bulgarian mumming traditions, this claim to fame, at least within Europe, is often recognized as a product of backwardness or lack of development. In other words, these pagan rituals are still extant in Bulgaria because the country is so far "behind" its European neighbors. Innovations such as incorporating women and children are ways to redefine these rituals as modern rather than patriarchal survivals. This helps validate and sustain the rituals *and* the masculine enhancement that is so much a part of the practice. Women mummers are a sign of progress or modernity.

The women I spoke to definitely saw it this way and, though not seeing it as gender activism, presented it in terms that promote gender equality. "Why shouldn't girls take part? The reasons for having only men were based on superstitious beliefs that people don't believe anymore." Moreover, even in the examples of re-enchantment I recorded, none insisted on a return to the parameters of former practices, such as the exclusion of girls. Another girl opined, "It's fun, and if we're in costumes and masks, what difference does it make if it's boys or girls." Following the insights of recent work on gender in Ukraine (Kebalo n.d.) and Russia (Honey 2006), which insist we define gender activism with indigenous (rather than Western) sensitivities, this would certainly qualify as such (see also Gal and Kligman 2000b). Many Bulgarian men welcome this "progress" not because it advances women's equality but because it both insures the continuity of these masculinizing practices in the absence of sufficient numbers of men and also diminishes the aura of traditionalism around mumming, allowing them to redeem elements of a traditional masculinity as contemporary. This parallels shifts in the organization of mumming toward self-management, as the state cultural workers so central to these activities under socialism have retreated from local influence, allowing mummers to present their activities as reflective of democratization and even civil society (see chapter 3). That prior leadership, by the way, was usually female, so democratic, self-management is often a return to *male* control (now possibly over female participants).

Another force is already coming from Westernization that is endangering the masculine image of these rituals through what Dennis Altman (2001) calls "global sex." This includes increasing awareness of a global gay culture through which some of the transgressive elements, especially transvestism, can be interpreted. This is clearly the reason why men are increasingly hesitant to perform the role of the bride. Given that the bride does not need to be convincingly female, and given that both of the places where I observed female brides had large numbers of participants, the purported difficulty in finding an appropriate male simply does not ring true. One participant admitted that it is hard to find a man to play the bride. In one of the pre-ritual organizational meetings I attended, a rather heated discussion ensued between the group leader and the man he suggested for the bride. The latter wanted to be a masked performer and not the bride, insisting that he was not suited for the role. When I questioned him later, however, he could not come up with any detail or particular characteristic that he lacked or possessed that would render him inappropriate. The inclusion of some women in mumming, especially in the role of the bride, has allowed men to redeem the masculinizing nature of the ritual by eliminating elements vulnerable to reinterpretation as homosexual (and therefore feminizing) markers in a global sexscape.

Such (mis)interpretations are less likely with regard to the lewd burlesque transvestites, precisely because their frivolousness as female caricatures links them incontrovertibly to the idea of inversion or reversal so beloved of ritual analysts and reporters. Not surprisingly, then, in areas where the idea of female brides has not been entertained, the transvestite bride is increasingly comic. Older mummers often complained that current transvestite brides are not convincing in their roles. One retired mummer was so distraught about this bastardization of mumming that he insisted on showing me what he had looked like as a bride. He pulled out a suitcase from under the bed in which the elaborate folk costume was lovingly stored and, with his wife's help, spent half an hour putting it on, adjusting each element with care to insure I appreciated what a mummer bride should look like. Indeed, I could not recall many brides I had seen in actual mumming events that compared, perhaps with the telling exception of one I saw in the 1980s. Current transvestite figures insist on making their underlying manhood evident to emphatically mark their performance as reversal and thereby deny any misreading of their actions as queer.

That such a recognition is spreading and is a postsocialist phenomenon can hardly be contested. It began soon after 1989, as Bulgaria experienced an explosion of sexually explicit information and images from a media completely unfettered by any censorship, including gay publications. This was to be subsequently restrained, but in the early years all sorts of sexual (mis)information and images proliferated. In the summer of 1992, on a crowded train to the provinces from Sofia, I was engaged in conversation by a middle-aged man in my compartment. Bulgarian trains have small enclosed compartments in which six to eight passengers sit on two long seats facing one another in rather close contact. If the trip is long, a fellow traveler will inevitably ask you something. In my case, my accented responses usually confirmed suspicions of my foreignness, leading to questions of origin. As usual, having been exposed as an American, which was still perceived positively in 1992, this curious man peppered me with questions about life in the United States. When I stood up to stretch my legs, the man jumped on the first opportunity to speak to me privately and followed me into the train's narrow corridor. There he broached the subject: he had seen news reports a few nights earlier about gay pride celebrations in New York and San Francisco on Bulgarian television. I had not seen the reports, but from his secondhand account it seemed that the free press, true to form, had focused on the most outrageous and extreme characters. He was genuinely incredulous and asked if the reports were true and if such things really happened. When I confirmed that they did, he then asked, genuinely befuddled, "Is this democracy?" Later, as the government of Philip Dimitrov became increasingly unpopular, I was commonly told, by way of criticism, that he and many in his government were homosexuals.

These examples illustrate an increasing awareness of a global gay culture (cf. Johnson 1998) that had not been fully appreciated in the socialist period. Certainly there were people with same-sex attraction (almost all closeted to some degree) who had access to information about gay life in the West. Foreign tourists, especially at the tourist meccas along the Black Sea, provided conduits of sexual information and relations. Among the straight, non-active homosexual and bi-sexual population, however, there was much less awareness. Until the 1990s the term "pederast" was the most common label for people believed to be homosexual. The term was still used in the 1990s, but I noticed a gradual replacement by "homosexual" and later even by "gay." By the time of my fieldwork in 2006 there was an indigenous contribution to this new global awareness in the persona of Azis, a wildly popular gender-bending, cross-dressing pop-folk Romani singer who "married" his male partner in October of that year. The point is that socialist restrictions served to insulate mumming rituals from an alternative interpretation that was spreading globally, and when it reached local Bulgarian villagers something had to give.

The shifts to female brides and comic transvestites are responses. Although no one in either case gave this as a reason for the switch, in villages where the bride is still a man I was assured on numerous occasions, beginning in the late 1990s, and with no provocation from me, that the figures had nothing to do with homosexuality. This preemptive defense confirms both the recognition of this new potential interpretation and the association of its origin in the West, where I came from. Of course, if one has to explicate this potential confusion, the value of the ritual statement is already compromised; the better alternative is to replace this element. Thus, reversing Judith Butler's (1990) famous formula, having a female bride removes the destabilizing potential of drag in order to shore up an already troubled gender.

Sex and Repression

The global gay dynamic is especially important, because beyond the issue of transvestism and drag performance, if one accepts even a modest psychoanalytic possibility, these rituals are saturated with elements of homoeroticism.[5] We can start with the phalluses used in several locations. The Kabile head mummer commonly prods men he meets with the large red phallus he carries around like a scepter. In Strandzha the single mummer, who is referred to by the slang term for penis, wears a large wooden phallus painted red amid his bells and regularly assaults other men with it. Another small phallic element is mounted to a short "barber stool" on which men are required to sit for a mock ritual shaving. Both of these activities are referred to as "kukering" so that the act of mumming itself is rendered as a mock sex act, often between men (Fol 2004:53).

Less obvious phallic implements, such as swords, shepherd staffs and long-handled hammers, are wielded in ways that also betray their sexual meaning (see figure 9). Mummers commonly use them to poke at other men's anuses. Later they end up holding the end of each other's "wooden" instruments (the same ones that have been prodding the buttocks of others) in mumming dances, especially in the finale at the village square and at festival performances. The implications of this are especially obvious in the case of long-handled hammers, as the Bulgarian word for hammer is a common euphemism for sexual intercourse. In Turiya the mummers greet each other with a choreographed routine that can only be described as a ritualized mating dance, including placing the wooden swords they are carrying between each other's legs and then using them symbolically to shave each other's faces, thus going from between their legs to their faces. In many villages the bride carries a distaff with a tuft of unspun cotton or wool tied to the top, often stuck, for convenience, beneath his belt in the front of his dress, creating a rather provocative image.

Bells are also part of this sex play. I have witnessed mummers using pelvic thrusts to swing the large bell hanging in front of their groin up between the legs of another, both male and female. This usually provokes the other person to step back, simultaneously confirming and refusing the symbolic sexual act. These mummers also seemed to prefer a resting position in which a large bell lay between their spread legs. This clearly sexualized stance is not simply accidental and goes beyond the previous suggestion of phallic exhibitionism to provocation and invitation. Most, if not all, of the observers are other males. The borrowing of bells is perhaps also relevant here. Bells are valuable, so they are not loaned casually, making the borrowing of bells somewhat less common than the lending of other costume elements. However, I also sensed a slight hesitation to wear another man's bells that may have further restrained requests for loans. This could be explained by the phallic interpretation of bells and the homoerotic implication of sharing them.[6]

In the village of Vasil Levski bells are accompanied by strings of colorful balls made of yarn hanging down the front of the costume. The mummers periodically fondled their own balls and asked other mummers if they wanted to feel them. The offer was always refused with disgust, often accompanied by graphic obscenities. Again, if there is any doubt about the emic symbolism of these elements, it would seem to be erased by the common invocations issued by the bride's escort at the collective kukeri finale: "Whoever doesn't like the kukeri can eat their bells. Whoever doesn't like the bride can eat her distaff!" In Mogila the kukeri did not use implements to make the point. Their horseplay involved pinching the men of the house they visited on the inner upper thighs (see figure 10). The pain involved made it impossible to mistake this as sexual overture, but the proximity to the groin clearly made it more than just the slap on the back or head common in other villages.

The transvestite figures are also homoerotic objects, as sexual activity from kissing to intercourse is continually attempted or mimed, and often in ways that tacitly or explicitly recognize the male sex of the transvestite. In Veselinovo the bride figure was regularly harassed by men grabbing his butt and then miming intercourse. In the village of Trapoklovo imitations of anal and oral intercourse seemed to be the dominant theme of the extensive horseplay that bordered on violence. In Mogila a man met the mumming group at his gate and insisted the "maiden" enter first, as he mimed intercourse with pelvic thrusts toward an imaginary figure in his grip. This bride was actually subjected to similar passion plays by men at several houses. In another village's festival performance the pretense of cross-dressing was explicitly denied by a contraption worked by a string around a transvestite's neck that simulated an erection under his dress. The erection was produced during the pantomime of intercourse with men in the group. With the exception of Turiya where the "granny" was mounted on top in the missionary position by multiple Arapi, most of the pantomime sex is from behind, suggesting anal rather than vaginal intercourse (again, if not confirming the homosexual nature of the interplay, at least leaving that possibility open). Oral intercourse is also commonly implied or simulated. In Mogila the bride would often step over men and boys sitting on the ground so that their head was under his skirt in a clear implication of oral sex. The sitting male immediately tried to extricate himself from the bride's clothing.

Mumming rituals provide protection for the expression of homoerotic desire in multiple ways. First, the traditional context demands the enactment. Homoerotic actions are not expressions of individual desire but are required to assure the vitality of the national culture and local livelihood. This calls for gratitude, not derision, and conforms to important masculine roles. Second, as previously suggested, the (intermittent) masking and (increasing) interpretation as reversal enables participants to deny the reality of their expressions. They are performances. Finally, the previously described masculine dimensions of the rituals provide a heightened context parallel to the wrestling ring or football field in the United States, where the extreme virility of the activity allows physical familiarities between men that are taboo or suspect in other contexts (Arens 1975; Dundes 1978). These elements were extremely important as avenues for homoerotic desire in the repressive socialist regime that denied and censored the option and thus confirmed them officially as play. In the postsocialist context they are increasingly recognized, especially by younger people, as potentially reflective of real feelings and the message is even more equivocal. The presence of women is a way to redress this new ambiguity.

This solution is not without contradictions, and this is why some men are less enthusiastic. The presence of women can dilute the hyper-masculine context, making homoerotic actions potentially *more* suspect. So the utility of women for male mummers may be limited to having a small number of female participants. A few exceptional (perhaps token) women provide cover, but too many women could threaten the masculine gestalt of the rituals. Also, the sexual impropriety surrounding the transvestite would be unacceptable if a woman was playing the role, and, in fact, it is noticeably reduced or absent when the bride is female. Probably, for this reason, the shift to a female bride is only common in the New Year's traditions, where the marriage ceremony is central and sex play with the bride much less evident. Indeed, a mummer in Batanovtsi in 2006 drew on this dynamic to defend his town's practice of having a female bride: "They say that a girl as a bride is not accurate or authentic, but I think it makes the custom *more* authentic. If it is a man it seems more like a joke, everybody is busy laughing and playing around with him, but if it is a real girl people are less distracted by the humor and focus on the original objectives and meaning of the custom." In this brilliant defense of female brides which turns the weapon of "authenticity" against the critics who invoke it, we also see the extent to which the gendered context for interpreting transvestism has changed. It now suggests, automatically, if not homosexuality then some degree of inversion and frivolity, even for those not intending that meaning. The male bride, so central to the ritual's efficacy in assuring abundance while asserting ultimate male power over fertility, is now rendered either queer or a joke, and must be replaced for the sake of the ritual's continuing efficacy and its utility in promoting masculinity.

Where sexual license has been more central and integrated into the rituals, the impact of switching to a female bride would be too extreme, and mummers continue to dragoon some man into doing it. As noted, these men respond by marking their masculinity and emphasizing reversal, but there is an added shift in how they respond to sexual overtures, notably a decreasing willingness to play along. Transvestite and male figures generally went along with the imitative sex play to some degree, much like a sexual performance, no doubt with sympathetic intentions for general village fertility (see figure 11). But recently there is increasing resistance, usually from the implied passive partner. In the village of Pobeda I saw two different men in the role of bride over the span of the ritual, and they presented different sensibilities. The older one indulged the sex play, even simulating fellatio and anal intercourse with his escort, the younger one eschewed these overtures altogether. This difference suggests an incomplete or differential spread of the sensibilities I am referring to, which maps onto generational difference, just as one might expect as global influences spread unevenly.

Increasing resistance from the implied passive partner actually high-lights a new masculinizing potential in these rituals, albeit for some men at the expense of others. In many locations the idea that same-sex activities be-tween men are emasculating is attributed only to the passive partner in these relations (see, e.g., Brandes 1981). Mummers' actions suggest a similar con-clusion, as the very people who refuse or flee from imitated threats of penetra-tion enthusiastically attempt to perpetrate the same on others. In short, then, a growing recognition of the possible reality behind same-sex enactments made it possible for individual men to enhance their own masculinity at the expense of other men, paradoxically increasing the value of sex play as other men become less willing to play along. These other men may also be mum-mers, but more often they are civilians whom the mummers encounter on the streets as they move around the village. As with other masculinizing ele-ments, the declining use of masks makes it possible for mummers to benefit personally from such masculine demonstrations and injects a physical com-petition that is masculinizing in its own right.

In this move the ritual shifts from a vehicle for repressed or, perhaps more accurate, previously undefined same-sex desire to a homophobic en-actment of men competing for masculinity among themselves (not unlike many masculinizing activities in the West). As the recognition of mumming activity as potentially homoerotic increases, its value for safely (that is, un-recognizably) expressing latent same-sex attractions is undercut. The same processes that bring this interpretation (globalization/Europeanization/ Westernization) have also exposed Bulgarians to more evidently macho con-texts, from extreme sports to extreme fighting. By comparison, mummers' actions no longer seem so extreme, thus reducing, somewhat, their value as examples of performative excellence. But these shifts have opened up a new value for demonstrating masculinity in mumming. Men now use their shared homophobia as a context that authorizes the achievement or enhancement of manhood by symbolically sodomizing others. The mummers demonstrate their masculinity by attacking non-mummers, who can compensate by at-tacking the transvestite bride. The latter is then on the bottom, literally and figuratively, without many options for redemption in terms of masculinity. This may explain why it is increasingly difficult to get a man to play this role and why it is still so important to have one do so in the areas where mumming traditions include significant sex play. In one village I witnessed a group of mummers, who had been up since daybreak refining their costumes, threaten to punish a latecomer by making him dress as the bride. The bride figure has shifted from a respected leader to a form of punishment.

The shrinking options for expressing homoerotic desire are also shaped by the experience of economic emasculation. The difficulties of the transition have made men less secure in their masculinity which dovetails with new recognitions of homosexuality to produce a threatening combination.[7] Neither force alone may have had the same impact; if men were still secure in their masculinity they would be less susceptible to anxiety over the possible alternative interpretations of mumming role play, and, without increasing awareness of alternative interpretations, the erosion of masculinity need not have threatened or affected extant interpretations of transvestism. The gender destabilizing forces of postsocialism make men more anxious, which affects how they respond to new interpretations of sexuality and gender. Expressions of latent homoerotic desire are acceptable/comfortable only when men are confident in their masculinity/sexuality. Homophobic interpretations are a product of increasing exposure to global homosexual possibilities in a context where previous masculine security is endangered and threatened.

I do not think the eclipse is complete. Rural Bulgaria is still a repressive environment when it comes to same-sex desire, so the possibility of its surreptitious expression is still crucial for some men, even if the mediums and activities must be redefined in order to maintain plausible denial. The homoerotic and homosocial nature of these rituals satisfies some men even while the homophobic assault serves others, producing a symbiosis of desperation. This is not to suggest that any of these men are homosexual in any way. In fact, I would argue the reverse—that such outlets are rather ineffectual for significant same-sex desire. In this sense the rituals are also hetero-normative in that they channel homoerotic desire through the validation of a more hegemonic homophobic masculinity. They are also just plain sexual. These rituals provide an outlet for sexuality generally in which men help one another by taking on symbolically the woman's role. As Weston La Barre (1962) showed in his classic study of snake handlers, under conditions of sexual restriction even handling snakes, the iconic phallic symbol, need not imply particularly homosexual leanings or desires when it is the sole outlet for sexual energy. In Bulgaria this possibility has been threatened by a sensitivity to new interpretations and a new binary, categorical understanding of sexuality that refuses the ambiguity of sexual expressions and labels actions as either straight or gay.

Alternatives Denied

The incorporation of women in mumming operates to sustain these masculine activities in multiple ways. First, women's involvement suggests a nontraditional practice that helps validate mumming as modern rather than a patriarchal holdout. Mumming traditionally denied the important contributions of women to society—a project Bette Denich (1974:260) characterized as the "patrilineal paradox," by appropriating female fertility through cross-dressing and insisting it was a male achievement through ritual action. This message is no longer tenable, as making money is the operative imperative and wives are often the only wage earner in a family. Women in mumming acknowledge women's subsidiary or supporting role without sacrificing the continuing centrality of men and masculinity. Given the difficulty of mounting the rituals with declining populations and resources, women's involvement helps sustain rituals that continue to be important for the assurance of a threatened masculinity in an economic context in which gender has been rendered more important to villagers' identities. At the same time the presence of women helps deflect the impact of new interpretive frames that arrived with the transition and threaten to recast the central transvestite elements as gay or homosexual while exposing the latent expressions of same-sex desire in sexual horseplay. In some ways the impact of postsocialist integrations has allowed homophobia to replace misogyny as the masculinizing muscle of mumming.

The meanings of transvestism and sex play in mumming have to do with the nature of the gender system within which they occur, and we can use changes in these symbolic meanings to probe deeper shifts in gender. The well-known sociologist of masculinity Michael Kimmel underlines the apparent truism of the co-determination of gender identity when he suggests that, "in all cases, masculinities are constructed in relation to femininities" (2007). It is indeed the recognition that masculinities are not only, or even centrally, about men but rather are implicated in, and authorized by, the structural dominance of men over women that moved the study of masculinity from its early position as a (chauvinistic) reaction against critical feminist theory to an important focus within the study of gender. Still, I believe mumming dynamics confirm that we need to acknowledge and attend to different degrees of integration or the different ways in which masculinity and femininity are related. The emic reinterpretations of mumming discussed here suggest a reorientation of a prior gender system along lines more consonant with Western models, specifically an increasing alignment of masculinity and femininity along a single gender continuum. In Bulgaria, in the 1980s, the experiences of masculinity and femininity were not so tightly interlocked. Instead, a rigid idea of gender grounded in essential/biological differences supported a gender system in which masculinity and femininity were perceived as autonomous systems. This granted all males a claim on masculinity, and although it clearly allowed for the possession of more or less of it, the lesser option, even in the extreme, did not imply femininity.

The notion that less masculinity implies femininity is a cultural stance that people who experience gender differences as more essential may not assume, and it may be a relatively recent development even in the West. This is supported by historian George Mosse's (1996:9) observation that the use of the term "effeminate" to imply an unmanly softness or delicacy only came into general usage in the eighteenth century. This development puts the onus on men to achieve their masculinity and makes the consequence of not doing so a dangerous feminization. In line with liberal individualism generally, men become *responsible* for their gender identity. This grants a hegemonic masculinity (Connell 1987, 1995) greater power and authority as the standard by which to measure individual achievement, while the contribution of this hegemonic man to bourgeois capitalism (Mosse 1996) may have merited the threat of feminization to promote it.

Some of these male images and expectations were evident in Bulgaria before the socialist period. Mosse (1996) connects them to the development of the bourgeoisie in late-eighteenth-century Europe (specifically Germany), and they certainly made their way into Bulgaria with other European influences. Indeed, this hegemonic model contains many of the images or ideas to which I appealed above to demonstrate the masculine potential of mumming. However, the acceptance of qualities common to *the* "image of man" (Mosse 1996) does not necessarily imply an identical understanding of gender generally. The increasing difficulty of finding a willing male to play the mumming bride may confirm the shift in gender, I suggest. When femininity and masculinity were perceived as distinct, men's activities could hardly feminize them, even if they acted like women. Masculinity and femininity were not two poles on a gender continuum but two distinct continua with some limited interaction. A new model of gender that connects masculinity and femininity along a single gender continuum makes the transvestite role potentially feminizing. This difference may be at the heart of the different understandings of masculinity noted by Matthew Gutmann (1997:386). He found different concepts of masculinity evident in the anthropological literature, one of which is "anything that men think and do" while another emphasizes male-female relations and what "women are not." Rather than a lack of conceptual rigor in this field, these views may actually reflect the different understandings of gender among the populations being studied.

Perhaps the continuum model of gender may, paradoxically, produce the multiple masculinities so beloved of contemporary gender researchers. The possibility of feminization puts one's gender identity always at risk and makes it imperative for men to claim manhood, and this requires alternative models for men not conforming to established or hegemonic images. This effort produces profiles of qualities and characters identifiable as distinctive, alternative sets, which can then coalesce into what Demetrakis Demetriou (2001) sees as a "masculine bloc."[8] This is not nearly so likely or important when every male is assumed to have a masculine gender identity, in which case what men do *is* masculine. The latter situation still allows for contests over what is most manly, and allows for change in gender systems as men attempt to acquire more of the benefits of a masculine identity by resetting the hierarchy of qualities in their favor; ultimately, however, there is less danger, as one cannot lose one's masculine identity. The latter possibility helps make the economic threats of postsocialism more threatening than the political challenges of the socialist period, and this explains why men need ways to validate their masculinity according to established hegemonic models. As previously noted, the men I am talking about have little power with which to establish an alternative masculinity.

Here is another reason to be cautious about notions of gender "crisis" and "cataclysm." The focus on the failure to meet existing gender mores can miss the extent to which the deficiencies are actually *created* by new Western gender expectations; it is not just the inability to fulfill old gender ideals but the additional installation of equally unattainable new ones. Both are going on simultaneously, and we must be careful not to let one overshadow the other. Kideckel (2008) recognizes this dynamic in Romania but primarily in relation to the instantiation of new feminine ideals. Notably no one has yet tagged this as a "crisis of femininity." This suggests that the notion of crisis may be doing unintended ideological work in diverting us from the dispossession that has occurred simultaneously, and, in this role, it also allows us to blame the victim: men's gender dysphoria can be attributed in part to their sexist (read backward) refusal to adopt new (read: modern/Western) gender ideas, when in fact it is the installation of those ideas already that endangers their manhood. This may explain the easy acceptance of women in mumming: it fits into a recently established ideal of gender relations and, in so doing, also helps revalidate the masculinizing possibilities of more traditional activities within the new field. Mummers' increasing concern for their physical appearance and the image they strike, which I have noticed over the years of my research, supports this claim. Watching men's prolonged preparations into perfecting their mumming costumes, and the meticulous vanity with which they don them before stepping outside, confirms that looking good has displaced many other ritual imperatives. It bespeaks a new male sensitivity that is already part of the gender landscape. This is also part of the explanation, as previously discussed, for entire villages changing their costume styles.

A possible conclusion of these observations is that an essentialist notion of gender as an inherent quality of one's sex may, within limits, allow greater flexibility to behavior than a model that recognizes only a circumscribed constructionism. In the former, one can act in ways antithetical to the masculine stereotypes and still be considered a man. I am not suggesting, however, that this provides a viable strategic essentialism (Spivak 1988), because the limits are too narrow for the progressive futures envisioned by feminist or queer activists and scholars. I am only insisting that a possible novel approach to improving and developing more equitable gender polities/policies, even if only as a step toward something more transformative, was missed by not recognizing prior gender arrangements or, at best, refusing them any validity or utility. This failure helped fuel the neo-traditional gender "backlash" that fascinated researchers after 1989, and widened the gulf that emerged between Eastern and Western gender activists and researchers (see Gal and Kligman 2000a: 98–103).

The foreclosure of alternatives is also evident in mumming messages about same-sex desire. As Massad has argued for the Middle East, the internationalization of a Western sexual ontology that incorporates the homosexual in the universally human risks "another subjective repudiation, a banishing of another *other*. . . . namely, those cultural formations whose ontological structure is not based on the hetero-homo binary" (2007:40; emphasis in the original). Here the difference may be less extreme for Bulgaria, as a nascent binary homo/hetero understanding of sexuality, evident in use of the term "pederast," already existed in the 1980s. Still I do not think that this Western model was fully developed or dominated the understanding of sexuality in a hegemonic way, and the possibility of a still proscribed same-sex desire was recognized *within*, rather than opposed to, an assumed naturalized heterosexuality. By replacing this with a more binary interpretation, global models have intensified homophobia, which authorizes Western models of redress. The human rights advocates implementing those solutions, according to Massad (2007:41) "are not bringing about the inclusion of the homosexual in a new and redefined human subjectivity, but in fact are bringing about her and his exclusion from this redefined subjectivity altogether while simultaneously destroying existing subjectivities organized around other sets of binaries, including sexual ones." That such efforts often come in the guise of "civil society" suggests a need to interrogate that talisman as well.

CHAPTER THREE

CIVIL SOCIETY AND DEMOCRACY

If Brezhani is snowed in, the village of Varvara in south central Bulgaria is a great alternative for ringing in the New Year. Although located on the northern slopes of the western Rhodope Mountains at 320 meters, it enjoys climatic (as well as scenic and economic) benefits from the closely adjacent valley. An evening wind prevents heavy frosts and ameliorates winters, making January access reliable. I went there in December 2005 to experience the festivities firsthand, having been enticed by the stirring descriptions I collected on an earlier visit in the spring of 2002. Although I arrived a few days ahead of the events, the village was already animated with excitement. I made my way to the chitalishte where a large poster covered one of the glass doors displaying more than forty pictures from past mumming celebrations (a useful archive for examining change). Inside I followed the voices of a women's choir up to the room where they were rehearsing. I enjoyed the music and waited for them to finish so I could talk to the director, who was also the secretary of the chitalishte and coordinating some of the New Year's activities. The ensuing conversation quickly turned into a group discussion, as all the women joined in with information about the festivities and repeated assurances that I was in for a treat. While they enlightened/entertained me, the secretary gave various directions to others, interrupting herself periodically to correct something she overheard the others tell me or to add a detail she thought I should know. A male mummer, here called a "dervish," showed up to ask if he could participate in some part of the event, having secured the appropriate costume, and another arrived to pick up part of a costume that had been left for him. The secretary reminded them both that she wanted the money box opened only in the chitalishte in front of several witnesses so there would be no question that anyone had taken some.

I stayed with the family of a sheep herder, known affectionately as *bai* Petko, who at sixty-six had long ago retired from mumming but was still an active booster and a fount of mumming lore. When I got to his house he showed off a favorite mask he had saved and kept upstairs, and then pointed to an empty, incomplete three-story house across the street, where, through the gaping holes still awaiting windows on the top floor, one could see several large, intimidating masks hanging from the yet uncovered ceiling beams. Half-finished multistory buildings were common in villages in the 1990s, as the gradual, informal construction strategy of rural homebuilders under socialism (Creed 1998:200–202; Kenedi 1982) disintegrated under marketization, leaving some villagers with unfinished constructions and insufficient funds. Those with funds often decided to use them to relocate to towns instead of finishing village abodes, which they might use instead as simply weekend/summer villas with no need for finished upper floors.

Petko then escorted me to another empty house, this one a tiny old traditional construction abandoned as a result of age and decay following the death of its elderly owners; its two primitive rooms, however, were enjoying a second life as a mask workshop for a group of adolescent boys. They were putting the final touches of paint on their masks when we arrived. The masks were striking and no mean accomplishments for boys their age. It was only with Petko's intervention that I gained access to what is otherwise off-limits: the masks are not to be seen until New Year's Day. He is a sort of mentor to the group and helps them with design and sometimes materials. He also loaned one of them a few bells from his extensive collection, which is stored on several wooden poles hung across the ceiling of a room in his barn.

Groups of young men work together on their mumming masks for months before the big day, brainstorming, developing designs, making prototypes, and finally building and painting the finished products. During this time older villagers prepare props, write scripts, and rehearse for the skits they will perform on the village square. In Varvara ritual authenticity takes a back seat to creativity and imagination. Their costumes are of the long-hair goat-skin variety, but their masks are unique. Forsaking the limits of traditional designs and mediums, most of the Varvara masks are newly designed and constructed each year out of wire, fabric, and other materials, often diverging radically from prior models (see figure 12). Unlike the somewhat routine enactment of traditional folk activities common to many mumming events (weddings, farm work, or the household greeting of mummers), Varvara skits are always fresh and often include political satire.

The actual festivities begin on New Year's Eve with family feasts in individual households. Bai Petko had slaughtered a turkey that his wife cooked with homemade sauerkraut. We were joined at dinner by their two married sons, Ivan and Dimitur, and their families, including Ivan's in-laws from a neighboring village. Dimitur and his family live with the father and mother in a three-generational household. He helps his father with the farm work and assists his brother in a village woodworking enterprise. Ivan lives with his wife and children in the nearby town so that his daughter, who attends high school there, can live at home (there are no high schools in most villages). After a few hours of eating and drinking, with folk music programs on the television in the background and animated conversation about subjects ranging from the family's sheep flock (Petko had to check on ewes about to birth several times), to the dire plight of the village economy (three factories had been shut down and nothing opened to replace them), to global geo-politics (including jabs at me as the de facto representative of Bush's Iraq policy), we greeted the New Year with a toast. Ivan then quickly disappeared and returned shortly in a blond wig, makeup, and a tightly revealing pink knit dress with its bust stuffed to the limits. Dervish day was here.

Ivan and I headed off to meet the group of mummers forming in front of a village tavern (itself packed with New Year's revelers). Dimitur stayed behind, never having had merak for the event despite his father's encouragement. The group we joined was a small subset of village mummers designated to canvass the village over night. It included a small wedding party (newlyweds and the groom's parents), a bear with trainer, a Gypsy couple, a few burlesque transvestites, two musicians (bagpipe and drum), and a few dervishes in long-hair goatskin costumes with store-bought rubber masks, and bells (one laden all over with bells). They visited homes throughout the night and into the next morning, rousing villagers and receiving money in return, as well as being treated with food and drink. Once they completed the canvass they returned to the village square, where the rest of the mummers and the public had been gathering since about 10:00 AM. They continued to approach the many visitors and relatives, who had come to see the festivities, for additional donations.

My experiences in Varvara, described in more detail below, convinced me to embrace an idea I had been harboring over years of observing and talking to mummers: that mumming in Bulgaria, both in the socialist and postsocialist periods, operated in many ways like that darling element of Western democracy supposedly missing from (post)socialist life—civil society. In what follows I use these observations to pursue two seemingly contradictory objectives: to advance the ongoing critique of the notion of civil society, but at the same time to suggest that civil society was more evident in Bulgaria than was often acknowledged. In fact, these are not completely contrary objectives, as the limitations of the concept are the reasons why parallel activities have gone unrecognized, and acknowledging these relations is a useful step toward redeeming the analytical potential of the notion.

Some may think this is beating a dead horse; I only wish it were so. The horse *has* been thoroughly beaten, especially by anthropologists (e.g., Goody 1998; Hann and Dunn 1996; Hearn 1997; Glasius, Lewis, and Seckinelgin 2004), but it refuses to die. As Chris Hann, an anthropologist who has followed the concept's career closely, recently observed, "ethnographic studies have had little effect on mainstream political science studies of the postsocialist countries, in which it has become common to address problems of democratisation in the language of civil society and to attribute virtually all social problems of the transition to a deficit in this sphere" (Hann 2006:159). This very paradox—the perpetuity and continuity of the notion in face of such potent critique—suggests that something important is at stake here, perhaps foundational to current systems of power. The persistence and attachment to the concept, more than the original fascination with it, demands continued interrogation. Still, in recognition of the power of the concept and its practical impact on populations where the extent of civil society becomes a measure of successful democratization, aid/credit worthiness, and even readiness for membership in international institutions such as the EU, it is imperative to show that civil society is more common in Eastern Europe than observers have often allowed (see also Cellarius 2004, chap. 6).

In short, this is a continued criticism of the term's teleological and ethnocentric baggage, while also recognizing its practical political importance within global systems of power (note the rise of the notion of "global civil society") and making an effort to redeem segments of East European societies within that system. So although I think the term is often unhelpful, and sometimes even detrimental, in explaining political dynamics in Bulgaria, I argue that particular relations related to ritual activities approximate the (ethnocentric) criteria of civil society. This dovetails nicely with Maria Todorova's (2009) recent research into the hero cult of Vasil Levski, which retains the term "civil society" but insists on its historical contextualization. She finds evidence of a nascent civil society in Bulgaria in the 1980s around renewed public interest and a state-sponsored investigation into whether Levski's skeleton might have been uncovered (and subsequently lost) during excavations in a Sofia church back in the 1950s. These efforts closely follow Hann's collective work and his charge that "it is worth paying closer attention to local ways of expressing similar kinds of virtues to those which Gellner and others have associated with civil society," which, he subsequently notes, *are often found in ritual* (Hann 2006:162–163).

To bring the argument full circle, I believe that the demonstration of these qualities resembling civil society forces us to ask deeper questions about *why* such activities are not commonly interpreted as civil society. This opens the concept to further and deeper deconstruction. Here, I fear, I find forces more nefarious than the simple Western bias and ethnocentrism exposed by other critics of the term. Although these are a big part of the problem, I also suggest that the graphic equivalences evident in mumming and other activities make this simple explanation insufficient—they are so obvious as to require active denial. This then exposes the civil society project as not just a well-intentioned misfiring but as a civilizing process for establishing governmentality. This conclusion builds upon Jonathan Hearn's (1997) analysis of Scottish uses of the civil society concept in the 1990s, which he interprets as efforts to compensate for the general lack of political engagement with the actual role of the state. Clearly this compensation serves a conservative agenda. In Bulgaria this was accomplished by dispossession, as indigenous avenues of civic participation such as mumming were denied in favor of alternatives more fitting with Western, neoliberal images, even as the latter were perhaps less effective for political expression. I conclude that this dispossession/replacement has produced a damaged notion of democracy that may take some time to fully rehabilitate.

Whose Civil Society?

The definition of civil society has shifted over its long history and is still significantly contested. It is commonly accepted to include the collection of voluntary organizations and institutions in a society that are beyond the family but not part of the state apparatus. Analysts differ, however, in determining if all such units should be included in the concept. For example, some theorists include religious organizations and political parties whereas others do not. Some include the free market itself as an element of civil society, but others exclude it, in one case recasting civil society as the sphere of interactions between the economy and the state, and including the family as part of civil society (Cohen and Arato 1992:ix). These debates are somewhat tangential to my argument, because the parallels I draw from mumming are with the types of organizations that are central to almost all definitions of civil society and also constitute the popular conceptualization of the term: the rich associative life which Tocqueville famously linked to American democracy.

The idea of civil society has a long intellectual and philosophical pedigree that hardly needs rehearsing here. The most recent wave of interest was largely inspired by East European dissident intellectuals under late socialism (see Kennedy 2002:44–90). Although intellectuals never achieved the "class power" that György Konrád and Ivan Szelényi (1979) predicted, the more narrowly defined subset of "scholars" retained a unique position in the socialist system (see Verdery 1991). They were in some ways privileged, but the actualization of that privilege through assumed compliance (whether actual or not) undermined their status as intellectuals, personally, locally, and in the larger cosmopolitan world in which most intellectuals imagine themselves. Not having an arena outside the state's organizational apparatus undermined the identity of free thinkers, which was a source of greater discontent for intellectuals than for most people living under socialism. For most others, family, friends and a surfeit of state-sponsored venues from social clubs to amateur cultural ensembles supplied a satisfactory subjectivity. In other words, the state's sponsorship of these venues was more problematic and unsatisfactory for intellectuals because they were defined by independent thinking. Their fascination with this issue resonated with the political assumptions of observers from civic-rich societies and confirmed rather simplistic stereotypes of socialism. Lest my attack on civil society, even as a concept, provoke accusations of being antidemocratic I defend myself with the words of Václav Havel, with the obvious irony intended: "There can be no doubt that distrust of words is less harmful than unwarranted trust in them. Besides, to distrust words, and indict them for the horrors that might slumber unobtrusively within them—isn't this, after all, the true vocation of the intellectual?"(cited in West and Sanders 2003:ix).

If we accept a generic definition of civil society as the collection of voluntary organizations and institutions between the household and the state, then we might start by asking, who becomes part of such a civil society? Where are the resources and possibilities for such a civic florescence to be found? My experience in Bulgaria suggests that it is most often in urban contexts where it is actualized by resourceful individuals with significant skills and abilities (see also Cellarius 2004:257). In the multitude of depopulated, economically decimated villages what should we expect by way of civil society? Here we might productively recall the etymological connection between the terms "civil" and "civilization." An earlier version of *Webster's College Dictionary* (1962) defines civil as "1. of a citizen or citizens" and "2. of a community of citizens, their government or their interrelations," but the third definition is "suited for a city dweller, not rustic or countrified; hence 4. polite; urbane. 5. civilized." Civil society is both the citizen's society as opposed to the state (as if they could be separated), but, equally important, it is the civil*ized* society as opposed to the other options of interaction and interest promotion/representation.[1] Taylor (2008) captures this link in relation to Hungary with the term "civic cultivation," which she defines as "the process resulting from struggles within civil society concerning the education of masses toward the practice of citizenship." Is civil society in Eastern Europe not then also part of a "civilizing process" (Elias 1978), revealing its promoters' orientalist (Said 1978), if not Balkanist (Todorova 1997), view of the (post)socialist world? Does the attention to civil society there, in fact, again privilege the urban over the rural, those for whom such a diversity of organizations/interests are more possible, and for whom the formalization of the relationships might be more necessary than in an already thick rural social milieu?

The proliferation of nongovernmental organizations (NGOs) in Bulgaria, many of which were inspired by the availability of funds to promote civil society, became a joke during the 1990s. One colleague told me, only half-jokingly, "Everybody has his own NGO." Implicit in this critique was confirmation of my own impression of many of these organizations: that they did not reflect grassroots movements or organizing among those most in need of political representation. Is such a civil society not, in fact, a means by which influence is limited to, or at least allocated disproportionately to, those with less to complain about or less reasons to mobilize? To the degree that the mechanisms of civil society become the means by which interests are represented and carried out, does this then render the actions of those with less time and motivation less consequential?

Clearly they have less influence than those who mobilize, but they may also have less influence than they had under socialism, when civil society was not the anointed venue of political representation. Certainly if one accepts the view of socialism advanced by many, that the state's omnipresence and responsibility made all kinds of quotidian activity politically salient and consequential, then the lack of participation in civil society institutions in the postsocialist context may well represent a loss of political influence for some people. Todorova (2009:100) suggests the same when she calls what happened after 1989 a "demobilization of civil society." Even if the more enfranchised mobilize via civil society to help the marginal or excluded, what are we to make of the representational authority of such actions and the cultural hierarchy they reproduce between those who speak and those who are spoken for? Postcolonial theory would certainly challenge a wholly benign interpretation of this outcome. Taken together these hesitations force us to consider whether the formalization of civil society in the postsocialist context might not lead to the disenfranchisement of some.

Civil society discourse in Bulgaria in the early 1990s was bound up with assumptions about capitalism (Creed 1991). Instead of political interest representation, the term was more often rhetorically linked to core qualities of capitalism, from inequality to work ethics. This link is not unique to postsocialism, for as Hearn (1997:36) notes, civil society is commonly used by the Right to justify the idea that states should be minimally involved in the economy. In the early postsocialist context it took on an additional role. The logic seemed to be that a rich civil society would not only reflect and politically represent diversity but, more important, would actually help differentiate what had been a rather homogeneous populace, and that this would help smooth the acceptance of inevitable economic difference, the specter of which threatened to derail the transition in a population with a strong commitment to economic parity. This is not surprising, perhaps, given the dual political and economic transition that was under way at the time, and the prior integration of political and economic forces under socialism. The unquestioned value of civil society, forged in the fires of socialist dissent, provided a valuable vehicle for delivering the less attractive economic demands of capitalism. Although it continues to operate as an accomplice of capital in the arena of market differentiation and consumption, much like the concept of community as interrogated by Miranda Joseph (2001), I believe that this earlier link to the economy has shifted significantly as a form of capitalism has become more ensconced in Bulgaria. The concerns raised here, however, caution against viewing the project even now as one of simple democratization; rather, they suggest that civil society has become partially a means of establishing governmentality.

The fascination with civil society continues and reproduces the urban-centric model that stresses formal and institutional means of influence over informal mechanisms, and which, in fact, views the latter suspiciously. Analysts tended to glorify the informal sector under socialism as a source of autonomy from the state. This was somewhat erroneous, since many informal practices were intricately linked to the state. Nonetheless, the image of informality generally celebrated the initiative, ingenuity, and even resistance of a "second society." Ironically, since 1989, the continuation of informality has increasingly become a problem, now often redefined as "corruption." Civil society is offered as the enlightened alternative. It is as if the unfortunate socialist prohibition on civil society justified informality, and now that the prohibition has been lifted, the informal sector is the problem and must be replaced by a sanctioned network of civil society. Apparently informal mechanisms are a poor substitute for formal mechanisms and valued only when the latter are unavailable. Or perhaps more revealing, informal activities are only valued when the state itself is devalued (as in the communist variant). When the state is defined as legitimate, the informal sector is seen as illegitimate, maybe because informality competes with or challenges the state whereas civil society complements it.

In Richard Rose's (1995) thinking, the different treatment is justified because civil society links people vertically, facilitating political influence on the state, whereas informal connections are primarily horizontal, constituting a "premodern" drain on time and resources. But this was not so true under socialism when much of the state apparatus was staffed by recently upwardly mobile individuals who retained informal contacts at the grassroots. Generational turnover, capped off by the collapse of the pervasive socialist bureaucracy and its *nomenklatura*, toppled this verticality, so the vertical advantages of civil society over informality may be valid since 1989, but such integration is not necessarily democratizing if the option is differentially available across the population. Informal links have become less vertical with the communist collapse, but civil society as the panacea excludes many of the neediest, including those with the most to complain about. Thus civil society, even in its useful positive value, can undermine participation and local influence in a way that facilitates governance. By contrast, informal activities exist in the current context as a potential critique of state failures, and, given the lack of venues for real political influence, these avenues must be examined in order to appreciate what is going on at the grassroots, regardless of their structural impact on the political system. Much as David Stark (1996) has rehabilitated the informal resources and networks of socialism as viable capital(ist) resources, we need to recognize the political utility of informal social relations and activities.

We must also consider how formalization facilitates postsocialist governmentality, which the simultaneous objectives of democratic and capitalist transition demand because they are so often at odds. One way to mediate this contradiction is through the focus on formal institutions that are themselves highly regulative as the means of interest representation. In other words, the institutions of civil society are much more predictable and usually operate within a state-defined framework, even though they are outside the state. Although not part of the state, they are formally sanctioned and regulated by legal restrictions, and therefore are much more controllable than informal mechanisms outside the state's purview. As previously suggested, they also tend, in the current context, to be peopled by the relatively privileged.

In a context where the economic policies of transition are so detrimental to large sections of the population, the image of democratization depends heavily on performative elements such as elections and a proliferation of civil society groups that seemingly verify the democratic transition simply by their existence and actions—another type of performative excellence. The actual influence of people on state policy is extremely questionable. From 1989 to 1997, as Venelin Ganev (2007) has described convincingly, the Bulgarian state was stripped of its resources and power by rapacious politicians who, motivated primarily by personal enrichment, succeeded in eroding the institutional levers of state control that might have restrained them. Although he does not pursue it, this perverse achievement obviously left the beneficiaries with little incentive or requirement to attend to the popular desires that got them elected in the first place, and it left their successors unable to do so.

A fairly peaceful democratic uprising in 1997 renewed hope in the possibility of responsive democracy, but a series of new insults immediately proved otherwise. World financial institutions such as the World Bank and the International Monetary Fund (IMF) took over the economy, installing a currency board and dictating austere economic measures that were widely unpopular. The NATO alliance brought Bulgarian state support for the American bombing of Serbia against significant popular opposition, evidently justified when one of the bombs fell on a Sofia suburb. Unrepentant, and still desperate for good relations with the United States, Bulgarian leaders brought the state into George W. Bush's coalition of the willing, even though few ordinary citizens were actually "willing" (as my dinner conversations in Varvara clearly confirmed). The decision to pursue EU membership basically turned domestic policy over to the *acquis communitare,* and even the many Bulgarians who supported this decision (some simply out of desperation following years of successive domestic disappointments) criticized various demands and noted the one-sided nature of the so-called negotiations.

What does it mean to experience the formative years of democracy in this way? What if people's voices, even in cases of widespread popular consensus, have no influence? I believe this experience has produced a shallow notion of democracy, appreciated as an apparatus of governance but not thought to reflect or respond to popular political sentiment. This is related to, but also different from, what other observers of postsocialist politics have coined "pseudo-democracy" or "Potemkin Democracy" (King 2001). These terms suggest only a partial or superficial democratization aimed primarily at satisfying Western donors. I suggest that even where democratization has been rather complete, the will of the people is still circumvented.

What is the value of a civil society if there is, in fact, very little (if any) substantive response from the institutions and agents of the state? Indeed, if Ganev (2007) is right, why should we be concerned about the existence of civic organizations as avenues of popular interest representation, when the state to which they present their interests is completely incapacitated? Civic organizations are reduced to mutual self-help organs to coordinate people's efforts to fend for themselves, which seems eerily similar to my experience of informal networks under socialism. Civil society then became increasingly crucial as democratic *performance,* while remaining less than completely effective as a democratic vehicle for the same reason that elections are: few real political options exist, and the state is unable to respond to divergent demands.

Politics as Performance/Performance as Politics

Perhaps because of the need to efface the performative quality of civil society in Bulgaria, performance in its more expressive sense is denied any connection to civil society, even when it operates in parallel ways with similar objectives. This deflection is no doubt encouraged by the fact that it fails to promote the underlying objectives of civil society: civilizing and establishing governmentality. To support this claim I return to the mummers to point out how their activities constitute relations and interactions that are indeed parallel to some of the expectations of civil society.

First, participation generates a subset of villagers who share a common interest in the ritual and who work to maintain it over time, through both participation and production of the necessary ritual paraphernalia such as costumes and masks. Although such efforts were supported somewhat by the state under late socialism, this was not the case until the mid-1960s, and the rituals were maintained independently for the first twenty years of socialist rule (sometimes in defiance of the state). Since 1989 the state, for all intents and purposes, has withdrawn, and the rituals have continued in many villages and have even expanded in some, although they've diminished in others. A few municipal governments have stepped in with support for festivals, but by and large the activities are removed from the state.

As noted in previous chapters, in several villages organizers and participants articulate this break by refusing to cooperate with the village chitalishte secretary—the public employee who organized such efforts in the past. The chitalishte remains the cultural center for the village and, as an important cultural tradition and practice, mumming would certainly be a legitimate involvement for the secretary. In many cases, as in Varvara, she remains a significant helper and promoter. In the village of Turnicheni, in 1997, the secretary was the primary agitator trying to insure participation in the face of economic crisis. In some cases mummers have separated from her influence because of disagreements over the event, but usually the rift comes down to resources. In short, the chitalishte no longer has the state funding that might be used to help the mummers or promote their event, and if the secretary still expects some of the collected funds to be used for books or others materials for the chitalishte, there is likely to be a crisis. Her organizing efforts or assistance can be construed as a contribution requiring compensation from the proceeds, so if those efforts are not essential, as they are not in most cases where the event is rather simple and routinized, the group would rather forgo her help to avoid any expectation of sharing the proceeds, leaving them to decide for themselves what to do with the money. The point is that many mumming groups now, as in the early socialist period, have no state connection, and, where the connection is extant in the role of the chitalishte secretary, we should not make too much of it. Indeed, many mumming enthusiasts reported to me that they made most of their own decisions among themselves during late socialism as well, with the secretary playing only a supporting role: "she helped organize additional performances at the square by singing groups and children, but we did everything else ourselves."

Looking at the role of culture houses elsewhere in the socialist world supports this conclusion. Researchers note the limited degree of Communist Party involvement in the cultural activities of local culture houses in various countries, including Poland, Hungary, and the Soviet Union itself (Taylor

2008; White 1990). In Hungary amateur art group initiatives shifted to the hands of the groups themselves in the mid-1960s, and they started their own associations and market coops in the 1980s, spurred by economic reforms encouraging cultural producers to be more entrepreneurial and self-supporting, granting even those that still operated within the culture house more autonomy (Taylor 2008). These reforms were less extensive and arrived later in Bulgaria, but accounts by mummers clearly suggest that they enjoyed significant autonomy in many villages. That the culture house was part of the state's administration of culture should not lead us to equate the activities which the culture houses organized or supported as de facto affiliates of the state rather than civil society. In some cases it simply provided cover: undocumented rock bands in Hungary were able to perform in culture houses under the cover of events sponsored by the Communist Youth League (Taylor 2008).

Although the varied and unclear relation of mumming groups to governmental cultural institutions in late socialism and postsocialism might explain the lack of recognition of mumming and related activities as civil society, this excuse does not hold up when compared to the focus on nongovernmental organizations (NGOs). NGOs are perhaps the most popular focus of civil society discussions in postsocialist Eastern Europe, owing largely to a self-fulfilling dynamic: originally funded and deployed to help instill missing civic traditions, their proliferation and growth became a measure of civil society. The organizations originally intended to educate or instruct gradually became redefined as evidence of success themselves. This might not be invalid were it not for repeated studies showing that NGOs, in fact, end up operating in ways that are far from the ideal image of civil society and often in ways contrary to it (Hann 2003; Mandel 2002; Phillips 2008; Sampson 1996, 2002). Hann (2006:156) constructively warns about the danger of focusing only on the new NGOs to understand civil society and even suggests that a naïve faith in the liberating potential of new NGOs has come to form a "new 'church'" (Hann 2004). These studies have also revealed that what passes for an NGO is often not completely separate from the state but instead is connected in various and complicated ways. If these relations do not invalidate NGOs as units of civil society, then why should the varied, often tenuous, connections between mumming and the state do so?

In a few Bulgarian villages ritual commitments in the face of other divisions have produced two or more groups of mummers, challenging simplistic interpretations of village solidarity, but also reflecting the potential of this activity to conform to particular interests and concerns, from neighborhood

Figure 12. Members of one of the several dervish groups in Varvara in 2006.

Figure 13. A young man in Kalugerovo, in 2002, prepares his long-hair
goatskin costume, as acolytes watch and learn.

Figure 14. A float joins the promenade of mummers in Varvara in 2006; these men subsequently performed a comic skit on the village stage.

to politics. In Sushitsa, a former village incorporated as a subdivision into the central Bulgarian town of Karlovo, mumming includes two subgroups with different costumes and distinctive gaits, but disagreements in the late 1990s ended up creating two different groups of mummers, each with its own two subgroups. According to the organizer of the breakaway group, the split was provoked by mismanagement of mumming activities by the chitalishte and also represented an effort to "resist commercialization" of the ritual. The group succeeded in obtaining official registration as a voluntary organization so they could receive invitations to festivals and have all other rights alongside the parent group. The organizer of the separatists insisted that there was "nothing political" about the division, by which she meant it was not related to party membership or support, but it clearly demonstrates how mumming commitments can be vehicles of expressing particular political interests (in this case challenging political patronage, corruption, and commercialism).

The Varvara example reveals less direct political motivations, but it is still illustrative. Here the mummers have always (according to living memory) operated in different groups, much like informal clubs. Membership in one group rather than another is completely voluntary and based on group compatibility, itself often reflecting neighborhood connections, but also friendship, age, and even political sentiment. The group of adolescents is obviously not concerned with politics, and older mummers deny that political interest has any role in mumming; one mummer did say, however, that "naturally" some of the friendships that bring mummers together in the same group are strengthened by political agreement. In other words, agreement on political issues is a factor that can strengthen a friendship, and strong friendship is a primary basis for group membership. These groups then work independently and secretly, and in fact compete with one another to make the best masks. All the members of a group make identical masks each year, which they show off for the first time on New Year's Day. The group emerges to promenade up and down the main road in the village until their time to perform on stage. On stage they show off the masks as well as their rhythm and stamina by jumping and dancing for several minutes. The masks of each group were impressive the year I observed them. In the past there was an award given to the best group; some people complained that there were no longer resources to give an award, but others said the awards had made what was a friendly competition ugly, and were glad to see them gone.

Although these groups are not sponsored by the state, mummers' commitment to the event often results in mummers making demands on village leaders for improvements or actions thought to be necessary for a more successful ritual such as repairs to the village square. Most village mayors feel compelled to support mumming activities, minimally through generous gifts when mummers visit their home or office, and perhaps in more structural ways such as offering organizational supports. Those who do not at least feign interest and support are subject to scathing commentaries by mummers and others that often include promises to throw them out of office at the next election (if not before). In the cases of mumming I witnessed firsthand, there was a direct correlation between the degree of the mayor's engagement and support and villagers' popular evaluations of the mayor. Anemic or unsatisfactory mumming rituals are often seen as a reflection of other village problems, which may be blamed on political leaders—local, national, and international. In 1997, when the country was on the verge of economic collapse, the mumming participation in many locations was weak. In the words of one villager:

"mumming is a celebration and you have to have spirit for it. There's no spirit now. It's like having a party with nothing to celebrate. You can do it, and get just as drunk, but it doesn't feel the same." In some ways the anemic performances actually deepened the collective depression evident throughout the country at the time, convincing villagers that something had to be done. Mumming is a socioeconomic barometer that can shape villagers' political and economic experience and provoke political action.

Mumming groups mobilize primarily for the ritual, including large meetings prior to the actual performance to assign ritual roles, as well as smaller gatherings to make masks and costumes (see figure 13). The group of mummers I visited in Brezhani is one of the most precise. They gather four times between October and the ritual event to critique the previous year's performance, propose new ideas and assignments, discuss proposals, and then vote on the final arrangements. Complete minutes of the meetings are kept in an official notebook of the group, and a final report of the ritual, including number of participants, amount of money collected, and how they fared in the intra-village competition with other mumming groups, is subsequently added as well.

Mummers also gather for other activities during the year. Several villages have special places that could be described as a club headquarters, where mummers might gather even apart from mumming events. Sometimes these are old abandoned houses where masks and materials might be stored and mummers might occasionally gather for card playing and drinking (e.g., Yardzhilovtsi).[2] In other cases these spaces are bars and taverns in a mummer's basement that might also serve non-mummers but whose core regular clientele is mummers (e.g., Brezhani and Gigintsi). Occasionally the space is assigned to mummers by the local government in the chitalishte, town hall, or other administrative building (e.g., Batanovtsi). In Batanovtsi the mummers have two sizable rooms in the large town hall, one a sort of storage area, the other a nicely furnished gathering room and museum, with large masks on exhibit and an amazing bulletin board around part of the room displaying media articles about the group, various awards, posters from festivals (both Bulgarian and international), and photographs of the group over the years (another useful archive for researchers). Such places have their own lexical designation in Bulgarian: *mechkarnitsa*. The word comes from the word *mechkari*, which, as previously noted, is derived from the word for bear and is used to designate mummers in several villages. A mechkarnitsa, then, is a gathering place or workshop for mummers. The term is not used everywhere, but it is common in the area around Pernik, even in villages where the mummers are not referred to as mechkari. The mummers of Batanovtsi, for example, referred to the fancy rooms described above as their mechkarnitsa even though they refer to themselves as survakari. Such physical spaces bespeak a degree of institutionalization.

Even where there is no designated physical space, mummers meet in other village locations. As previously noted, a banquet is very common, sometimes in the wake of the actual event but more often at a significant interval following the ritual. In the former case mummers consume the food they have collected, and in these villages they typically receive more perishable food items such as eggs, salami, fruit, or cheese. In the latter case most food offerings are nonperishable items such as dried beans, and the food for the banquet is purchased with the collected funds. In both cases the collected wine or brandy is also consumed.

In all such meetings of mummers that I attended conversations were never limited to mumming discussions. Politics was a common topic, and mummers often came up with creative suggestions for resolving village and national problems. Many proposals were violent, but others sounded more reasonable. Engagement with mummers over the period spanning preparation to finale reveals the events as an important context for producing political discontent and sometimes turning it into an organized force. Although collective meetings of mummers are not regular events, compared to the famous Philadelphia mummers whose frequent meetings and activities insure recognition of civic significance,[3] participation in Bulgarian mumming forges bonds that are tapped regularly in everyday life.

Mumming groups also mobilize to organize, plan, and participate in festivals. Mumming troupes are occasionally invited to foreign countries to perform as living "folklore." More often commitment to the rituals brings together groups from different villages through the sharing of costumes and joint participation in one another's rituals. As was evident in chapter 1, mummers from distant villages commonly exchange invitations and participate in each other's events. Some villages even coordinate the dates of their celebrations in order to facilitate such interaction and cooperation. As noted in the previous chapter, the mining village of Eleshnitsa is fairly unique in conducting mumming events on Easter, and though participants report that they have "always" performed on Easter, they also acknowledge that the timing allows more men to participate. They can do so because "many startsi don't have their own costumes" and the scheduling allows them to borrow expen-

sive elements from mummers in other villages who have completed their activities and won't need them again for several months. These relations, like
those within a village, can be quite strong and are tapped for needs well beyond the ritual, including mobilizing labor, finances, and political influence.
Indeed, since costumes are highly valued, loaning and returning can significantly increase both the depth and breadth of trust between mummers.

Such connections were particularly useful in the socialist context noted
for its vertical rather than horizontal integration. Indeed, there were few formal
avenues for coordination and interaction across socialist villages, especially
those that were not in the same municipality or county. Moreover, the latter
often included villages with a history of conflict. These historical antagonisms
were reproduced as they found themselves competing for the resources dis-
tributed among them from the county seat. Mumming provided an important connection to other villages that might be more open to other types of
cooperation. These links also facilitated the spread of information censored
by the state media. Mummers reported to me that they often returned from
festivals or visits to other villages with significant news they never would have
known otherwise. This included information about agricultural experiments,
such as new crops and new organizational forms, that they might anticipate
coming their way, which in turn gave them a heads-up on the kinds of ideas
circulating among higher-level government planners. They also heard about
the effects of Chernobyl radiation on agricultural products in some areas, and
they could then avoid buying produce from those regions.

The network of mummers, in fact, accounts for the success of my fieldwork. I regularly asked mummers I spoke with about other villages with mumming traditions. In most cases I not only was told the name of the village but
the names of other mummers I should talk to there. It is a dense social network, and, indeed, were it not for the fact that some mumming groups have
antagonistic relations (usually those in neighboring villages), one might call
mumming a nationwide fraternity with local branches. If one accepts this
analogy, then the civil society parallel is obvious. I also believe that the socialist state's involvement actually increased the parallel, as the organized festivals helped participants to see their disparate and distinctive traditions as
part of a single activity. The generic use of the term *kukeri* testifies to the increasing recognition of unified activity. Varvara's figures are not kukeri but
rather dervishes; moreover, because they celebrate on New Year's, the popular
term survakari would seem to be a more appropriate substitute. Yet, although
dervish is still the most common term, villagers often refer to them as kukeri,

and, in fact, the front of the chitalishte had a large banner reading "Village Varvara wishes you happy kukeri days."

In mumming rituals, as well as festivals and travel abroad, mummers clearly constitute the equivalent of village booster clubs. They also contribute more directly to village improvement, as some of the funds collected may be designated for village needs such as repairs to the village fountain or purchase of supplies for the kindergarten or chitalishte. Of course, for those who believe in some supernatural effect from these rituals, mummers provide an invaluable contribution to the village's well-being. In villages that have been hit hard by emigration, mumming groups operate much like expatriate organizations in which villagers return to carry on the rituals, bringing material and social benefits with them. The village of Gigintsi, where I accompanied mummers in 2002, has a population of less than 200, and nearly 20 mummers kicked off the event on the 13th (although somewhat fewer for the village canvass on the 14th), despite frigid temperatures and daunting snowfall. Most of them came from Pernik for the event, including several teenagers who had been born and raised in Pernik, the sons of village expatriates. The story in the nearby village of Svetlya is even more extreme: there more mummers are predictably mobilized than in Gigintsi from a population of just over 150 full-time residents. At the festival in Pernik, Svetlya is one of the larger mumming groups participating, sometimes as many as a hundred mummers, comparable to the size of groups from villages with 2,000 residents.

While villagers may participate in festivals organized by elements of the state, they insist on describing mumming as a grassroots activity completely removed from the state. They even minimize the former socialist state's support and emphasize instead how villagers kept the ritual alive despite state prohibitions during the Stalinist years. The continuity of mumming after communism collapsed and the state withdrew all support confirms that state assistance was perhaps not essential even under socialism (and thus mumming may have operated much like civil society then as well). Nonetheless, political leaders from the district or county level may still show up at festivals and even individual village rituals if they are sizable. This is not an official political forum, but in a context where village(r)s are often off the political radar screen, these visits provide interaction and communication between political leaders and villagers, granting the former a chance to see and hear about local conditions firsthand while providing villagers a chance to observe and evaluate their political leaders.

Some mumming events include satirical political skits in which explicit political messages are part of the performance. The events I witnessed in Var-vara in 2006 illustrate this nicely. As the bridal couple, along with the bear and his trainer, continued to circulate among the growing audience, and the masked mummers continued to promenade up and down the main street, the program got under way on the stage directly in front of the chitalishte. It started with folk singing and dancing by the group of village women I had heard practicing when I first arrived at the Varvara chitalishte. Now decked out in folk costume, they were satirically introduced as the Philip Kutev Ensemble, one of the most famous professional folk ensembles span-ning the socialist and postsocialist periods (see Buchanan 2006). They were followed by the reenactment of the mummers' household greeting. By this time a "float" had appeared and joined the pedestrian parade going back and forth on the road by the chitalishte, distracting the audience (see figure 14). It was a flatbed truck hauling an old, beat-up Bulgarian Lada (the Fiat-style car produced during the socialist era), accompanied by a motley crew of young men dressed in wigs and sexually provocative medical costumes. A sign over the car identified it as "The Newest S-Class" complete with a Mercedes logo.

Back on the stage, a collection of middle-aged and older women replaced the singers to enact a scene at a Bulgarian border crossing. Two women were dressed as men in the roles of a customs officer and a border guard. The hilarious skit consisted of various women trying to cross the border into Greece. The officials examined the documents of each, finding problems with all of them. Each refusal elicited a sob story from the woman in an effort to persuade the guards to let her pass. The first woman could not find work in Bulgaria but had a job lined up in Greece; the next one had a sick son already working there and she needed to help him; the last one claimed that her entire village had already relocated to Greece and that she had to join them, bring-ing the last village hen with her in her hands. The guards were not persuaded. Then a man with a large box showed up and, when told there was a problem with his documents, he began pulling out money, making it clear what kind of "papers" one actually needed (and the previous supplicants lacked) to get across the border. After bribing the guard he was told he could cross, but the customs officer insisted that she had to inspect the box. The man frantically dialed his cell phone (no doubt trying to contact higher connections to inter-vene), but before he could mobilize them the officer had already opened the box to find a provocatively dressed young woman, clearly destined for sex work in Greece. The obvious allusion to the traffic in women was complicated and broadened when she was found to be carrying gold and narcotics. The action became a bit frenetic and hard to follow at this point, but in the end this windfall discovery, which the border officials divided between themselves, was enough to cover the bribes for all the women and everybody was allowed to go to Greece. The audience laughed heartily in the face of what I thought was a rather grim ending. When I pointed this out to the man standing next to me, he looked at me strangely and said: "It's a *happy* ending, everyone gets out of the country."

This was followed by another skit enacted by the young men on the float, which got rather lewd. The dilapidated "Mercedes" was presented as a lottery prize, and the burlesque medical personnel took to treating two other transvestite figures for mad cow disease and bird flu (both having been major European scares at the time, with bird flu actually having been detected in Bulgaria). The sign indicating bird flu, however, was "abbreviated" replacing one letter in the word for bird with a dash, making it actually read "pussy flu." This required a gynecological exam conducted by a man in medical attire with a tensile wig, prominent bosoms, and a fire extinguisher between his legs. The treatment is obvious—the hose from the fire extinguisher was put between the patient's legs and blasted off in spurts simulating an orgasm. With the patient cured, the actors proceeded to perform the "first transvestite wedding in Bulgaria," which was explained as happening "by the order of the EU." This was intended as a jab at the EU's immoral pro–gay rights demands, and it vividly confirms the increasing recognition of a global/Western gay consciousness as suggested in the previous chapter. Some members of the audience were clearly uneasy and embarrassed by these sexual elements, but overall the public responded positively to the skits.

The extent of political commentary in Varvara's enactment, like its masks, is unusual. In fact, this combination has earned the derision of residents of a neighboring village who dismiss these activities as "Varvarski kukeri" (Varvara mumming), and then use the same term metaphorically for any activity done in a frivolous, unconventional way. But political elements are often present as adjuncts to more traditional mumming practices in many villages, and they sometimes attract media attention amplifying their political impact.[4] Moreover, as I have noted elsewhere, mumming groups and symbols can be mobilized for political purposes (Creed 2002a; see also Benovska-Săbova 1998). During the extensive protests in January 1997 in Sofia, student groups tapped into mumming symbolism for one of their most effective protests, donning bits of mumming costumes and performing in front of the parliament in order to "drive out the evil forces." More recently, in January 2008, a demonstration organized by environmentalists to protest development in the Pirin Mountains engaged actual village mumming groups. Their call for action was addressed directly to mummers: "kukeri" was the first category listed in the call for mobilization, followed by "spelunkers, mountain-climbers, skiers, snowboarders, alpinists [and] optimists." The subsequent description of the event promised that "a powerful group of mummers will help us to drive out the dark forces in state government, because everybody knows that living traditions want a living nature." Clearly the fact that the Pirin Mountains are home to many mumming groups (recall Brezhani from the previous chapter), and the traditional link between mumming and fertility, which is essentialized as "nature," make them a powerful concentrated symbol for this particular political effort.

The point is not that mumming groups are political organizations but, rather, that these apolitical civic organizations have potential as vehicles of interest representation and protest. Even in a civic-rich society like the United States, these activities can be recognized as politically threatening. In 2003 a comic group of Philadelphia mummers was pressured by the mayor and a Catholic cardinal to scrap their planned presentation in the annual mummers' parade. The parody, titled "The Devil Made Me Do It," poked fun at the then expansive priest sex-abuse scandal in the Catholic Church. In all likelihood mummers were even more significant in the socialist context, as every action had political potential. Although many aspects of life may have been de-politicized by the communist collapse, many continue to carry potential political significance because politics remains an anathema. The popular abhorrence of politics and embrace of an "anti-politics" is often traced to the politicization of everything during the socialist era, but it was certainly sustained, if not compounded, by the shameful and ineffective actions of politicians in the postsocialist era. In twenty-first-century Bulgaria, politics in any form at any level is popularly eschewed. Almost all involvement in partisan politics is vulnerable to accusations of influence seeking and corruption, because the postsocialist political field has remained dominated by these objectives. Ethnographers working in such contexts have argued that cultural forms and activities take on much more political significance. Obviously the shame of formal politics does not foreclose political opinions, so we must look elsewhere for their candid expression. In short, politics must be disguised, so what better place to look than mumming.

Amico (2007) suggests that music plays an important role in defining and presenting gay male identities in Russia precisely because the shame of politics undermines the standard forms of activism found in the West. We risk missing the significance of a Russian gay identity and its political influence by measuring it in terms of the civil society organizations that dominate gay activism in the West, specifically because such activism is seen as political and thus very uncool. Rather than the politically tinted avenues of civil society, Russian gays establish communities and identities through music. Taylor (2008) makes a related argument in Hungary focusing not on gays but on populists. She documents a history in which populist writers constituted a political movement in *pre*socialist Hungary, precisely because politics was seen as potentially corrupting, and people sought guidance instead from the spiritual and cultural. Various populist efforts that shaped progressive activists were organized around folk culture, such as the caroling scouts who share some similarities to Bulgarian mummers. She suggests that the dance house is also a cultural practice with political effect/affect, first as an avenue of resistance to state socialism and then as a nationalist force in postsocialism. I am not positing such broad claims for mumming but simply suggesting that these examples justify paying attention to what mumming might be doing.

Modern Complications

Mumming involvement produces groups of villagers with shared interests whose participation in mumming benefits the village in various ways and provides an avenue of interaction and cooperation not only with fellow villagers but with mummers from other towns and villages as well. These activities provide access to politicians at local and county levels and can be an avenue of interest mobilization and representation. This is not a sophisticated analysis, and that is just my point. It does not take great acuity to see the attributes of civil society in these activities, and yet they are not included in such discussions or analyses. This is partly because analysts and politicians interested in civil society usually do not pay attention to "cultural" events. At the same time mumming groups are hardly omnipresent, which suggests a limited degree of influence at best, so I do not want to make more of this avoidance than the data merit. Still, mumming is not the only example. Todorova reached the same conclusion in the more explicitly political context of the debate over the possible discovery of Levski's grave. "As long as they were not *seen* as directly challenging the existing political superstructure (either ideologically or personally), some kind of civil society and public debate were tolerated and even encouraged from the late 1960s on" (Todorova 2009:107; emphasis in original).

When these avoidances are added together they suggest that something was distracting attention. The focus on civil society produces a veiled critique (intended or not) of informality, which operates to deflect attention from activities lacking formal and permanent structures (such as mumming), despite the time, effort, commitment, and resources they mobilize. To the degree that elements of civil society are institutionalized or actualized, they further undermine the influence of informal activities, which are then defined nearly by default as insignificant, frivolous, or trivial. Obviously the hesitancy to see a parallel to civil society is also a way to deny the significance of the political commentary included, much as the comedy of American late-night television simultaneously expresses criticism in a way that renders it less threatening as satire or comedy (just for fun), even as it acquires more importance as a source of political information for the population. The general tendency to ignore informal activity in relation to civil society should provoke inquiry into how the latter may configure popular political influence in ways that have consequences. I believe it does so in ways that civilize citizens assumed to lack the prerequisites for democratic participation while simultaneously funneling participation into arenas and institutions that help promote governance. If this is so, then, for some people, it is hard not to see the move to civil society as a form of silencing even as it empowers.

Recognizing the civilizing mission of civil society exposes its link to another powerful project: modernity. To some degree the need for civil society is founded upon teleological assumptions about social evolution from the direct, dense, and significant contacts of *gemeinshaft* to the instrumental, formal, or abstract social relations of *gesellschaft* and the parallel shift from mechanical to organic solidarity, in the context of political evolution toward the assumed pinnacle of political organization, representative democracy. Mumming is unable to function conceptually as civil society, then, because in the eyes of many observers it is quintessentially premodern. As already recounted, mention of my interest in mumming to urban politicians or even urban intellectuals (other than folklorists or ethnographers) often provoked embarrassment. The link between civil society and modernity disqualifies particular activities or venues that are, for whatever reasons, interpreted as premodern. Seeing mumming as premodern is overdetermined by its purported antiquity, abetted by the fact that it is performed in "backward" rural areas (of a country whose hold on modernity is itself tenuous). This pertains despite the fact that the rituals have shifted significantly in response to modern demands. At the same time the incorporation of mumming as a prime piece of national(istic) folklore since the 1960s also works against the image of civil society as a vehicle of diverse interest representation distinct from the state within a Western framework that automatically links the national to the state.

Vigorous efforts to build civil society go on while promising or potential cultural venues for collective representation, such as mumming, are ignored or denied, and other cooperative institutions are actually being liquidated (i.e., cooperative farms). This combination can be understood when the overall objective is not just to produce mechanisms for civic participation but to (re)constitute the autonomous individual who is then free to actualize his or her interests via collective organization free of the restraints of "culture" or entangling social relations, fitting a Western, if not neoliberal, model of political participation. Obviously removing these restraints also opens the society to effective administration and the unfettered operation of market principles.

The possibility that mumming operated differently and provided an alternative way of input and influence was confirmed in one of the many evocative conversations I had with mummers, this one with a middle-aged man from the village of Cherna Gora. I asked him my usual questions about why he participated, to which he gave a common reply: he could not really explain it, the desire was inside him, "some people have it and some don't." I pushed on and asked if he thought there was any material benefit from the ritual in terms of abundance. He paused thoughtfully, turning his pack of cigarettes over and over on the table, and then said, "I won't say there is, but I can say it is just as effective as voting." This synthesis captures better than any analysis the civics lesson of this chapter. I suggest it is more than just analogy; it shows how mumming is linked to the civic engagement and opportunities for expression that have been monopolized, discursively and practically, by the ideas of civil society and electoral politics, in a place where politics is discredited and democracy is a shallow performance.

While anthropologists have generally been critical of this civil society discourse, many have supported a complementary argument: the idea that socialist society was highly atomized. I turn to this trope of (post)socialism in the next chapter.

CHAPTER FOUR

AUTONOMY AND COMMUNITY

Approximately thirty kilometers due north of Varvara, across the valley defined by the Maritsa and Tolpolnitsa rivers, sit the adjacent villages of Lesichevo and Kalugerovo. Mumming here, as in Varvara, is one of the most anticipated events of the year, although it occurs later in the winter. Varvara residents associated this difference with geography, saying that villages north of the Maritsa River celebrate at Lent (specifically cheese Lent) rather than New Year's. While this distinction pertains along the western origins of the river, it does not hold as the river flows eastward. Mummers in Lesichevo are called dervishes, as are those in Varvara, but in Kalugerovo they are known as *dzhamali*. The costumes in both villages are similar to those in Varvara—long-hair goat skins (although, as noted in chapter 2, this is a recent innovation in Kalugerovo where mummers previously wore sheepskins). The masks in Lesichevo and Kalugerovo, however, bear no resemblance to the diverse and elaborate Varvara constructions. Instead, they are fairly uniform and create a more seamless connection to the costume. They are made of the same long-hair goat skin, sewn into a cap that flows down the back and sides of the head. The face is an embellished fabric flap with holes for the eyes (see figure 15). This design is especially convenient for the extended eating, drinking, and socializing that characterize Lesichevo practice, as the flap can be lifted up easily over the head and out of the way for the duration of the mummers' lengthy visit.

In Kalugerovo there are numerous brides, dressed not in traditional folk costume but white wedding gowns with veils. In Lesichevo there is no bride at all and no musicians. Although this is uncommon in mumming practice, it is by no means unique. As in a few other villages the bride's central role is replaced by a black-faced Arap. I discuss this recurrent element further in the next chapter; here I focus on other dimensions of mumming elaborated in Lesichevo—the practice of mumming in small groups and the ritual elaboration of conflict. The former element was evident in Varvara, where groups worked independently in secret to design and build their masks, but the village canvass was still a single group of mummers representing the collective village. In Kalugerovo and Lesichevo there is no unified village canvass; instead, different groups of mummers, each with approximately three to seven members, wander around the village independently of one another. There is no concern to cover the entire village and no assigned territories. Household visits in Kalugerovo are primarily confined to the evenings; during the day the young men prefer to spend time at public places or intersections where they can hold up passing pedestrians or motorists for "donations." This insures that they get cash instead of food and drink, although at one intersection staked out by a large group of mummers, I overheard one tell another: "I told you this work had died," referring both to the limited traffic and the meager sums they were collecting. I must say, however, that compared to mummers in other villages they were not nearly as aggressive in forcing the cars to stop, and those that did were often let go without a donation if they declined. Compared to similar efforts in villages like Yardzhilovtsi, these younger men were simply "not serious," as a couple of my friends expressed it. In Lesichevo, by contrast, the house visits were central. They consumed most of the day and were generally more extended than in any other village I observed, made possible by the fact that not every household was visited.

These two villages are also unusual for the free reign given to force and violence. Although many mumming traditions include symbolic enactments of violence, such as minor slapping and pinching, in Lesichevo and Kalugerovo, as in some other villages, the physical force goes beyond the symbolic to the downright painful, with victims sometimes suffering severe harm. I was warned about these villages by informants in Varvara. The son of my host there once went with some friends to Kalugerovo for the mumming event, but they left quickly because they were getting hurt: "After getting some lumps and some bruises we decided that this is not for us." When I observed activities there in mid-March 2002 I didn't get bruised, but I am sure it was in deference to my status as a foreigner because there was aggression all around me. When a mummer spotted someone he knew, a rather violent attack usually ensued with the mummer attacking and hitting the observer mercilessly. The victim sometimes resisted and tried to hit back, provoking a more extended battle that occasionally escalated into an exchange of blows that teetered on street fighting. This was considered inappropriate for the victim who is expected to "take it." The more common and more socially appropriate response was for the victim to shield himself in a defensive posture and try to get away.

In Lesichevo I spent most of the major day of mumming activity with a group of four mummers I joined early in the morning as they dressed. This was actually the second group I tried to join that morning. I had planned to accompany a group of seven younger mummers, some of whom I had met on an earlier trip to the village and who assured me that I would have the most fun with their group because it was the largest in the village, and, as one of the young men put it: "the more dervishes, the more friends to visit, the more brandy!" This logic should have been a warning. When I arrived at their meeting point early in the morning, they were already so drunk that I could hardly communicate with them. Though my language skills were partially to blame, the level of inebriation was the main problem. While members of other groups had been preparing and repairing their costumes for days, these procrastinators had stayed up all night to finish the job. The skins must be soaked in advance to rehydrate the hides so they are malleable. Only then can they be repaired and re-sewn into the component pieces: legs, sleeves, and a vest. They must then be dried out long enough for the hair to dry, so that it bounces and flows to maximum effect but not so long that the hides rigidify again. Mummers actually wear skins with the hides moist, adding to the discomfort, especially in cold weather. The drunken mummers insisted that doing much of this work the night before was part of the fun of the event (a fact other mummers attributed to their youth). Of course, this meant that they were also drinking all night.

The drunken mummers were nothing if not animated, insisting that I try on various hats and masks, and talking to me incessantly and simultaneously in loud voices—no doubt in a misguided effort to help me understand their slurred speech. One tried to help by speaking Italian, which he had learned during several months of working illegally in Italy. That I do not speak Italian seemed not to deter him in the least. No one tried English, or, if someone did, I didn't recognize it. Luckily sober helpers arrived to assist in the final stage of dressing; I doubt they would have managed otherwise. One of these help-ers told me that "the boys" would be "like this" all day and recommended that I join another group to get a more representative impression of the custom. Difficult as it was to turn away from this curious train wreck, I eventually heeded his advice. I still had the privilege of observing the younger group at a few houses during the day when they crossed paths with the group I accom-panied, and, surprisingly, they seemed less incapacitated despite having been treated to brandy at several houses by this point. I can only hypothesize that the accompanying food offerings and regular physical exertion helped neu-tralize the alcohol.

The alternative group included four men: three were middle-aged, in their late thirties to late forties, and the fourth was a younger man in his early twenties. Three others assisted the four with the difficult process of dressing. These mummers were also drinking, of course, but seemed nearly sober com-pared to the other group. They assembled at the home of one of the dressers who was usually a mummer himself. When I asked him why he wasn't dress-ing this year, he reported that he had broken his leg two consecutive years in mumming altercations and so was taking this year off. And this from the more sober group! I knew I was in for something different here, and I will admit to some concern about my own safety.

Dressing is a complicated procedure; the individual pieces of the costume that are prepared in advance are actually sewn together by the dresser on the mummer's body. After all the seams are complete, which can take half an hour or more, the mummer tests the costume by jumping and strutting, re-turning to the dresser with complaints that it is binding in one place or shift-ing too much in another. The dresser makes the necessary adjustments until the mummer is satisfied. Mummers are literally sewn into their costumes and cannot take them off unless they cut the seams. This meticulous stitching ex-ceeded the efforts of mummers in other villages with similar costumes. The difference harkens again to the violence of Lesichevo mumming, as the pieces would easily be ripped apart were they not stitched securely and tightly. In fact, one dresser accompanied the group all day with a big needle threaded with what looked like rawhide to repair the seams pulled apart in the aggres-sive fighting and jumping.

The various groups of Lesichevo mummers are defined by friendship. By default, this generally creates a particular age profile for each group but not perfectly. Most groups had at least one member outside the modal generation. I spoke to mummers in several groups, and they all confirmed that friendship was the basis of group formation—men joined mumming groups with their friends. These groups were also less territorially defined than those in Varvara, although, in several cases, personal relations overrode neighborhood there as well.

Some groups include a mummer described as the "shover" (*butach*), a man dressed in folk costume whose ritual role is to harass and shove the dervishes, provoking them to fight, which does not take much as they are willing combatants. The Arap figure sometimes acts as their defender, which gets him into fights with the shover as well. The shover is especially prominent at the village square in the afternoon when all the mumming groups gather together and dance nonstop for hours around the square. Prior to this gathering, the shover's role is filled primarily by the host of each house the mummers visit (and in a few cases the host is actually dressed in folk costume for this performance).

The mummers set out to visit the homes of their friends and relatives. For the group I accompanied, this amounted to twelve houses. The weather was pleasant, so all the meetings took place outside. Had the weather been bad, I was assured, they would have been invited inside. At some houses a table was already partially set with food. Others were less prepared, and the food did not appear until the mummers were there. Upon arrival they begin shouting to the owner who eventually emerges. The mummers then greet their hosts with a short dance and blessing: "To be alive, to be healthy, everything to produce for you, even from dry stones . . . the good God to provide for the throat."[1] They also hit the hosts on the rear with their swords. Mummers reported enacting other activities at some houses: jumping over children and the elderly (if they can bend down) to ensure health, holding children while jumping with them for the same purpose, and hitting fruit trees with their sword to insure fruit. The group I accompanied performed none of these activities, but I did witness hosts pulling out hair from the mummers' costumes which is later tied with a red thread and placed in the joints of either the fence or the house to ward off evil, a meta-ritual adaptation of martenitsi practices (described in chapter 1).[2] The mummers feign resistance to these efforts or irritation if they are accomplished clandestinely.

The mummers sit down and are treated minimally to pickled vegetables (the only vegetables available at this time of year) or perhaps more elaborate fare, including banitsa. Wine was offered at some houses, but the traditional and typical offering is warm sweetened brandy. This must be heated for the visit, so it sometimes takes a few minutes to produce and must be consumed in situ. This almost necessitates a more prolonged social event than the wine or plain brandy found elsewhere, which can be quickly swigged or poured into vessels to take along. Usually offered hot, the brandy may require some cooling and slower sipping, which goes along nicely with the extended stays of Lesichevo mummers. These are lengthy socializing events, half an hour was the average.

At two of the households our visit overlapped with another group of mummers. On one of these occasions we were joined after we were well into our visit at the house, and the other time we coincidently arrived at the intended house at the same time as another group. These larger crowds made the event more festive, including socializing between mummers from the different groups, but the overall experience was much the same. In the case where both groups arrived together they also left together and continued for some time in a single larger group on the street, separating again to enter different houses further down the lane. Thus some houses are visited by multiple groups, whereas others may host only one or two and some none at all.

When the mummers finally leave the house, the men of the house often accompany them to the street whereupon they begin wrestling with the dervishes (see figure 16). This varied in intensity from obvious pantomime with little actual contact to intensive fighting. No punches were thrown, but there were aggressive take downs and painful falls. As previously noted, this is the main activity at the village square later in the afternoon, where all the groups gather and dance their typical step in a circle around the square. They are constantly engaged in fights by both costumed "shovers" as well as men in the audience. Already drunk from a day of drinking, the dancers move around the square in a circle while also spinning themselves (a unique movement perhaps not coincidental to their local designation as dervishes). As it continues for hours, mummers step out and rest, but it is hard not to suspect that at this point they are in a quasi-altered state. Not surprisingly, it is here that some of the more extreme physical injury, such as broken limbs, occurs. There are no other organized enactments at the square, leaving one to surmise that conflict itself is the central mumming project.

The mummers of Lesichevo perform, in an explicit way, the nature of social relations I had experienced living in various Bulgarian villages. I had already made this association with previous ritual events, so my Lesichevo experience in 2002 was more of a capstone confirmation than an eye-opener. The nature of social relations I refer to here is one in which conflict and tension are paramount, but rather than signifying a lack of cohesion or collectivity—

what some have described as a pervasive "atomization"—these conflicts testify to the extensive relations and expectations that produce recurrent disappointment and, more important, are actually a component of community relations. This suggestion continues the previous chapter's critique of civil society, which is assumed to be missing not only because the socialist state suppressed such organizations, but also because it destroyed the social fabric of society, forcing families in on themselves. Ironically, although these two arguments enable each other, anthropologists have largely challenged the former while supporting the latter.

I am concerned, however, that my critique of the atomization argument (as well as the civil society discourse) not be taken as support for the contrary model of Eastern European/(post)socialist society mentioned in the previous chapter, which I find equally problematic. This model, also common across the social sciences, suggests that socialist citizens wove extended and dense webs of kinship and informal interdependencies which they relied upon to get goods and services otherwise in short supply and to evade the obstructive and pervasive bureaucracy. In many cases, usually among the well-placed, these networks became the foundation of postsocialist "mafias." How can these two seemingly contradictory models of socialism coexist: one in which people are ensconced in webs of relations so extensive that they survive the system that spun them to entangle subsequent democratic efforts, and another in which citizens are so bereft of social relations that they lack a place to start building civil society even after the causes of their atomization have disappeared? I think mumming helps us understand how these different factors articulate and, in so doing, exposes underlying assumptions that may have helped produce these scholarly models. I suggest that both views share some similarities and that our expectations about social relations, specifically ideas about community and modernity, account for the appeal of these models beyond their empirical reality. In other words, we have to look at the epistemological bases of these ideas to understand how they acquired such acceptance, especially given their potential oppositions.

The culprits are the qualities that haunt our very understanding of collectivity, most evident in the notion of community, which, more often than not, carries assumptions of harmony and homogeneity that one might call "romantic." I have demonstrated the continuity of these ideas despite numerous challenges and corrections in a previous publication (Creed 2006), and I do not intend to repeat that argument here. Instead, in the remainder of this chapter, I review the specifically East European consequences of this romance: the atomization thesis and the fascination with informal networks. I then use mumming activities to suggest a more distinctive/nuanced understanding of social relations, missed by those focusing on civil society, atomization, and informal networking.[3] My broader claim is that these two models miss the rather complex way that tension, conflict, opposition, incorporation, affiliation, and cooperation interacted for Bulgarian villagers, obscuring a cultural resource that could have been exploited for a different cultural construction of democracy and political participation.

Images of East European Social Relations

Romantic ideas about community have had a major impact on anthropological research in Eastern Europe. Early work in the area, sometimes based on historical reconstructions or the ill-conceived study of culture at a distance, focused on what might be considered paragons of romantic community such as the Russian communal village (*mir*), the Balkan extended communal family (*zadruga*), and pious Jewish small towns (*shtetls*) (Mosley 1940; Zborowski and Herzog 1952). These traditions fit nicely with the evolutionary view of community because Eastern Europe was seen as the backwater of the continent and the logical place to find the vestal community that had been destroyed by Western urbanization and industrialization. Fieldwork in the area was limited by cold war considerations to Yugoslavia where the community study method shaped much of the work (Halpern 1958). By the 1970s East European political reforms were opening borders for researchers in Hungary, Poland, and especially Romania, where Ceaușescu's efforts to establish his independence from Moscow led to a more open foreign policy. The first ethnographic reports, however, tended to verify the community model. John Cole's (1976) analysis of Romania, for example, emphasizes the reliance between neighbors and kin in the Romanian countryside, replicating an image that Eugene Hammel (1968) painted earlier for Yugoslavia by emphasizing extended ritual kinship relations and obligations of godparenthood. This view was also important to indigenous scholarship of the region, as it provided a native tradition supposedly compatible with, if not productive of, socialist cooperative policies (Krustanova 1986; Skovierová 1988).

By the 1980s a new perspective was gaining momentum. Social commentators, inspired by the same dissident critiques that revived the idea of civil society, turned their attention to the destruction of social linkages throughout East Europe. Sociologist Stepan Nowak posited that such destruction had created a "social vacuum" in Poland (cited in Wedel 1992:9). Chris Hann

(1985:98) suggested a rural variant by noting that socialist administration in Wisłok was "not conducive to village unity" and calling his ethnography *A Village without Solidarity* (although he also documented significant integration via religion [1985:100–117]). Istvan Rev's (1987) classic piece on Hungary popularized and christened the argument by claiming that villagers had became distrustful and atomized as a result of collectivization and the prohibition of political organizing. The ironic advantage of atomization was the promotion of everyday resistance: silencing the public sphere dispersed politics and infused every action with political potential, the sheer bulk of which forced the system to respond. However, since "the peasant understood that the only way to success was through strictly individual, silent action, the community was undermined. . . . Both the working of the centralizing state and the successful individual resistance against it helped to undermine the basis of communality. The price of changing the political system was a change in the community" (Rev 1987:348).

This thesis reaches its apogee in David Kideckel's (1993) ethnography of a Romanian village where a poetic rephrasing of the position provides the title of the book: *The Solitude of Collectivism.* The evocative phrasing, however, is somewhat misleading, since individuals were not alone but rather were ensconced in tight-knit families that were isolated from one another. In this view, the family became the bunker against total(izing) socialist regulation. Faced with state control in every other arena, people retreated to their families as the only location of trust, fulfillment, and commitment. In dealing directly with the state these family units became increasingly isolated from one another so that the local community became a mere bureaucratic entity of the state composed of atomized families pursuing selfish interests. The parallel with Edward Banfield's (1958) notion of "amoral familism," which he coined to explain the lack of community relations in a southern Italian village, is not lost on Kideckel, who actually invokes it, albeit with qualification (1993:136).

This model has become almost accepted wisdom in accounts of socialist Eastern Europe. Martha Lampland's (1995) analysis of a Hungarian cooperative farm suggests that the process was abetted by the commodification of labor that transformed traditions of community labor exchange into commodity relations. Nancy Ries (1997:64) notes the anti-communalism of Muscovites toward neighbors, which is echoed by Beth Holmgren's (1995) claim that home provided Russians a psychological and moral refuge from the restrictive Russian public space. Svetlana Boym (1994) takes this a step further, pointing out that even the household could be too communal for those Russians forced to live in multifamily apartments. Here the kitchen as a communal meeting place was yet another case of forced communality to be avoided. This, then, is one explanation for the particular problems of democratization after 1989: the collapse of the socialist state left atomized families with limited connections and little social capital (e.g., Tausz 1990).

Of course, family commitments need not be antithetical to community ones. As anthropologists have shown in different parts of the world, family and community relations can also reinforce each other through cultural institutions such as the MesoAmerican fiesta system (Cancian 1965) or political structures such as historic European village councils and assemblies constituted from representatives of village families (Roseberry 1991; Stahl 1980; Worobec 1991). The socialist state, however, attempted to limit political and cultural relations that might integrate families, a process Kideckel calls "chopping" (1993:78–80).

As suggested, this rather popular model seems to contradict another interpretation that blames current difficulties on a surfeit of face-to-face relations and networks at the grassroots (Åberg 2000; Rose 1995, 1999). Alena Ledeneva (1998) notes both pros and cons to this latter interpretation, in *Russia's Economy of Favours*, but the pervasiveness of the relations she describes provides other analysts all the evidence they need to explain postsocialist difficulties. This view, which is evident in the fascination with post-communist mafias (Creed and Wedel 1997; Humphrey 1991; Kaplan 1998), is graphically captured by Rose's (1995) image of an hourglass. According to Rose, the Soviet Union had "a rich social life at the base, consisting of strong informal networks relying on trust between friends, relatives, and other face-to-face groups. Networks can extend to friends of friends, too." At the top there is also "a rich political and social life, as elites compete for power, wealth, and prestige. Yet the result is not a civic community but an hour-glass society, because the links between top and bottom are very limited. The narrow midpoint of the hour-glass insulates individuals from the influence of the state" (Rose 1995: 35). Rose has less faith than Robert Putnam (1993) in the transformation of such informal networks to formal ones, so these dense relations are cast as "negative social capital" that prevents state consolidation and blamed for the Russian malaise.[4] Rose subsequently acknowledges that informal social capital can have benefits such as improving the health and survival chances of poor Russians (Rose 2000), but that is apparently not enough to redeem it, and others claim that it is even counterproductive to health (McKeehan 2000:1309).

In fact, both views maintain that these societies were atomized: anthropologists see the separation at the level of individual families separated from one another, whereas political scientists see atomization between larger networks of people who still lack the institutional or formal connections that are the sine qua non of integration and civic culture. Thus Rose claims that despite a wealth of (negative) social capital Soviet citizens were atomized, and made more so by the geographical scale and massive population of the Soviet Union. The ability of such distinctive, even contradictory, views of grassroots social structure to produce similar atomization arguments is partially a result of scale: what appears to be a collection of antagonistic families from a village perspective looks more like a cohesive unit from the vantage point of the state.

Convergence can also be traced to parallel ideas about community. Both viewpoints replicate an evolutionary and romantic model of communal decline. In the family bunker model, socialist development destroyed community relations in much the same way as its capitalist alter ego did, but it also suppressed the civic and voluntary associations that replaced such primordial attachments in the wonderful world of Tocqueville. In the excess connection model, these societies are associated with the continuation of face-to-face relations and networks, but this renders them premodern or even antimodern by default (Åberg 2000; Rose 1999). The continuing and expanding networks of relations between family members acquire a negative valence. Community is not seen by some because it is based on conflict and competition instead of romantic consensus; those looking from a different scale see community solidarity but define it as antimodern because such uniformity is associated with the rural "past." Those who are more ethnographically inclined, equipped with cultural relativism and local experience, see the conflict and diagnose atomization. Those without these experiences sustain images of Eastern Europe as previously backward and socialism as hardly modern, leading to assumptions of continuing "premodern" forms of association such as thick social relations. But either way it seems that Eastern Europe is doomed to be lacking or retrograde. This lack, however, was the product of misrecognition.

Ironically ample evidence exists to challenge these models. Daphne Berdahl's (1999) observations from the former East German border village of Kella—a place of exceptional state surveillance within a rigid socialist polity—suggest that community relations existed under socialism and may have suffered more from unification with West Germany than from socialist atomization. Free time, lack of conveniences such as telephones, and participation in church activities reproduced village social relations and local identity prior to 1989; all diminished in the first years after unification. Tone Bringa (1995) delineates *two* communities—Catholic and Muslim—in the Bosnian village she studied a few years prior to the wars. As in Kella, religious practice and activity is central to community identity and relations, but Bringa also describes a common shared "village community" based on customs of hospitality and labor exchanges for house building. The latter is especially notable because villagers avoided communal work efforts organized by the village council just as one would expect on the basis of the atomization argument, but they did participate in work exchanges between households as rural families clearly did in Hungary as well (see Bell 1984; Sik 1988). Even Kideckel gives indications of community connections when he suggests that Romanian villagers were concerned about how "friends and neighbors might react" to them joining a political party (1993: 226).

The atomization argument is also challenged by gender studies that refuse the dichotomy between public and private upon which the thesis depends. These views insist that the private is political, and indeed Eastern Europe has provided some of their best evidence (Kligman 1998). In their essay on gender and postsocialism Susan Gal and Gail Kligman emphasize the parasitic relations integrating family and the socialist state so that "the ideological opposition between state and family (public and private) and the valorization of the family as authentic and honest that are so common in public discourse in the region contradict the much more complex set of practices that linked families, household and states" (2000a:70).

The linkages were thick in the Bulgarian villages I visited, although I would call them symbiotic as well as parasitic. Bulgaria is an important case to add to the mix, because it was thoroughly secularized in the 1980s and the existence of community cannot be based on religion as the other examples cited above allow. Ironically I went to Bulgaria in January 1987 (months before Rev's important publication) with the explicit goal of documenting atomization, or what I called at the time the "individualization of households." I found plenty of fractured and selfish relations to support my thesis, but as I gathered more and more evidence the characterization seemed less and less valid. I dropped the idea in order to pursue what seemed to me the more complex and contradictory nature of village social relations. I returned from the field at the end of 1988 only to find everybody else talking about atomization, and by the time I finished my dissertation, in 1992, Kideckel's manuscript was in press. As reported above, this model also provided a handy excuse for transition difficulties after 1989, as it blamed the socialist system for destroy-ing the social relations needed for democracy, and thus it acquired even more authority expos facto.

I recount this intellectual biography here, because I believe my decision to abandon my hypothesis in the midst of potential empirical support and growing popularity is perhaps the best evidence that it was an incomplete characterization. I still agree with Rev's conclusions about the power of vil-lagers to transform the system that oppressed them, and I have documented how everyday economic practices affected this (Creed 1998), but these prac-tices relied upon community interactions in multiple ways. The areas of agree-ment provoked me to wonder more about the disagreements, and this led me to the underlying assumptions of the atomization arguments. I began to think that the conflicts that helped demonstrate socialist amoral familism were, in fact, part of what it meant to be a community in the village. Villag-ers looked atomized because analysts saw them through the romantic notion of what they thought a community should be. However, conflict, selfishness, and autonomy do not negate the significance of community if the community is constituted on the basis of such relations. This seemed to capture Bulgarian village life better, for despite all the conflicts and efforts for family autonomy, the village remained, using Fran Markowitz's (1993) felicitous phrasing, "a community in spite of itself," which was central to practical life as well as so-cial identity.

Both before and after 1989 village families strove for self-sufficiency and economic autonomy. Under socialism this was driven by the economy of shortage (Kornai 1992) and perpetual uncertainty about what villagers could acquire from the state's poor distribution system. People were forced to rely on themselves. After 1989 a subsistence strategy became even more essential because villagers lost their state jobs and had no other income or support be-yond their newly restituted land. Subsistence production provides a degree of self-sufficiency for the productive unit and reinforced the family unit over the individual, but family units have always been dependent upon one another. This was most evident in what was known as the "personal sector" of socialist economies.

I have documented these relations in detail elsewhere (Creed 1998, esp. chaps. 2 and 5), a small sample of which will suffice for the point at hand. Vil-lagers produced most of their own grain needs on plots of corn and wheat al-located for personal use by the collective farm, which also provided much of the mechanized cultivation. The village bakery was fairly reliable and cheap, so most wheat was used as feed for sheep and goats that provided wool, milk, cheese, and meat for household consumption and sale to the state. Maximum wheat production, however, required personal connections with tractor drivers or their supervisors to assure timely plowing, planting, and harvesting. This privileged some villagers over others, but most families had some connection that could facilitate the process, and this dependence assured that they maintained these important relations through reciprocal assistance or gifts. The goats and sheep that consumed the grain in winter were pastured collectively by neighborhood for the remainder of the year. Each village household provided a shepherd for a number of days based on the number of animals. The shepherd of the day took the milk from all the animals so that he or she could make cheese. Cheese making would hardly have been worth the effort with only the milk of a single family's animals.

Major events such as weddings and house construction could never have occurred without a significant network both to acquire needed materials and help with the work. Similar exchanges have been documented in Hungary (Bell 1984; Sik 1988) and Bosnia (Bringa 1995). As Robert Minnich (1979:82) recognized so perfectly for rural Slovenia, household autonomy is only possible through interdependence. Of course, villagers were sometimes paid for the labor or products they provided, but in an economy of shortage even selling your labor or goods was a favor, so relations with suppliers had to be maintained through other exchanges. These relations followed a hierarchy of preferences in which kinship was the most common and desired connection, but neighbors, friends, and colleagues were also important relations of cooperation. These relations certainly diminished under socialism. The Bulgarian villagers studied by Irwin Sanders (1949) before World War II exhibited a greater number and variety of labor exchanges and interdependencies between households. To oversimplify, what happened in the subsequent decades was a shift from dependencies between households to dependencies upon state assistance, which inspired the atomization thesis. Many of the needs uniting families in the 1930s were subsequently supplied by socialist institutions such as the collective farm and the machine tractor station, but these units operated largely with village personnel through village social relations, such as those with tractor drivers, so the relationship between state and household was still mediated by other village relations. The much cited direct state-household axis actually cut through other village households. Thus household autonomy was an objective that no village family could achieve, and consequently atomization was hardly complete.

Still, apart from collective herding that was very routinized, attempts to solicit help in socialist Bulgaria could be quite difficult and often generated conflict. The same relations that villagers depended upon provided the potential for conflict when desires were not fulfilled—which was often the case. Villagers who were tapped for favors complained about those who asked for them; the latter complained if the people they asked refused or took too long to comply; and, if any exchange actually occurred, the equivalence, whether in cash or kind, was a constant bone of contention for both sides. These disputes can be seen as examples of growing atomization, but they can also be viewed as community relations in a context where the village remained an important basis of identity and survival, in part because exit was prohibited. Indeed, the state severely limited urban migration after the massive rural exodus of the 1960s, itself provoked by earlier collectivization. By the 1980s villagers had to have permission to migrate, and desirable urban locations had strict limits. Most rural Bulgarians continued to identify one another by village of residence, and one's village of origin remained central to the identity of urbanites as well. In such a context, as conflicts became more common they simply became more elemental to community conceptions. In an ironic way, complaints verified the expectations, even if unmet, that linked villagers together in a community, albeit one understood in terms of potentially antagonistic families. These relations may not have survived the transitions of the 1990s, but it is clearly inaccurate (if not disingenuous) to blame current problems on socialist atomization. Indeed, village families have become more atomized since 1989 as a result of urban migration, unemployment, and impoverishment, and family relations have become more central as other relations have receded in tandem with the resources needed to sustain them (see also Berdahl 1999; West 2002).

In short, I am not questioning the evidence of atomization. Those who have reached this conclusion are far too good as ethnographers to have gotten "the facts" wrong. I am also not suggesting that atomization proponents define community in explicitly or intentionally romantic terms. In fact, they do not really define the term at all, which may be the source of the problem. Without specification, the underlying assumptions still inherent in unqualified notions of community can lead to interpretations of conflict and autonomy as atomization instead of a local variant of community. I believe this is what happened in the case of Eastern Europe. It is no surprise that East European intellectuals such as Nowak and Rev reached the same conclusion, as they were trained in the same enlightenment tradition through which the

Figure 15. Group of dzhamali in Kalugerovo in 2002.

Figure 16. Following a house visit in 2002, a Lesichevo dervish and a villager wrestle on the street outside the latter's home.

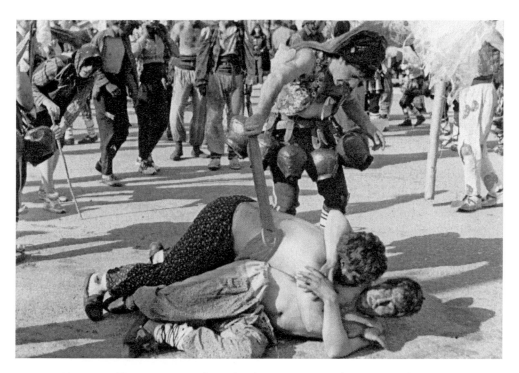

Figure 17. Two Arapi wrestle under the supervision of a starets at the Turiya mumming finale in 1997.

community concept acquired much of its romantic connotation. Of course, I also accept that local investigations of community notions may validate the atomization thesis in some places.

I am not advocating the opposite view of Eastern Europe as extensively integrated, which may be implied by analyses emphasizing social networks (Åberg 2000; Ledeneva 1998; Rose 1995; Wedel 1986). In fact, extensive integration through personal networks is negated by the conflicts that such relations engender. Connections create as much division as cohesion and cannot have the corporate consequences such descriptions imply. Despite having face-to-face relations villagers did not see their interests as uniform or collective, even in periods when many of them felt threatened by outsiders, as during collectivization and restitution/privatization. This does not mean, however, that they did not have a sense of community—conflicts can be indicative and constitutive of community.

This conclusion evolved from my observations of social relations but was confirmed by the analog I recognized in East European ritual events. It was in the quasi-ritualized context of pig-sticking that Minnich (1979) found the relationship of interdependent autonomy he documents for Slovenia and that I find most compatible with the social relations I witnessed in rural Bulgaria. A similar opposition in togetherness is evident in Bulgarian wedding rituals, where Carol Silverman (1982) documents the symbolic extortion of the groom by the bride's family, and the compensatory theft of items from the bride's house by members of the groom's retinue (for similar symbolic ransoms, see also Genchev 1988; and Ivanova 1984).

Funerals are perhaps the most frequent ritual elaborations on the village/family interface. As elsewhere in the Balkans, Bulgarian village conflicts provide material for funeral laments, the recitation of which clearly reinforces the sense of community (cf. Danforth 1982; Kligman 1988; Seremetakis 1991). Laments also emphasize the futility of accumulation which is itself a veiled commentary on the selfish interests of families (Kligman 1988). Death rituals are expressly defined by family relations, but their fulfillment maintains community connections—regular visits to the cemetery at specified times produce a collection of individual families, sharing the experience of mourning distinctive family losses (Danforth 1982). Not to do so is to court the ire of the deceased's soul, which can impact the village as well as the family, so fulfilling family mortuary obligations is a community responsibility. The fascinating wedding of the dead, or funeral-wedding (Genchev 1988:5; Kligman 1988), seeks to ensconce the unmarried deceased into another family matrix partly because villagers can only relate to one another through family-defined units. In Bulgaria this juxtaposition of family and community, conflict and collectivity, is even more explicit in mumming rituals.

Reconciling Autonomy and Networks

The descriptions of mumming provided in previous chapters would seem enough to refute the concept of atomized villagers, as they fit easily into a Durkheimian model of ritual solidarity. I do not deny this "function," and in the villages where the rituals have retrenched only to the collective gathering at the village square, the message of solidarity often predominates. The same reading can be made of a number of mumming cases where multiple mumming groups have consolidated into a single unit, as has happened in both Batanovtsi and Purvanets. Moreover, as David Kertzer (1991) has noted, ritual enactment itself creates solidarity through joint practice. However, in the more extended mumming complex, such as that of Lesichevo, these demonstrations of solidarity and goodwill are interwoven with clear representations of conflict and household autonomy, providing a more complete appreciation of village social relations.

First, the nature of masking itself is indicative of another reality. Despite the masks, villagers often recognize the participants, and in many villages participation is traditionally associated with particular families, making identification likely even with masks. Still the mask and costume deemphasize these village connections. The masks need not fully conceal the participants in order to transform them. The headdresses deflect rather than disguise the participants' family and household identifications, making it possible to dissociate their actions and interests temporarily from that of a particular household. At the same time the very need for a mask is testimony to the fact that such a separation is difficult and that kin connections are paramount, requiring rather extreme measures to overcome. That masks are no longer always worn in many villages but rather carried, perched on top of the head, or left on the side of the road is not only an effort at individuation as suggested in chapter 2 but is also a recognition that the effort to displace family identities is ultimately futile, even while the effort is necessary. This contrasts markedly with the role of masking in Newfoundland mumming, where complete anonymity and subsequent revelation through the guessing game is the central objective (Handelman 1990). In Bulgaria the message is not so couched or hidden; even masking conveys a direct statement about family and community.

The very sequence of the ritual, which follows a pattern similar to many other calendric rituals, narrates the same plot line. Costumed actors are ritually transformed into a village entity at the village square (itself a symbol of the village) or some other central location, and then move to household units, verifying their independence, incorporating them only individually, and in situ, into the collective celebration. Solidarity is demonstrated not simply (or even centrally) by a collective village gathering but by the visit to each separate domestic space by a small subset of residents whose disguises embody the mythic, usually unseen, amorphous, and potentially monstrous aspects of community. The "exchange" of blessings for produce implies household dependence on the supernatural intervention of mummers, but it also includes a counterstatement of household autonomy, since the agricultural products given to the mummers demonstrate the householders' success as autonomous family farmers. These offerings of food and drink are presented and evaluated as evidence of the hosts' domestic and farming skills. It is thus impossible to disentangle the circular relations of autonomy and dependence—villagers demonstrate their independence in the very process of soliciting communal support, and mummers can only extract communal offerings in exchange for a household/family blessing.

The canvass of households also exposes evident conflicts. In some villages not all households are visited, and those who refuse to receive mummers are likely to be labeled stingy or unsocial. Often unrelated town residents with villas in the village watch the mummers go by with neither side initiating interaction, dramatizing the rural-urban tension rife in Bulgaria (Creed 1993, 1995). In villages where most households are visited, not all hosts receive the mummers with equal enthusiasm. Some view mummers as petty extortionists who must be paid off to prevent them from wreaking havoc on household property—a threat that was purportedly realized more in the past. In these cases the visit itself exudes resentment on the part of the host. Mummers are sometimes resentful when their hosts include a young man, which can be read by the mummers as a refusal to join their ranks, and thus a tacit criticism of their actions. In such cases even a warm reception includes potential conflict, demonstrated by the mummers physically abusing the "offender." Reception may be enhanced by kin connections between participants and hosts, reminding the mummers that family has not been totally eclipsed by their ritual status. In fact, the ritual is most animated when members of the host family are also mummers, which threatens the symbolic division between mummers as representatives of the community and individual families. In many such cases the increased conviviality is countered by more exaggerated enactments of conflict in the form of fighting, theft, and destructive behavior. These actions effectively reassert opposition in those cases where it is least structurally apparent.

It is no coincidence that bachelors, rather than older men or younger boys, are often the ideal actors for this assignment. Since they may soon marry they are potentially ambiguous or liminal in relation to existing village households. At least one son, ideally the youngest, is expected to live patrilocally with his parents after marriage, but other options exist, including living neolocally or even matrilocally, so bachelors' household affiliations are fluid and uncertain. Those of unmarried women are perhaps equally uncertain, but patriarchal attitudes cast them as adjuncts to household heads. At the same time the dominant domestic ideology does identify the household as a feminine sphere, so it is not surprising that women should be excluded from the symbolic representation of a community that is juxtaposed to individual domestic units. The traditional exclusion of women from the "public arena" is partially to deny or minimize the presence of the domestic context in the *collective* village space occupied (indeed created) by the mummers. Women are too intensely associated with the domestic sphere to be able to ritually transcend it, even with the aid of masks and disguises. The increasing involvement of women as mummers discussed in chapter 2 reflects the erosion of this ideology by socialist egalitarianism, female employment, and Westernization/Europeanization, but the association of women with the household is still strong and may represent another counterweight to the expansion of female mumming participation.

The centrality of the bride figure to the ritual underlines the significance of women in the family, and women become the central focus of mummers' attention within each courtyard, demonstrating the significance of the household to the community (cf. Kligman 1981). The domestic/female must be displaced to establish *communitas*, but that very symbolic creation focuses on domestic units and women! The irony is the essence. It is also important that the female ritual figure usually appears in a family-based ritual role. This is most explicit in the survakari wedding, but it is also evident in other mumming celebrations where the female is usually associated with either recent or impending marriage or recent childbirth. The family symbolism is further affirmed by some of the gifts handed over to the mummers, which are symbolic of dowry/wedding or christening gifts. This is especially apparent in the village of Lesnovo, where the transvestite bride drapes a handkerchief over the shoulder of the host or hostess, just as a bride would do to a guest at her wedding banquet. However, instead of keeping the gift as a wedding guest would do, he or she puts money in the handkerchief and returns it to the bride who takes it while performing the standard kissing of the hand. Following widespread wedding practice the hosts might also pin some currency on the dress of the bride. Many other elements of mumming reference or replicate wedding rituals, including the symbolic shaving of mummers and hosts which mimics the ritual shaving of the groom in wedding preparations, and perhaps even the ritual plowing as some regions report a tradition, now extinct, of harnessing a bridal couple to the yoke (Genchev 1988:61). Prior to the widespread adoption of the white wedding dress in the village of Boyanovo, the headdress of a recently married woman was given to the kukeri bride to wear.

This tradition is revived somewhat in Kalugerovo where the mummer brides now wear modern white wedding dresses that may have been worn by real brides, although cheaper costume versions are also made specifically for the event.

So mummers as *community* figures tap into the symbolism of *family* ritual to acquire community offerings. Apparently the community can only be affirmed through the manipulation and use of the family. As noted in the introduction, I refer to these events as meta-rituals since they consciously reference and manipulate other rituals, and thereby underline the centrality of the component at the same time that they provide a different message. That mummers depend upon family rituals to affirm community relations encapsulates the kind of community they are affirming—one that is constituted in large measure by the distinctions and possible antagonisms between families. This is not an argument about the nature of parts (families) to the whole (community). To suggest that the community is constructed out of families is to privilege structure over relations. The community here is the tense and conflict-ridden interactions resulting from the combined autonomy and interdependence of village households, and this is the clear message of mumming.

The ritual inauguration or climax at the village square does bring component households together at the symbolic nexus of the village. The same blessings that have been repeated at each household are repeated a final time, as one chronicler puts it, "in the loudest voice possible so the whole village hears" (Stamenova 1982:38). The repetition reminds listeners again that the blessings issued for their households are, in fact, inextricably connected to village blessings. The ritual is often concluded by a folk dance (horo), which is itself symbolic of the connection between villagers. Villagers join the mummers, and the ritual morphs into a standard village folk dance characteristic of other ritual celebrations. The mummers' horo becomes a village horo.

Even at this collective finale, however, the conflicts continue in the form of symbolic bride theft and physical skirmishes between mummers and onlookers. In terms of the latter, the village of Lesichevo may be the most explicit, but jousting and fighting is evident in many finales. Theft or seduction of the central female figure is a leitmotif in most pre-spring activities and some New Year's practices as well. Throughout the mumming activities, whether at the square, en route between houses, or inside the courtyards of village houses, men who are not mumming try to steal the bride or, in more ribald practices, have pantomime intercourse with him. When he is visiting their yard they try to get him into the house itself. Mummers are kept busy retrieving him. They take the job seriously and have been known to break doors and windows to get the bride back. They always follow such efforts with a ritual flogging of the thief. In the Rhodope village of Orehovo, where there are two transvestite "maidens," they are also punished by the Arap after he retrieves them, reportedly for not being more diligent in avoiding or resisting such efforts. The attempt to steal the female symbol of fertility and bounty is, above all, a representation of the selfishness and envy that separates village households: the desire to monopolize and keep all the benefice the female figure represents in one's own house. The same interpretation holds for efforts to have sex with the transvestite figure. One of the most explicit representations is that by Turiya mummers described in chapter 2. There the central female figure is a grandmother with a baby and, although some men imitate sex with him during the house visits, when the group arrives at the square for the finale he is continually seduced by various Arapi, which provokes his jealous Arap escort to ignite the crude straw tent in which the illicit liaisons are taking place.

Mummers are charged to prevent such efforts and to punish those who persist. The lesson is clear, but equally clear is that no one takes it to heart and that such attempts will continue. The perpetual enactments are not repeated simply to drive home the prohibition but also to demonstrate that such selfishness is intrinsic to the village community. Moreover, people gain luck and fertility from the theft and short-term possession of the bride even though they are ultimately thwarted. What appears to be a demonstration for the purpose of moral instruction is also a contribution to the ritual objective of household fertility and well-being. Theft is expected and has individual benefits, just as it does in villagers' daily lives (Creed 1998:197–200). In some cases the mummers, who represent village interests, are thieves themselves; for example, in the village of Boyanovo the mummers are treated with food, drink, and money, but they go to the chicken coup directly to "steal" eggs. The eggs could be presented as gifts, but instead they have been left in the coup intentionally to represent the important role of theft in community relations and to suggest that what is not given will be stolen.

The same concern with selfishness is evident in one of the blessings commonly offered by mummers at both individual houses and at the village square: the wish for agricultural prices to be low (Stamenova 1982:29). This hope highlights two factors. First, it privileges the subsistence sector of the village economy over commercial activities. Low prices follow from an abundant harvest, and an abundant harvest is more important to subsistence producers than market prices. The blessing is also another chastisement of the family farmer who might wish to benefit more from both abundance and the high prices that would follow if fellow villagers did poorly. The mummers as embodied community insist that the fertility they summon is not for one family alone, which would allow it to profit differentially. So their wishes must be qualified by the insistence that prosperity has to come from collective fortune not individual advantage. That this qualification is necessary is evidence of the divided interests of village households.

In the village of Orehovo the collective gathering at the square includes the Arap leader reciting a list of transgressions by villagers or families. Those who have stolen, lied, practiced magic against others, or violated property boundaries by plowing and planting in a neighbor's plot are publicly named and chastised, along with the village drunks. This threat may operate as a moral incentive during the year, as people might not want to risk being called out for such behaviors, but, for those who are, the public declaration is hardly an avenue of reconciliation and instead tends to generate more conflict.

Perhaps the clearest demonstrations of opposition are the episodes of ritualized conflict. As noted in chapter 2, mummers are fighters and often are armed with symbolic weapons. In several villages with mumming traditions there are myths of mummers' graveyards, where mumming groups supposedly met and fought to the death. According to commonly held lore, mumming groups were not supposed to cross paths, and if they did they had to fight. Today such battles are continued symbolically through festival competitions, which some mummers treat with the seriousness of life and death. These battles are largely perceived as conflicts between different villages, reinforcing the association of mumming with the village and supporting the idea of community solidarity against outsiders. But there are elements of ritualized battle and conflict within villages as well. The village of Yardzhilovtsi maintains two large mechkari groups representing two different parts of the village, and they are not allowed to cross into each other's territory. The culminating event at the ritual square is basically a competition between the two groups to see whose wedding is nicer, whose musicians play better, and whose masks are more impressive, but, most important, who makes the most noise. Similarly, in the villages of Brezhani and Eleshnitsa mummers are organized into a few neighborhood groups that only canvass their own area, and then compete at a gathering on the square. Organizers in Eleshnitsa told me that they just prepare the stage and let the groups decide everything else for themselves because "they don't like each other," which makes any collective coordination hard to manage.

In other villages, such as Lesichevo, multiple mumming groups overlap in the territory they cover, but the constitution of the groups still illustrates the vectors that divide the village, usually those of generation and friendship. Evidence of any village solidarity is limited to the village square after the canvass, when all the groups join together and conflict in the form of wrestling and fighting is the central activity. The structure of the ritual itself reveals a community that is only rarely together or collective. Mummers share an experience but not collectively. They move in separate, distinct, and autonomous groups that might come together and share events at one house but then branch off again on separate tracks, perhaps meeting up later with a different mumming group at a different house. A sort of fragmented unity is also evident in that all groups may visit the same house, making these houses/yards loci of the larger community, not at a single time but only over time with different groups overlapping, just as the varied interests of individuals and families within the village diverge most of the time and come together only briefly in specific instances. The overall implication, however, is one of collectivity, even though it is reflected in a way that mirrors the villagers' everyday actions. The man who had his leg broken two years in a row and decided not to tempt fate again in 2002 opted instead to help out as a dresser for a group that included the very man who had broken his leg the previous year!

In Lesichevo the most aggressive fighting took place on the street as the hosts escorted the mummers out of the yard (see figure 16). There was some roughhousing in the yard, especially hitting the host with the wooden swords (on the rear), but the more serious fighting occurred on the road in front of the house. It is more spacious there, and combatants are less likely to damage the yard. Village yards are usually fully utilized for practical purposes, and fighting could easily destroy grape trellises, break tables and chairs, or stomp down perennial herbs and seedlings (as previously noted, this is actually expected in some villages). But the move to the street is also symbolic and helps us refine the atomization argument. The atomization of households is not a complete separation of relations but rather an inside-outside distinction mistaken for exclusion. In other words, outside the household and yard the *same* people who had just been treated hospitably with food and drink inside find themselves at loggerheads. This enacts an inside-outside opposition, but the larger point is that the "inside" is contextual and permeable, with friends and neighbors moving in and out of it. It is not a notion of household autonomy that is rigidly delineated but one that is flexible and porous.

Some mumming groups in Lesichevo, as noted, include the figure of a traditional peasant with whom the masked figures fight constantly. In other words, here the conflict between mummers and hosts is incorporated symbolically into the mumming performance itself—mumming now becomes a meta-ritual reflection of itself, highlighting the centrality of the refracted theme of conflict. According to Fol's (2004:57) descriptions from Strandzha, the mummers there "appear to be in continuous conflict with people without masks during the house-to-house procession." In the village of Turiya the final ritual battle between masked startsi brandishing wooden swords and the Arapi could easily be viewed as a conflict between the community and "outsiders," if it were not for the different and equally central roles the Arapi have played throughout the day, many of them clearly representing the village. Indeed, some Arapi even wore vests with the name of the village sewn in large letters across the back, and they also end up fighting among themselves in the finale (see figure 17). In the shifting contexts of mumming allies become foes, just as they do in the unpredictable drama of everyday village life.

Mumming events not only represent conflict, they also generate it. A common conflict is over the roles individuals will play. The growing difficulty in finding an appropriate man for the bride discussed in chapter 2 is one such bone of contention, but other roles can provoke the same. Although the number of masked figures and Gypsies may be unlimited, other roles must also be filled and there can only be one of each. Sometimes no one wants to fill these roles and someone must be cajoled or forced to do so; at other times multiple individuals want to play the same role and someone must be denied. In either case conflicts may result. I saw more than one argument over the priest figure in which the man who wanted to play the priest was challenged by other mummers who insisted he was not suited for the role, usually because he did not look the part or was insufficiently versed in the relevant Orthodox rites or simply was a poor actor. In one case no one else wanted to play the role, and so it was an outright rejection rather than a preference; the insulted mummer then refused to participate in any role. Occasionally I witnessed conflicts with the musicians. Musicians in some villages are paid out of the proceeds that the mummers collect. Elsewhere they are strictly volunteers. In Varvara, in 2006, the usual bagpipe player insisted for the first time that he should be paid, following the practice of "other villages." When the organizers told him that they would get someone else to do it for free, the musician insisted that they could not replace him because he had performed there for twenty years and it was his role. Eventually he relented and agreed to continue playing for free rather than be replaced.

Mumming can generate conflicts between villagers who think they should lead the event or between leaders and mummers over how heavy-handed leadership should be. Leaders are usually agreed upon collectively, although certain individuals have likely advantages in this decision, including those with more to contribute such as talented and prolific costume makers; those in positions of village leadership, like the chitalishte secretary, are also advantaged as they can use their position to encourage participants—in one village it was a lawyer, in another the local policeman. Usually it is a person who has earned the position through devoted activism in the ritual. I spoke with mumming enthusiasts in Batanovtsi who were not participating precisely because they had bad relations with the new group leader. Yet they were in the audience at the mumming inauguration on January 13 and then drove to a neighboring village to observe the joint meeting of mummers—they simply refused to submit to the leader's direction.

Mummers or villagers may get angry with participants who are not performing their role adequately, especially at festivals where they compete for awards as a group. Formulaic mock battles can escalate into real fighting when one combatant decides the other has crossed the line from horseplay into aggression. In Pobeda I witnessed a major conflict impinge on the collective communal village finale. As part of the comic performance, one of the mummers selected to pull the plow acts recalcitrant and is disciplined and replaced. In this case the mummer took offence at the extent of the punishment and nearly came to blows with the peasant character. It was clearly not a scripted conflict but a real one. All these possibilities become more probable with more drinking, which itself is a possible bone of contention as some mummers see the event as an occasion for drunkenness while others insist on more discipline (although not sobriety).

In many villages the event has led to conflicts between the mummers and the secretary of the chitalishte, who, as previously noted, was officially responsible for village cultural activities during the socialist era. The conflicts might be aesthetic or organizational, but as explained in the previous chapter, they are usually financial as mummers increasingly insist on keeping the collected money for their own use rather than contributing it to the chitalishte. In Batanovtsi just the opposite happened: the chitalishte was chosen to receive some funds that in prior years had been given over to the kindergarten. Some explained the switch on the basis of fairness and the need to spread the benefits around local institutions. Others insisted the switch had to do with sour relations between the kindergarten director and the new mumming leadership.

Not surprisingly money is a potential source of other conflicts as well. Suspicions arise about skimming funds, and elaborate techniques are employed to guard against embezzlement. In many villages the boxes used to collect the money are made with only narrow slits for inserting coins and currency, with no way to open them without destroying the box. They are also sealed with stamped tapes so that any tampering would be obvious. Regardless of how the money is collected, important protocols surround the opening and counting of the money. This usually involves a group of people so that there are plenty of witnesses. Despite such precautions, it is always possible for someone to make accusations against the whole group of counters ("Who do you think decides who will observe it?" I was asked, when I once mentioned the transparency of the counting protocol). Even if there is no chance or suspicion of skimming, conflicts may still arise over what to do with the money. Villages have established traditions, but, increasingly, mummers are challenging these conventions, often based on their knowledge of what mummers in other villages do.

The declining role of the chitalishte secretary as the obvious authority has opened up new possibilities for organizational conflict between participants. Conflicts also emerge over ritual innovation, with some villagers insisting on "traditional" practice and others embracing novelty. The traditionalists use the festivals and the expectations of the ethnographers who judge them as the justification for their concern with authenticity. They usually carry the day at festivals but not in village practice where innovators are freer. Any of these conflicts can escalate to the point of group division leading to two antagonistic mumming groups, as in the previously mentioned case of the Sushitsa suburb of Karlovo, but more often they end with a disgruntled individual or group refusing to participate.

Such conflict, of course, is not always solely about mumming, which provides a convenient vehicle for expressing other ongoing tensions in the village. In the village of Gorna Vasilitsa, the division of the village into upper and lower halves was reflected in antagonisms between individual mummers from the two different divisions. But a greater conflict erupted when the chitalishte secretary moved the finale from the soccer field in the upper part of the village to the village square located in the lower village. In 2002 this change did not produce a divided celebration, but a few mummers from the upper half of the village refused to participate. They saw their hosting of the finale as an important recognition of their neighborhood's significance, which is usually overlooked because the administrative buildings and institutions of the village are all located in the lower half of the village. This both reflected and exacerbated existing strains in relations between mummers in the upper half of the village as some continued to participate.

A final type of conflict emerged around the role of competition. While competition between villages is one of the central motivating factors at festivals, the possibility of intra-village competitions between mummers is extremely contentious. Some mummers want rewards for the best costumes, best performances, or best groups within the village, whereas others eschew this option as debasing the ritual or undermining its collective purpose. Oral histories from older mummers confirmed that organized competitions with awards to individuals or groups within the village were innovations copied from the festival system and only began to show up in the 1970s. Still, in many places such competitions became important and the subsequent lack of resources for prizes was commonly cited as an explanation for declining participation in the 1990s. Conversely, in Eleshnitsa the growing enthusiasm for the ritual was attributed by locals to the increased need of villagers for the continuing, albeit modest, cash awards offered by the village administration. A jury of village officials watches the performance of neighborhood groups on the square and makes cash awards to the best group(s). Former jury members told me that they had tried to spread the limited cash awards over various groups to help more of them but that the mummers preferred that one group get it all (preferably their own). One of the organizers said that she had asked not to be on the jury, because all those who don't win "hate me for the whole year."

Other villagers, however, ridiculed the notion of having intra-village competitions, saying that it was a "village" or "folk" holiday and insisting that awards created bad feelings. One Lesichevo resident dismissively labeled the option "Kalugerovo work" in a jab at the inauthentic nature of the neighboring village's ritual, where modest individual awards are given. By contrast, villages like Yardzhilovtsi and Varvara, where the ritual finale is obviously a competition between different mumming groups, do not give awards, leaving it to villagers to debate which group was the best. These discussions can provoke conflicts for nearly the entire year after the event, as it is a common topic of conversation. Even in the villages where organizers have discontinued or resisted local prizes in order to underline the collective nature of the ritual, this decision itself becomes a source of conflict and debate.

Implications

The conflicts evident in Bulgarian mumming by no means eclipse its collective character, and though themes of conflict may predominate in some villages, in many others the communal nature of the ritual is overwhelming. One need only witness one of these rituals to recognize that Bulgarian village households are not thoroughly atomized everywhere. Still, the interpretations pursued here suggest that mumming does far more than simply reinforce the village unit; it verifies, affirms, and even produces the very contradictions and atomization it seems to redress. The rituals do not simply assert the value of community over the family; instead they show how in the context of a village these two concerns are intertwined and interdependent, if primarily through their opposition. I believe the representation of these tensions in a ritual form that is still so clearly symbolic of the village community (a quality especially evident at the festivals) suggests that they are more than just the negative fallout of either socialist or postsocialist policies but rather constitute the very nature of social relations as locally conceived and experienced.

Mumming thus represents relations in a way that our social scientific categories cannot easily express. This analytical difficulty stems in part from a romantic shadow haunting the concept of community that implies harmony or consensus, combined with an urban bias that emphasizes choice over inevitable associations such as village residence. I have suggested that this view of community has shaped our understanding of East European societies under socialism leading to both exaggerated images of atomization and distorting claims of a densely integrated grassroots. Mumming rituals demonstrate an alternative idea of community in which inevitability, conflict, and divided interests combine with interdependence, interaction, and cooperation in a way that is hard to conceptualize or capture with Western social models. As a result, the existing potential of this conceptualization for new models of participatory democracy were missed, and standard Western models for interest representation and civil society were deployed to fill a void that was actually not a void at all. Again, these new models may eventually provide avenues for democratic participation, civic cooperation, and political engagement, but they have already proven to be a very long and painful road to those destinations. Of course, pain was assumed to be necessary (as in the very conceptualization of shock therapy), but I think that assumption reflected the lack of recognition of cultural resources that could have been redeployed in ways that would have made the transition more civil and less shocking. The failure to recognize the nature of grassroots social relations led to accusations of either atomization or nepotism which validated remedies such as civil society and decollectivization rather than alternative avenues that might have been less painful and protracted. The most dangerous consequences of this same blindness concern ethnic relations and nationalism, which I take up in the following chapter.

CHAPTER FIVE

ETHNICITY AND NATIONALISM

In the winter of 2002 I began to focus pointedly on representations of Roma in mumming. Not having worked on Romani issues previously I began first with local scholars who had. By that point Romani studies was a burgeoning field for Bulgarian researchers, justified intellectually and politically by the dearth of attention under socialism. As Isabel Fonseca (1996:129) notes, socialist political prohibitions on conducting and publishing research on Roma were reproduced by the capitalist profit motive after 1989, as publishers doubted the market for academic tomes on Roma. But Romani studies did enjoy a benefit Fonseca misses—the backing of foreign aid from Western countries in support of NGOs concerned with minority rights. In this period the line between NGOs and scholarship blurred, as scholars, like everyone else, tried to stabilize their eroding economic position by selling their knowledge and skills to the new and well-funded nongovernmental sector. As the apparent antithesis of state-dominated socialism and the foundation for the much vaunted civil society, NGOs were the darlings of Western sponsors. Some scholars formed their own NGOs to tap into the new resources. Others were hired or financed by NGOs to carry out research, which the NGOs helped publish and used as evidence of their accomplishments for their sponsors. In most cases these scholars remained in the employ of the state, constituting one of the many linkages between the purported nongovernmental and state sectors.

Consequent to this flurry of activity in the 1990s, there were several specialists in Romani culture and performance for me to meet. Regardless of
their areas of research, they, like all Bulgarians, were familiar with mumming
rituals and festivals. Several of them assured me that Roma did not participate in these rituals except as paid musicians. Although exclusion by ethnic
Bulgarians was acknowledged as a possible explanation, most of these commentators gave more weight to Roma's disinterest in mumming, which, as
one specialist observed, "is not part of their culture," or, as another put it, "it
is not a Gypsy tradition." I was skeptical of this cultural essentialism, because
the history of Bulgarian folklore is full of examples in which Roma adopted
Bulgarian folk practices and rituals previously not part of Romani tradition.
However, I did not doubt the substantive claim that it purported to explain.
Indeed, I could not really imagine that Roma would find these rituals appealing precisely because of the derogatory Gypsy representations in many of
them. Alternative explanations for disinterest, even if implausible, seemed to
render the phenomenon itself more factual. A few specialists challenged this
orthodoxy, assuring me that Roma certainly participated in various mumming roles, but they had not observed such involvement personally nor could
they recommend a place where I might. Their lack of evidence only seemed to
confirm that such cases were exceptional and minor.

It was with this conviction that I arrived in the village of Gorna Aleksandrovo on February 10, 2002. I had begun the day talking with mummers in
the village of Topolchane right outside the city of Sliven in east central Bulgaria as part of my effort to select a village in the area to observe a few weeks
later at the beginning of Lent. One of my informants happened to mention
that they were mumming that very day in some villages down the highway.
This was a shock because, as mentioned in chapter 1, ethnographic discussions linked kukeri events to Lent with almost no discussion of the rather extensive juggling of dates that characterizes current practice. The colleague
with whom I was traveling and I immediately looked at each other with the
same thought—we had to go. I promised the informant to return to Topolchane later in the month to observe their own celebrations (which I did), and
we hurriedly departed for the aforementioned villages.

We headed east from Sliven and stopped first at the village of Trapoklovo, mentioned in previous chapters for its extremely aggressive mumming
activities with heavy (homo)sexual symbolism. We then continued east a few
more kilometers to Gorno Aleksandrovo. Upon locating the mumming party

there it was immediately apparent that we had stumbled upon something different. Having witnessed numerous mumming celebrations by this point, this group immediately impressed me as even more enthusiastic and energetic than usual, especially given that it was already early afternoon and the participants had been mumming since morning. My colleague registered the same impression. Moreover, when the mummers realized that we had come specifically to observe them, they immediately began to perform for us (or, perhaps more accurate, for my camera). They made no appeal for money or offerings, as often followed such attention in other villages; instead, they continued to dance for an extended period before taking off for another house.

Costumes here are similar to those described for the village of Mogila (see chapter 1)—traditional peasant folk leggings, a tunic-like top, often embroidered, with a beaded leather harness supporting a large collection of small thin bells. Masks are mostly hoods covered in colorful sequins, but, as in nearby Topolchane, there are a few larger ones in which cloth is wrapped around a frame made from two poles extending up on each side of the mask, creating a sort of flat fabric canvas that is decorated with small mirrors, jewelry, lace, braid, and other accessories. Most mummers wore their masks constantly, which, as noted previously, is also a bit unusual. In addition to the masked kukeri, the group of approximately thirty included a bridal couple with a transvestite "bride" and her "betrothed," a bear and bear trainer, a priest, and various other figures including Gypsy-like figures, seductive transvestites, the hero from an Italian television serial being shown at that time, and four men in military camouflage with the label "otryadnik" on their backs. Otryadniks were early socialist-era volunteers responsible for monitoring and promoting order and discipline in their neighborhoods. They performed a similar role with the kukeri, keeping them in orderly lines and dictating their route. They were especially central when the group returned to the village square in the late afternoon for the ritual finale.

The mumming group canvassed the village entering the yards of some houses to jump vigorously around and receive the requisite treats of wine, food, and money. They were sometimes greeted by the home owners at the gate to the yard, with a pitcher of wine and a platter of food (small sandwiches or banitsa); at a few places the home owners had set up more elaborate banquets on the street in front of the house, complete with tables and chairs and much more food. The wine was passed in pitchers or metal pails from person to person in a communal drinking exercise. When the vessels were drained, the host quickly refilled them. The most unique element in these visits was the collection of money. Rather than the man or woman of the house giving the cash to the bride or costumed kukeri leader, the money was collected by a man in street clothes who carried a notebook. When he was presented with the money, he dutifully wrote down the amount in the notebook beside the donor's name, and the donor then confirmed the entry with a signature. This precise accounting is perhaps the most extreme response to the concern with embezzlement discussed in the previous chapter.

At the first house visit I observed, as soon as the kukeri raised their masks to drink the proffered wine, I noticed that more than one of them looked like they could be Roma. The physical qualities that supposedly distinguish Roma from ethnic Bulgarians are, of course, like those that purportedly separate racial categories everywhere: they fall along a continuum that makes it impossible to definitively distinguish discrete racial/ethnic groups. Although some individuals at the ends of these continua embody the physical stereotypes of ethnic Bulgarians or Roma to a degree that makes the observer fairly confident in an ethnic assessment, many more do not, and I have met many Roma that I might have assumed were ethnic Bulgarians and many ethnic Bulgarians that I would have guessed were Roma. Ethnic Bulgarians denied this ambiguity and attributed it to my foreignness, as if my vision and powers of observation were compromised in the same way my speech and verbal comprehension were limited by not being a native. So I turned to the large crowd of onlookers following the group of mummers (many of whom were Roma) and asked a woman who I thought was ethnically Bulgarian whether there were "Gypsies" among the masked kukeri. "They're all Gypsies," she replied coldly.

That one short sentence completely upended my assumptions about Roma and mumming. I was dumbfounded. Further observation and investigation moderated the shock, as her assessment proved to be a significant exaggeration. Several ethnic Bulgarians were participating, including the bride and groom figures as well as several masked figures, but, in sum, the vast majority (perhaps two-thirds) of the mummers were Roma.

The predominance of Roma in mumming reflects the increasing percentage of Roma in the village population, as many ethnic Bulgarians moved away during the collapse of the agricultural economy in the 1990s. Most of these families moved to the city of Sliven, indeed a few of the kukeri I spoke with lived in Sliven and had returned to the village, where they still have relatives, for the festivities. Apparently the depopulation trend has continued: villagers in 2002 estimated the population at one thousand, but by 2007 it was barely six hundred. Already in 2002 the majority were Roma. Many arrived in the village after collectivization, encouraged or forced to settle there to work in the expansive vineyards planted by the new collective farm. Collectivization provoked massive migration from many villages. The newly industrializing state was glad to have these new urban workers, but it eventually found itself short of farm workers as well. The settlement of Roma, whose peripatetic lifestyle was anathema to socialist control, into depleted villages solved two "problems" at once. When collective farms were dismantled after 1992 they lost these jobs and had no claim to the land, which was returned to its former owners or their descendants. Still, many Roma had built homes in Gorno Aleksandrovo during the socialist era, and facing discrimination by potential urban employers, they stayed put in greater numbers than their ethnic Bulgarian co-villagers who had more opportunities for employment in towns, thereby increasing the proportion of Roma in the village population. They then stepped in to fill the depleted ranks of the mumming company as well.

Gorno Aleksandrovo was the only village I visited where Roma predominated in a mumming event, but I subsequently observed Roma fulfilling various mumming roles in several other villages. I was told by multiple informants from Semchinovo, the village next to Varvara, that the Roma there regularly stage their own separate mumming celebration just for the Romani quarter of the village. The event mimics the traditional village model. Here the dervish tradition among ethnic Bulgarians has diminished over the last several years, with only a few young people going around the village to select houses on December 31 and then joining the Varvara celebrations on January 1. The Roma, however, muster a large group of masked participants that canvass all the households of their neighborhood. They use the collected money to make up packets of treats for every Romani child. The village natives who recounted this to me were clearly impressed with both the Roma's activism and how they used the money. They also saw it as an indictment of ethnic Bulgarians in the village who could no longer produce a respectable dervish day.

What are we to make of Romani participation in, and even in some cases the apparent co-optation of, rituals that often include enactments of derogatory Gypsy stereotypes? Various factors can explain this seeming paradox, including mystification and resistance, but neither of these popular models seems to mesh with my experience of these events. Michael Stewart's (1997) classic ethnography of Hungarian Roma comes closer by showing how Roma have reworked and inverted negative stereotypes such as dirtiness and thievery into valued elements of Romani social and cultural distinction and even superiority over non-Roma. Roma represent the world in such a way that the stereotypes are not actually demeaning; the failure of non-Roma to recognize this is evidence of their inferiority and shamelessness. In this sense the question itself only seems reasonable in a non-Romani worldview, and this may explain the perplexed responses I received from some Roma when I asked it (see below). It does not, however, explain other responses.

Searching for other answers exposes nuances in the nature of Bulgarian-Roma relations. This chapter, then, uses mumming as a window onto the nature of ethnic dynamics in rural Bulgaria and discovers a different type of relationship than the forms usually assumed to pertain between ethnically defined groups. This builds upon the discovery in the previous chapter of a distinctive notion of community among ethnic Bulgarians and suggests that this notion can incorporate village Roma as well, albeit in an even more ambivalent way. This suggestion dovetails with Rogers Brubaker's (2002) critique of the tendency to take groups for granted in the study of ethnicity. He calls this penchant "groupism" and defines it as "the tendency to take discrete, sharply differentiated, internally homogeneous and externally bounded groups as basic constituents of social life, chief protagonists of social conflicts, and fundamental units of social analysis" (164). When applied to ethnicity this has deflected attention away from the connections between ethnic Bulgarians and Roma in individual villages in favor of the generic and exclusive categories of "Rom" and "Bulgarian." I suggest that mumming rituals were not offensive to some Roma precisely because the rituals reference and demonstrate a larger message about the nature of local ethnic relations that is inclusive, despite being discriminatory and derogatory. Stewart's (1997) insights into Hungarian Roma would suggest that this inclusion may be appreciated not for the begrudging tolerance it offers Roma but for the options it provides Roma for reproducing their distinctiveness—that is, it provides Roma social access and materials for the manipulation of non-Roma. Thus Roma may ironically value the ambivalent inclusion represented in village mumming as a way to access resources and relations that they need to sustain their distinction.

The idea of a local Romani inclusion supports, but also radically qualifies, the recognition of a distinctive "Bulgarian ethnic model." In this formulation, as characterized by Antonina Zhelyazkova (2001), "each of the numerous ethnic and religious communities in Bulgaria is able to maintain its own integrity, which is accepted by the others as necessarily different. . . . 'Otherness' is accepted calmly and without prejudice, as something known, as a familiar strangeness, which blends into everyday experiences and is therefore not perceived as threatening." By way of qualification, I believe mumming reveals plenty of ethnic prejudice; it also shows that relations between ethnic categories have different experiential contexts so that it is a mistake to attempt to explain Bulgarian-Turkish relations in a single "ethnic model" along with Bulgarian-Armenian or Bulgarian-Roma relations, even if they exhibit some similarities. Zhelyazkova (2002) recognizes that lived experience is formative: "The positive element in accepting ethnic and religious diversity stems from the centuries-long experience of cohabitation and is linked to the generally stable informal relations among the different communities," but then fails to recognize how that very logic might nuance the nature of relations across different ethnic groups. Her model also intimates a degree of acceptance that comes too close to what Robert Hayden (2002) calls positive/active tolerance, in distinction to the more passive understanding of the tolerance that accommodates competition and antagonism. I believe mumming shows Bulgarian-Roma relations to be much closer to his model of antagonistic tolerance. Unlike Hayden's model, however, I do not see this type of relationship as particular to ethnic relations; rather, as I hope the preceding chapter demonstrated, it is also characteristic of relations between ethnic Bulgarians in the same village. I suggest, then, that the crucial link is the recognition of the importance of village/place identities and their interaction with ethno-national ones. The insistent privileging of the latter to the exclusion of the former in analyses of this part of the world is an example of Balkanism par excellence (Todorova 1997).

The sighting of a begrudging and locally delimited inclusion in mumming is based on extensive research with ethnic Bulgarians, not Roma, and I make no claim of insight into the constant and varied experiences of ethnic discrimination for Roma themselves. In other words, this view is one that many ethnic Bulgarian villagers express (in ritual and everyday life) toward Roma, and is not necessarily shared by Roma. However, I did speak with enough Roma in the contexts of mumming rituals to suspect that this inclusion is useful to Roma who recognize it for what it is and are hesitant to jeopardize it, especially for the more exclusionary alternative offered by Western models of ethnic relations. It is the potential of this ambivalent inclusion that has been missed and is in danger of being displaced by a more segregated understanding of ethnicity. This is not an apology for Bulgarian racism toward Roma, which is deep-seated, pervasive, and horrendous in its manifestations and consequences (Silverman 1995; Vassilev 2004). Moreover, the message of inclusion is only a subtle undertone or complement to the more exclusionary actions and discourses expressed by the same people. Indeed, it must be ferreted out by an interpretive ritual analysis. The latter, then, is only to suggest that particular elements in this profile could have provided the bases for building novel and more equitable relations, and that they were missed when relations were seen only through a Western and urban lens.

The next section presents some of the Gypsy images in mumming rituals in three villages with very different mumming traditions in three different parts of the country. I then address responses by Roma to such images and, following their lead, offer in the subsequent section interpretations that look beyond the obvious offense to an ambivalent local inclusion, I hope without eliding the underlying and foundational racism and prejudice. I conclude by wrestling with how this local inclusion compares to relations between ethnic Bulgarians and other minorities, and how it articulates with more exclusionary discourse and practice on the national level.

Gypsy Representations

In the village of Turnicheni, in 1997, three young men dressed and described as "Gypsies" were one of three primary groups separately canvassing the village to collect money. The other groups included a young man in a horse costume accompanied by his trainer/tender (although the horse seemed to be in charge), and a trio consisting of a transvestite "virgin" in folk costume escorted by two "dervishes" dressed in old military costumes, commonly associated with the rebels of the April Uprising against the Turks. The masked mummers, here called startsi, do not participate in the canvass but rather join these groups at the finale on the village square. The Gypsy group included a young man wearing ill-fitting pants and no shirt, his face and upper body blackened with ash and soot, carrying a loom beam with a red ribbon tied around the "head." He accompanied another young man playing the role of his wife, dressed in a ragged dress with a blackened face and leading around their child at the end of a long chain, played by an adolescent in rags, also with a blackened face.

The trio entered the yard of each village household and began moaning: a loud "o-h-h-h," followed by an "a-h-h-h," repeating the sequence louder and longer each time until someone emerged from the house with wine, sausage, and money. The wine and sausage were offered to the mummers, and the money was put into a sealed bank carried by the female figure in a hand-basket. In return the mummers rubbed the proprietors on the cheek with their soot-covered hands, which left a black mark. The mark served as a sign that the person had contributed, and I noticed several villagers sporting these marks as they went about their business later in the day.[1] To insure a nice mark, the mummer rubbed his hand across his own blackened face first, a practice that forced him periodically to replenish his own makeup. Every several houses he would grab some straw from the animal pen in the yard and set it on fire while moaning. The fire burned down quickly and cooled while the group was being treated; the mummer then used the ashes to touch up his face before moving on to the next house, leaving the owners to clean up the remains of the ashes.

With the canvass completed the couple then showed up at the village square where they entertained the gathering onlookers, including several Romani families. The main activity was to run around the square moaning and threatening to smear soot on anyone who did not run away. The transvestite figure now carried the loom beam which he periodically threw up in the air, but its main use was as a nutcracker. The couple would sit down on the pavement and take out walnuts from their basket and proceed to crack them on the ground with the loom beam and then eat the nut meat. A Bulgarian man standing next to me commented, without provocation: "just like Gypsies." After other mummers arrived, the Gypsy couple began to interact with the "virgin" trio, grabbing the virgin and running around the square with her, which provoked her dervish defenders to come to her aid and assault the Gypsies, temporarily driving them away.

In other mumming traditions we find greater numbers of Gypsy figures playing a more peripheral role. This is especially true of some villages around Pernik. In the village of Yardzhilovtsi, in 1997, numerous figures were referred to as "Gypsy" with a variety of roles. The village is large, currently home to about twelve hundred residents and has an extremely active mumming tradition, boasting two large mumming groups that cover two different halves of the village. The mayor bragged that Pernik officials usually send observers interested in the ritual (people like me) to his village. Each of the two village groups included several diverse Gypsy figures. As is common, they were responsible for collecting and carrying the gifts in kind: wine, brandy, eggs, beans, flour, fruit, salami and sausage, and so on. This, of course, replicates the everyday role of many landless rural Roma as menial laborers for ethnic Bulgarians. These are often younger participants, although in Yardzhilovtsi adult men also performed Gypsy roles, probably because of the large number of roles to be filled, including, for example, manning barricades at all the roads leading into the village, where Gypsy guards demanded a "toll" from cars entering or leaving. All these Gypsies had darkened faces, either with soot, ash, black makeup, or a dark makeshift ski mask with holes for eyes, nose, and mouth. Costumes were typically dirty, ragged clothing, sometimes worn in several layers, with a bandana around the head. Female Gypsies (played by either males of females) might also be pregnant or carrying a doll, conveying the stereotype of Roma as having many children. They may also be better dressed and adorned with jewelry similar to the fortune teller motif well known in the West, and sometimes blended with the sexualized imagery of burlesque, but these were exceptions to the prevailing abject image. Physical infirmity was also a common element of Gypsy costumes, most commonly the hunchback and the crippled man on a crutch. Bandages often symbolized some injury.

The village of Pobeda in southeastern Bulgaria is noteworthy in that there was, arguably, only one Gypsy figure in two days of mumming by three groups of mummers: two groups on the first day covering different parts of the village and a slightly different group to finish up on the third day that included some new participants as well as some who had participated in one of the two groups on the previous day. I say "arguably" because a few people referred to some comic figures as "Gypsies" even though they were not in any way marked as such, and indeed some of them had an explicit alternative identity (written on their costumes). One man, masked with a plain light-colored striped scarf covering his face and wearing ragged ill-fitting clothes, carried a broken plastic snow sled strapped to his back and a sign indicating his membership on the Bulgarian Olympic team (a clear swipe at the country's global athletic competitiveness in the Winter Games taking place at that very time). Another was a Taliban figure (this being the winter after September 11, 2001). Two male transvestites were dressed as sexually provocative women but not marked as Gypsies. Only the bear trainer was an obvious "Gypsy."

At the finale on the square, however, a whole caravan of Gypsies arrived, complete with a covered wagon. The stereotypical markers of Gypsies were clear here, including the wagon itself, which bespoke their transience. Only a few had darkened faces, but the rest presented other obvious Gypsy elements: ragged and mismatched clothing, an unkempt appearance, pregnancy, and a baby carriage. Their actions confirmed the imagery: they pulled their wagon to a spot just slightly off the center of the square, took out a large black pot and some straw, and proceeded to build a fire. For the entire time they were on the square, they danced around the area of the fire and wagon to chalga music. This Gypsy spectacle provided the counterpoint, with the obvious moral evaluation, to the other major group performing on the square—the traditional Bulgarian peasant family. The latter also arrived with a cart, this one pulled by a man in a donkey costume. The image here, however, was that of industriousness, as the cart was loaded with farming tools and the central activity that ensued was the enactment of the agricultural cycle as described in chapter 1. While Gypsies danced and cooked, Bulgarians worked.

Some of these Gypsy elements and images are found in mumming events across the country. For example, the bear figure is nearly pervasive and is always accompanied by a bear trainer, who regardless of dress or makeup is assumed to be a Gypsy. Training bears to "dance," usually to music provided by the trainer, was an exclusively Romani occupation, associated specifically with the group of Roma known as Usari. These trainers and their bears could often be seen in large cities and tourist towns where they performed on the street for tips. The practice was outlawed after 1989, but the prohibition was only sporadically enforced. More effective was the action of animal rights activists (funded by the Brigitte Bardot Foundation and the Vier Pfoten Association in Austria) who set up a refuge for the bears and paid Roma to relinquish them. The transfer of the "last three dancing bears in Bulgaria" to the refuge was a publicized event in 2007. In mumming rituals the bear characters do not dance so much as wrestle with the home owner, allowing the latter to demonstrate his strength and virility. They also often "walk" on the back of villagers to cure pain and insure general health. The trainer, usually with a fiddle, is universally assumed to represent a Gypsy. In some cases he will have a blackened face, but not always. He is usually not marked by other negative images such as ragged and dirty clothing, no doubt because of his distinctive role as mediator between Gypsies and ethnic Bulgarians.

In accounting for the Gypsy presence in mumming I recognize that much is explained by the stereotypes of Gypsy fecundity. They are often represented with a baby, as mentioned, and also, perhaps, as pregnant. As such, their appearance in fertility rituals is easily understood as basic contagious magic. This is more explicit in locations where a Gypsy woman is a central figure, such as Orehovo, but the inclusion of Gypsy figures even as supplementary characters owes something to the assumed link between Gypsies and fertility. Since the demographic transition in the early twentieth century, spurring human fertility has not been a major concern for most ethnic Bulgarians, most of whom are more focused on preventing pregnancy (the country has one of the lowest birth rates in Europe), but most want at least one child, so difficulty conceiving can be an issue, and fertility for crops and livestock has become ever more central to rural livelihoods. This Gypsy value reinforces negative stereotypes of Roma even as it attempts to tap them for the benefit of ethnic Bulgarians. The interpretations offered here are not intended to replace or supersede this obvious link but rather to suggest that the way these images of fertility are incorporated also tells us something about the nature of social relations.

Romani Responses

The most important indication that something more than just degradation of Roma is present in these rituals is how the rituals are received by the Roma themselves. This reception is evident in their participation in mumming, but it is also seen in their involvement as public observers of mumming activities and their comments when asked directly about the rituals. In many places, as already described, Roma participate in the rituals in various roles, from musicians to masked mummers and even "Gypsies" (Manova 2002). Although no Roma ever described his mumming persona as "Gypsy" to me, I observed many Romani children in makeshift costumes nearly identical to the costumes of Bulgarians explicitly labeled Gypsies, including having soot-marked faces and, in one case, a Rom performing as the bear trainer, an exclusively Gypsy occupation.

The participation of Roma as musicians can be easily explained by the payment they receive for their services. There are also material incentives for other roles. In some villages, such as Lesnovo, the Gypsy-like figures, called *plashilki* (as well as "Gypsy" by some ethnic Bulgarians), are all young Roma and they keep the money they acquire as a group (see figure 18). They are only given coins, however, and consequently never collect very much money, so each year they let a different participant keep it all. This method, which they themselves devised, also insures continual participation, as each child has to participate several years before reaping the benefits for him- or herself. In other cases mummers divide the proceeds, but even if they do not, the prospect of free food and drink during the event and at subsequent banquets is a material incentive. These are all certainly benefits but hardly sufficient to account for participating in an event experienced as odious and offensive.

Material incentives also do not explain why Roma are regular observers of the ritual activity and in some contexts provide the majority of the public.

Even in villages where Roma do not participate in the rituals and mummers do not visit Romani homes, Roma come out with their families to watch the activities of mummers as they pass through or near their neighborhoods. In almost all cases I observed they appeared entertained and amused by the antics. They are also often engaged by the mummers who might chase them or threaten them with one of their ritual weapons or try to grab a child. In Topolchane a trip with the mummers through the large Romani quarter to visit a few of the houses, including those that had a mummer participant, brought everyone out of their houses into their yards and the street. Roma also turn out in large numbers at the village square for the ritual finale. Romani vendors may also be seen selling toys, trinkets, and food in villages where the final performance attracts large crowds, although here material incentives are obviously the motivation. One might be tempted to explain Romani presence as a form of resistance, an insistence on being seen in reality and not as ritual caricature, indeed, as a challenge to the Gypsy images of mumming while bearing witness to the derogatory treatment. One who has seen the interactions, however, would probably not make this argument. It also runs counter to the explanations that Roma give for various engagements.

I spoke with Roma observers on a few mumming occasions, always starting conversations with a question about their general impressions of the activities. No respondent initially expressed umbrage at the Gypsy images. I then asked them directly whether they found the references to Roma in mumming insulting. In villages where the identity of Gypsy-like characters was more ambiguous, I even inquired about other mumming traditions where the Gypsy intent was explicit (as in those described in the previous section). Most of the Roma I spoke with acknowledged their awareness of these examples, even when local traditions or enactments did not include them. Their responses ran a gamut, from insistence that they did not understand the question to incredulity that I really meant to ask what I had asked to evident amusement. Even direct, leading questions did not prompt village Roma to express offense, perhaps because I was also a *gadja* (non-Roma), clearly fascinated with the rituals, speaking to them in Bulgarian and with no relationship of trust to any of them.

A few general responses were repeated regularly. For example, mumming was frequently dismissed as mere frivolous merrymaking and therefore absurd to take seriously enough to be insulted. In the words of a young mother watching the survakari in Batanovtsi with her child and husband: "This is play, people having fun; nothing is serious, so how can it be an insult?" An-

other common response, perhaps more evident where Roma were not mumming participants, was that mumming was rather foolish behavior, demeaning to the Bulgarians. These Roma seemed to share the derogatory judgment
of the stereotyped activity and images but saw it as an indictment of the actors rather than the imagined referent. This point was made most directly by
a middle-aged male Rom watching a small festival in Yambol while some very
explicit, black-faced Gypsy figures paraded by: "Why should I be insulted? I
don't act or look like that. They are the ones that should be embarrassed, I'm
laughing at them!"[2]

The most frequent response suggested that if there was offense, it was too
minor to merit notice compared to the serious discrimination suffered daily.
In other words, any potential insult was insignificant compared to the real
racial discrimination that occurred, and to complain about mumming only
trivialized those serious offenses by creating a conceptual parallel. Not surprisingly, the most common, serious complaints concerned job discrimination. Since 1989 the situation for Roma has deteriorated dramatically, a major
problem given their precarious economic situation during the socialist era.
As noted, most lacked any claim to land in the system of restitution devised
by the state, and with the associated high unemployment, they found it impossible to find jobs. As one man watching the mumming group pass by his
house in Batanovtsi put it:

> Offensive? My God, we have so many offenses, how could you think that this
> is a problem? Work is the problem; it is hard for us to live or provide for our
> families. Whenever there are jobs the Bulgarians always offer it to a Bulgarian,
> never a Gypsy. That is where we feel the insult, not here. Before the changes
> there was a shortage of workers and we could always find some work, but now
> they will not allow us to do the same work they sought us out for before. Even
> jobs they used to refuse to do, calling it Gypsy work, they won't hire me to do
> now. They only hire Bulgarians.[3]

As compelling as this man's analysis was, it did not necessarily elimi-
nate a possible link between the Gypsy representations in mumming and
job discrimination. Indeed, the derogatory stereotypes performed in mumming, notably sloth, theft, and sloppiness, may account in part for discrimination against Roma in the job market. When prodded with this possibility,
the same informant said that it was not stereotypes that kept them out of
work but rather employer connections to other Bulgarians. "I've done some
of these jobs before, and did them so well that they use to seek me out to work

for them. So they know I am not lazy and do a good job, but they still won't hire me now, because there are Bulgarians, friends and relatives (*blizki*), who need the work."

Such insightful critiques also deny the utility of false or insufficient consciousness as the excuse for limited Romani offense. Though this might explain the Roma who claimed not to understand my concerns, the more likely explanation is Stewart's (1997:235) documentation of the Romani worldview that makes my questions nonsensical—namely, that derogatory stereotypes are in fact positive values. None of these explanations sits comfortably with the other two responses presented above, which recognized discrimination and yet denied the link to mumming. To suggest that they are only partially politically conscious is to privilege a Western sensitivity or interpretation a priori. In contrast, it is important to note that Roma are intensely aware of the parallel between their social position in Bulgaria and that of other marginalized ethnic groups elsewhere in the world. The association with African Americans is particularly strong (cf. Lemon 1995). This may have been privileged in part by the knowledge that I was American, but in some cases I obtained evidence of the analogy before an informant knew where I was from (although obviously recognizing me as a foreigner). Romani youth valorize cultural products associated with African Americans, notably music genres such as hip-hop and rap, justifying their preferences with the social parallel between their plight and that of African Americans. Roma of all ages know about and idolize Martin Luther King Jr. He was often mentioned in exchanges I had with Roma, sometimes with simple admiration of what he had accomplished for African Americans and at times with the more explicit desire for a Romani version, for example, "We need a Martin Luther King here."

I pressed a few of these commentators with the link again, suggesting that many Americans (black and white) had found black-face performances in American popular culture, including mumming in Philadelphia, a disturbing symbol of racism despite mummers' claims to the contrary (Welch 1970:135–144) and that the cessation of such activities had been an important part of the African American struggle in the United States. This seemed to puzzle the two Roma with whom I discussed it; one simply shrugged and offered no further defense, and the other responded that these activities must be different than Bulgarian mumming. There are likely Roma with whom I did not speak who find mumming performances offensive. Donna Buchanan (personal communication) notes that professional Romani musicians, by dint of their association with an ethnically driven occupation, may find it harder to deflect ethnic stereotypes, making them more offensive. To state the obvious, Roma are hardly homogeneous, and different subject locations affect the experience of offense. Still, that some do not see mumming as insulting, when they do see other behaviors by ethnic Bulgarians as such, should warn us against making a wholesale parallel with Euro-American uses of black face. Although the parallels are undeniable, and recognizing them may come with Roma's increasing political mobilization, apparent similarities should not blind us to subtle differences.

Alternative Interpretations

If we accept the argument from the previous chapter that mumming reflects a community that is ambivalent and conflictive, then it is easy to see Roma as part of such a community and Gypsy representations in mumming as statements of that ambivalent and unequal inclusion. Indeed, if mumming enacts village social relations rather than reversing them, then we have to entertain the possibility that the inclusion of both Gypsy images and Romani participants in mumming is indicative of a social inclusion of Roma in the village. In analyzing a Moroccan variant of mumming, Paul Silverstein (n.d.) shows how Jewish elements have been transformed by Amazigh activists from derogatory and exclusionary inversions into positive demonstrations of Philo-Semitism. I cannot push the argument that far in Bulgaria, as the images of Gypsy inclusion are also explicit statements about *how* they are included, which is in a discriminatory, derogatory, and marginal way. Still, it is an inclusion quite distinct from models of ethno-national exclusion, and this nuance has been eclipsed.

Gypsies are important figures in many mumming rites. In a few villages, such as Orehovo in the Rhodope Mountains in southern Bulgaria, a female gypsy figure (*tsiganka*), portrayed by a man, is one of only a few central figures. Here, as in other villages such as Turnicheni, mumming is not a massive collective activity but rather the affair of a few individuals who fulfill a discreet number of roles. There are five characters in the mumming party: an Arap, an old man, two transvestite maidens, and the transvestite Gypsy. To have a Gypsy in this select group speaks significantly to what the community is like or how central the image of the Gypsy is to the community embodied by the mummers. In the vast majority of villages, however, the Gypsy figures are both more numerous and more marginal. Although they are not the central figures of the ritual, they are essential. In many villages mumming rituals must have Gypsy figures in order to be considered complete or successful.

Some of the actions and performances of these Gypsy figures speak clearly to Romani inclusion. In Pobeda the group of Gypsies appears at the village square separate from and prior to any other mumming figures. Subsequently they interact only occasionally and tangentially with the Bulgarian peasant family, attesting to extensive ethnic segregation. Only the bear and its trainer move back and forth between the two groups, replicating a pattern of interaction in which Roma with particular occupations or skills operate as brokers between these usually segregated populations. Still, both groups are eventually encircled by the spectacularly masked kukeri who symbolize and protect the village; being within that circle, albeit separate from the Bulgarian peasants, is a statement of (marginal) inclusion.

One obvious reason for inclusion is to showcase the superiority of the Bulgarian peasants, who are themselves represented in somewhat derogatory ways as simple (minded). The ritual suggests that ethnic Bulgarians need the Gypsy stereotype to valorize their own identity. As Shannon Sullivan (2006:157) notes, the "Roma's alleged wildness is necessary to *gaje* life because *gaje* life is defined in opposition to it." This is especially important given a commonly cited national inferiority complex in Bulgaria famously encapsulated in the term "Bulgarian work" and embodied in Pobeda mumming by backward peasants and the Bulgarian Olympian with his cracked plastic sled.[4] Ethnic Bulgarians need the Roma to provide the low Other that elevates their own national image to something superior (Stallybrass and White 1986). This is particularly significant for rural Bulgarians who suffer an additional inferiority as the most backward segment of the national population. Stewart's (1997:chap. 7) discussion of the mutually constituting nature of the "peasant" and the "Gypsy" in Hungary confirms the dialectic between these categories. Mumming performances such as those in Pobeda suggest that ethnic Bulgarian villagers recognize and value this contribution. Following Stewart, we might suspect that Roma also value this opposition for their own cultural validation.

This interpretation, however, is far from complete, because the ethnic Bulgarians I know were constantly mixing their disgust and criticism of Gypsies with begrudging admiration. Gypsies are lazy but clever and sly (*hitur*)—a valued characteristic often attributed to Bulgarian heroes (both historical and fictional). Of course, they are also often acknowledged for their skills as craftsmen and musicians. This oxymoronic condition is captured well in the common Bulgarian expression, "Nice work, but it's Gypsy." The ultimate negative stereotype, however, that always seems to overwhelm any positive attribute is their proclivity to steal. But theft is also one of the most common complaints leveled against ethnic Bulgarians by their co-nationals (Creed 1998). Anyone who gets ahead is suspected of theft, from village entrepreneurs to national politicians. When I confronted one friend with this apparent similarity between Roma and ethnic Bulgarians, he attempted to clarify it for me: "True, Bulgarians steal, but Gypsies cannot *not* steal." One way to read this evident essentialization of Gypsy behavior is that Bulgarians chose to steal whereas Gypsies can't help themselves. Where the greater blame lies in this comparison is certainly debatable.

A common role of Gypsy figures in mumming troupes is to collect and carry the food and alcohol donated to the group. In addition to gifts in kind, they also ask for and receive money. Both roles speak to the expectation of providing for village Roma. In the village of Cherna Gora, the group of several young Gypsy characters descended on the homeowners after the other mummers had departed and begged vocally, "for the little Gypsies, something for the dear Gypsies."[5] This is a powerful symbol of inclusion. The expectation that villagers should help the Roma makes these Gypsy characters compelling solicitors for the mumming troupe. If we acknowledge that mummers rely symbolically on the cultural appeal of wedding gifts and religious offerings to solicit the bulk of their money, then we must accept that the other pleas and requests they issue are also culturally resonant and valid. Begging Gypsy figures are not just ridiculing Roma, although that is undeniable; they are using the sociocultural claims that village Roma have on their non-ethnic co-villagers in order to extract more money for the mummers.

Irony and hypocrisy are rife, as ethnic Bulgarians complain about village Roma asking for handouts in other contexts and yet traffic in this expectation for their own benefit as mummers. Fieldwork in rural Bulgaria over several years has exposed numerous interactions between village Roma and ethnic Bulgarians that replicate Gypsy receptions in mumming. I have been present in different households when village Roma appeared, sometimes selling homemade wares but many times seeking handouts. At times they were sent away empty-handed, explained with a simple dismissive "Gypsies," as if the very word was sufficient to convey the whole story and exchange. Many times, however, I observed Bulgarians making significant efforts to find something to give them, including used clothing, food, or money.

An alternative motive for these gifts was sometimes made explicit: "Now you're here asking for food. Where were you when I needed someone to hoe my corn?" Roma provided manual labor as well as horse services for rural

Bulgarians, and because the proffered wage was usually not attractive (or even useful in socialist times), an economy of favors paralleled and supported these labor arrangements. This link between service and favors was not exclusive to Roma. In Varvara the owner of a large collection of mumming bells teased a young man who wanted to borrow some of them with a similar taunt, threatening not to let him borrow the bells because he had not helped in the farm work the previous year.[6] The point is that, in villages, many Roma participate in work relations that establish or demand other social obligations, although the responsibility to give to Roma was not limited to explicit economic reciprocity.

In Lesnovo the plashilki are all given coins, much like the Gypsies of Cherna Gora, but without explicit begging. In this case they are all Roma. Villagers save coins for the purpose and give out handfuls. It is obvious that this appeal traffics in the obligation or expectation that villagers give to begging or needy Gypsies, especially when they provide a service in return, as they *are* doing by mumming, which dispels evil and invites abundance. In other words, the Gypsy figures are important to mumming because they are part of the village and they invoke the social obligation to provide for village Gypsies. Of course, the way they are included again speaks volumes: they are given food and coins rather than the larger amounts of money given to the central mumming figures, and they follow behind the main group; as one young ethnic Bulgarian dressed as a Gypsy in Cherna Gora put it, "Gypsies are always last." In Lesnovo a few hosts attempted to avoid the onslaught of Romani mummers by hurling the coins on the ground so the young Roma would scatter to retrieve them. Although this manner of dispersal was the exception, it vividly captures the condescending way that Roma are included. These are certainly not ways that deserve validation and reproduction, but they could have provided bases to build upon rather than receiving the same destructive impulse that characterized the political economy of postsocialism.

Another reason to nuance our interpretation of Gypsy imagery is the aforementioned denial of its accuracy by both participants and observers. In many cases characters that Bulgarians might call "Gypsy" do not exhibit any of the typical Gypsy stereotypes. In other cases these stereotypes are blended with non-Romani images. This is most evident in the case of burlesque or lewd transvestite figures who might have a darkened face but whose ostentatious sexuality is not a stereotypical quality of Gypsies for Bulgarians. Indeed, Roma are more likely associated with female sexual propriety and the lack of sex appeal. Consequently these figures are more likely to be called promiscu-

Figure 18. Young Roma as plashilki in Lesnovo in 2006.

Figure 19. The survakari goup in Batanovtsi in 2006 included Gypsy figures and Roma mummers.

Figure 20. An Arap in Lesichevo, in 2002, having his face blackened by a helper.

ous women or prostitutes rather than "Gypsy" despite their darkened face. But, like other figures with darkened faces not intended to represent Roma, their blackened skin makes "Gypsy" a reasonable or possible designation in a highly racialized context, especially when forced to create generic or general terms for these figures. In other words, the use of the term "Gypsy" for these rather indeterminate figures is an effort to place them into a single category for the purpose of description for the ethnographer. In fact, sometimes informants only resorted to the term "Gypsy" after failing to come up with a more fitting or accurate generalization for me.

The appeal of "Gypsy" as a generic rather than descriptive term reflects the homogenization of these rituals and the significant influence of the Pernik region. As noted in chapter 1, the Pernik festival has helped define mumming practice and this has also granted the villages around Pernik, which are disproportionately represented in the festival, a strong influence over the generic images of mumming, especially those distinguished as survakari (New Year's rituals). These villages have some of the most explicit Gypsy figures, and since "Gypsy" works well as the supplemental category of mummers there, it is often applied less precisely and less appropriately elsewhere. In short, observers not from a given location or not involved in mumming there might use the term "Gypsy" to refer to characters that local villagers or the mummers themselves do not. For some, this misnomer works to distance the practices from disrespect to actual Roma since the performers are not "realistic" in relation to accepted Gypsy stereotypes. Here the signifier seems explicitly decoupled from the signified.

As noted, other terms also exist for comparable figures, notably "Arapi" and "plashilki." The term "Arapi" was used for more mysterious and unreal characters or Islamic-inflected figures, although the latter might also carry some of the same markers as Gypsies. "Plashilki" was often used to characterize many of the figures that might include Gypsy-like figures. They were not usually as scary as the name implies, although some might be, and they might also wear masks rather than makeup, connecting them to other frightening mumming figures. They might also get the name from the overall objective of the mumming troupe to scare away evil, or perhaps from the fact that bystanders are afraid of being marked by soot. As pointed out earlier, the masked children mumming in Lesnovo are generally called plashilki, even though, or perhaps because, they are all Roma. They do not pool the pittance they collect with the ethnic Bulgarian mummers collecting bigger sums, but, given the exclusiveness of the mumming group to a particular age set, their inclusion is still symbolically significant. Most fascinating, many of them wore white masks. Thrilled to find what I assumed was resistance— the use of "white face" by Roma as a retort to the use of black face by ethnic Bulgarians—I asked why they wore white masks. The recurrent answer was that it was the only material they had or that other markings drawn on the masks showed up better on white fabric. Indeed, a few young Roma wore black masks but still referred to themselves as "plashilki."

Tsvetana Manova (2002) has documented a case of a young Rom self-avowedly performing the role of a Gypsy. She suggests that by masking himself, even as a Gypsy, he made himself part of the mumming group, reversing the everyday exclusion and alterity of Roma. I suggest, however, that this ritual role is in fact much like that of his everyday life—an unequal inclusion.

Roma are easily incorporated into mumming in roles that conform to their expected social position: as Gypsy-like figures (whether called "Gypsies" or "plashilki"), as musicians, or even as other masked figures so long as they remain a minority. When Roma predominate among central mumming roles, as in the village of Gorno Aleksandrovo described at the beginning of this chapter, anti-Gypsy sentiment becomes more evident.

Yes, unfortunately, the Gorno Aleksandrovo mumming story is not one of idealized ethnic tolerance and integration. As the mumming troupe made its way around the village, two dissonant narratives played out. The dominant one was indeed a rather inclusive story enacted by ethnic Bulgarians welcoming, treating, and embracing the predominantly Romani mummers. On the side, literally and figuratively, was a different commentary provided by ethnic Bulgarian observers who were accompanying the troupe both to enjoy the festivities and observe how their neighbors feted and tipped the performers. This story was also joined by a few of the ethnic Bulgarian mummers. The mummers constantly pleaded with me to take their picture, but occasionally ethnic Bulgarian mummers nabbed me when the others were distracted and asked that I take a picture "of just the Bulgarian mummers" (not a large group as previously noted). As word spread about who I was and why I was there, a few ethnic Bulgarians approached me to convey their discontent at the predominance of Roma in the ritual, comparing the current activity negatively to the past when it was almost entirely Bulgarian. As one man put it, "Ah, then there was something. Now, only Gypsy work." When questioned further, however, he had trouble pinpointing the exact differences, eventually settling on the greater number of mummers in the past and their greater discipline. He then pointed out that many villagers greeted the mummers at the gates to their yards or put the food and drink out on tables along the street in front of the house, so that the mummers could not see what the villagers had in their yard and house. I did not have to ask why: if Gypsies spotted something desirable, it was assumed that they would return later to steal it. Another man told me that the mummers had to write down the monetary contributions so meticulously and conspicuously because otherwise the Gypsies would steal part of it.

I jotted down all these comments in my notebook, but from my general experience in various villages over time I recognized a general loosening of ritual discipline as the entertainment value of the event overshadowed its supernatural objectives, even when Roma were not predominant. Similarly greeting mummers at the gate or setting up tables on the street to treat them were no more common in Gorno Alexandrovo than in many other villages I visited without Romani mummers. The former was often an effort to minimize the property damage mummers might inflict on the fully utilized yards that had often been recently planted and perhaps covered with elaborate plastic domes to insure early produce. If the household intended to put out a large feast, the yard was often too small to accommodate it, and so the street was the obvious alternative. Three different observers in Gorno Alexandrovo, all ethnic Bulgarians and old enough to be retired, assured me that the written accounting of monetary donations had been part of local practice as long as they could remember, so it could not have been a response to recent encroachments by Roma.

Every ethnic Bulgarian I queried in Gorno Aleksandrovo, including those volunteering anti-Gypsy commentary, were glad that the Roma were keeping the ritual alive. Indeed, many older villagers loaned Roma their mumming costumes, making it possible for many more Roma to participate than could afford to do so on their own. So ethnic Bulgarians bemoaned the predominance of Roma in mumming and yet embraced them as mummers, expressed gratitude to them for maintaining the vitality of the ritual, and even facilitated their participation by providing costumes! This is a perfect encapsulation of the complicated nature of Bulgarian-Roma relations. It is not a case of reversal or "mere" performance, with the real story of antagonism recited by a baleful chorus in the background; rather, both are part of the total experience of ethnic relations and reflect an ambivalent incorporation.

Inclusion, albeit always unequal and marginal, was the more dominant theme. Moreover, the contrary commentary was not motivated solely by anti-Gypsy sentiment (just as the inclusive performance was certainly not devoid of it). It was also a critique of the political and economic forces that had depleted the village of ethnic Bulgarian mummers, as well as a partial performance for my benefit, inspired by nationalist sentiment. To the degree that mumming rituals have become associated with Bulgarian nationality, as they undeniably have, some villagers were concerned how I, as an American, a Westerner, might interpret the predominance of Roma. The link of mumming and nation was obviously troubled by the strong Romani presence, which required explanation.

A similar defense was needed regarding local identity. While modern mumming is authorized by its national associations, the more explicit and visceral connection is between mumming troupes and a local/village identity. This created the danger that I might interpret the predominance of Roma in mumming as indicative of a Romani village. In fact, this was somewhat the case demographically in Gorno Aleksandrovo, but not politically, as ethnic Bulgarians held all village administrative posts, including that of elected mayor. Ethnic Bulgarian villagers, especially men who had been mummers in the past, were not anxious to accept the implication of the current profile of the mumming troupe, preferring instead the identity of the village reflected in past mumming practice. For them, criticizing the Gypsification of mumming established their earlier experiences as the authentic and valid mumming practice, and therefore the true reflection of village and national identity.

In a sense, they were almost performing racism to counter the evident message of mumming. It was as if their extreme embrace of Roma in mumming necessitated a counternarrative. I doubt that they commented so strongly and explicitly on the racial/ethnic dimension when no outsider was present; I provoked its expression. Although my presence did not create these sentiments, which are deep and strong, for some villagers it may have granted these sentiments pride of place over the more ambivalent ones evident in the actions and comments of others that day. The implications of Roma mumming had to be countered precisely because mumming carries such recognized and acknowledged meaning. It is the very centrality of mumming, the premise of this book, that required some villagers to offer a counternarrative and produce racist discourse. Here is a clear warning against any romanticization of the marginal and begrudging inclusion evident in mumming: it tends to morph easily, if not inevitably, into a standard categorical racism when the demographics shift in favor of the minority.

A related dynamic seems to be associated with absolute absence. As noted, the use of the term "Gypsy" to identify various mumming characters and the degree to which they performed common anti-Gypsy stereotypes varied significantly across the country. Both correlated *roughly* with the absence of Roma in the village or their limited participation in mumming. The more explicitly derogatory representations were found in villages with few or no Roma. Silverstein (n.d.) notes how absence authorizes the presence of masquerade identities in Morocco, promoting the expansion of Jew face and the erasure of black face in a context where Jews have left and blacks (Iqbliyin) are increasing. Bulgarian villagers also alluded to such a link. Although Turiya villagers refer to their dark-faced mummers as Arapi rather than Gypsies, two different villagers attributed the vitality of their ritual traditions to the fact that Turiya is a "pure Bulgarian village."[7] As pointed out, the villages around Pernik have some of the most explicit Gypsy imagery and these villages usually have few Romani residents. A mummer in the village of Gigintsi said of his village, "Gypsies and storks are not allowed." Storks are an omen of good luck, so one interpretation seems to be that the village has neither good nor bad extremes. The lack of storks is offset by the lack of Gypsies. The absence of Romani co-villagers perpetuates experiential ignorance and grants political license to continue or reinforce negative stereotypes.

Somewhat conversely, we might also think about more explicit anti-Gypsy performance in villages without Roma as sour grapes. Although villages with many Roma are assumed to be impoverished by that very fact, those with no Roma are sometimes even poorer. There are historical reasons why some parts of the country have more Romani residents, including the actions of the socialist government in settling populations of Roma, but whenever I asked about why there were few Roma in a village or district I received the same answer in the form of a question: "Why would they be [or stay] here?" Many ethnic Bulgarians assume that Roma, with their peripatetic traditions, lack of possessions or land, and apparent willingness to live in deplorable conditions are completely mobile and can simply pick up and leave places that are economically inhospitable. Their evident role in the petty cross-border trading that exploded after 1989 (Konstantinov 1996; Konstantinov, Kressel, and Thuen 1998) confirmed this assumption for many Bulgarians. So while a significant population of Roma is usually cited as a major problem for a village, the lack of any Roma could be a tacit sign of even greater distress. Roma from around Pernik probably moved to town or even Sofia, which is not that far away, to escape these impoverished villages with few options for making a living. As one man from Yardzhilovtsi explained when I asked why they had to have Gypsy figures in mumming: "it is not that you have to have them, but there is nothing valuable without Gypsies." The presence of Gypsies testifies to the value of the ritual and the place. In this sense we might rethink the previous interpretation of the comment from the man in Gigintsi that storks and Gypsies are not allowed. It could be an acknowledgment that the village's lack of luck and prospective is confirmed by both the lack of storks and the absence of Roma. This region offers more evidence of the suggested correlation, as places closer to Pernik, such as Batanovtsi, which is only one train

stop away and nearly a suburb of the city, have Romani residents, fewer derogatory Gypsy figures among the mummers, and a few Romani participants
in the mumming troupe itself (see figure 19).

The most compelling support for the model of local Roma inclusion suggested here came from the village of Varvara, not in the actual mumming
activity itself but in the concomitant New Year's tradition in which young
children use decorated cornel branches called *survachki* to hit the back of
adults, wishing them a healthy prosperous year. The children are usually rewarded with money. The elaborate mumming activities in Varvara, described
in chapter 3, brought out a large number of observers on New Year's Day from
neighboring villages and nearby towns. Romani merchants also came to sell
toys and trinkets from tables they set up near the village square. Their wares
included artificial survachki covered in flashy colored aluminum. So while
people were milling about and watching the mumming activity, children were
circulating among the crowd tapping adults on the back with their survachki
(both homemade and newly purchased) and collecting money. Ethnic Bulgarian children usually restricted this activity to adults they knew (friends of
their parents, relatives, neighbors, teachers, etc.), but young Roma were less
discriminating and tapped almost everybody they encountered. They also received much less for their efforts, getting only coins whereas ethnic Bulgarian
children sometimes were given paper money.

Not all Romani children, however, were treated the same. Although villagers accepted the greetings of some and dutifully dug into their pockets for
coins to give them, they aggressively shooed others away. I had already noticed this discrepancy when I happened to be standing next to a village acquaintance as he chased off a young boy about six years old who was headed
toward him. Without provocation, he turned to me to explain his behavior
(itself an indication that his refusal required justification), and said, "He is not
ours." By this he meant that the child was not a village resident. As he elaborated, families of Roma had boarded the train from the neighboring town
of Velingrad to work the crowd gathered for the festivities. This distinction
was made by most Varvara residents who recognized and treated the Romani
children from their own village but refused all others. One man kept telling
the latter to "go back to Velingrad" whenever they passed nearby. For many
visitors this distinction was not obvious or even relevant, so the Roma from
outside managed to collect some coins, but I witnessed several cases in which
villagers informed their visiting friends or relatives which Roma were not
from the village and the guests obliged by refusing to tip them. Villagers felt

compelled to treat "our" Roma albeit less generously than ethnic Bulgarian children but had no compunction about dismissing, even deriding, those who were "not ours."[8]

Although the possessive pronoun "our" invites accusations of a patronizing paternalism, or even ownership, this was definitely not the case. "Our" (*nash*) is commonly used in Bulgarian to signify inclusion. It might be used for members of the same family, members of the same village, members of a person's social network, or members of the same nation. The actual extent of inclusion is contextually determined, but none of them has the paternalistic notion of ownership. In this usage it would be more accurately translated into English as "one of us." The common use of the pronoun by ethnic Bulgarians for Roma from one's village conveys directly the possibility of inclusion represented in mumming. Of course, this local inclusion is also the basis of a more general discrimination. The notion of "our" Gypsies may create a connection that bridges continuing racism within villages, but it also validates the broader disregard for all other Roma. It works both ways at the same time. This helps explain how local village inclusion can exist, while broader surveys suggest that over 70 percent of ethnic Bulgarians have unfavorable opinions of Roma (Vassilev 2004:49).

To conclude with perhaps the most highly charged (at least for an American observer) element of racist representation, a dimension of even black-face makeup is worth cross-examining. Of course, the most obvious is that Roma are not black (although they have embraced the notion for political reasons which I discuss below). The effort of ethnic Bulgarians to make them black in mumming is partially an effort to racially distinguish themselves from Roma who, as I have noted, are often not as physically distinctive as many ethnic Bulgarians insisted (or, perhaps, wished). This distinction works, to a degree, to make Bulgarians more European in the face of a self-image as partially "oriental" because of their geographical location and their five-hundred-year history under Ottoman control. This interpretation mirrors Michael Rogin's (1996) analysis of black face in American minstrelsy and early Hollywood movies, which he suggests Americanized and whitened the Jewish and European ethnic characters who performed these roles. Black makeup implied that the characters were not black, helping to establish that they were white. Similarly, negative Gypsy representations such as the use of black face are primarily a defensive response to the aforementioned national inferiority complex. This one conveniently legitimates the parallels Roma draw strategically and successfully with the struggles of African Americans, so that they might find "blackening" politically expedient. This Romani strategy, in turn, casts ethnic Bulgarians as parallel to white Euro-Americans, which they find reassuring and validating given their ambivalent conception of themselves as (white) Europeans.

Other figures represented in black face, especially the Arapi, are often positive characters. In the famous case of Turiya they are ambivalent figures, much like Gypsy figures discussed here. They escort the transvestite figure (and baby) but are also the main culprits trying to seduce her in the finale. They are also marked as Islamic by the fezzes and shalvari (billowy pants) they wear. As Mary Neuburger (2004) has noted, these are the standard cultural markers of Islam for Turks and Pomaks in Bulgaria, and potent symbols around which significant ethnic-based political struggle has centered in the past. When I asked villagers and participants about these figures, no one could identify them beyond the term "Arapi" or locate them geographically. Some said they were "like Gypsies," referring to the more well-known imagery of Gypsies in other mumming traditions, but they did not call them "Gypsies." Like the latter their faces are commonly darkened unevenly with ash. However, Arapi in other villages, such as Lesichevo, Kalipetrovo, and Orehovo, more fully embody their designation. In these villages their entire faces are blackened, and not just with soot but with a dark-black greasepaint or polish (see figure 20). In these cases they are the leaders of their respective mumming troupes and are unambiguously benign, indeed positive, figures. The horse figure from Turnicheni also had a soot-blackened face without racial implication. This is not to deny the racist foundations of black face but to suggest that we cannot assume such a derogatory meaning and intent translocally or ahistorically.

Local and National Identities

As variant instantiations of an iconic national folk practice, village mumming authorizes an exclusionary nationalist project, but at the same time, in many of these instances, its local message allows for ethnic inclusion of Roma. Although this may seem contradictory, it may instead reflect the articulation of different dimensions of identity. It suggests that local identity in Bulgaria is not a diminutive refraction of national identity but rather a continuing affiliation that sometimes works at odds with national identity. As noted in chapter 1, villagers identify mumming with Bulgarian national identity and explain their involvement as a contribution to sustaining the nation culturally. But their actions clearly attest to a local identification and attachment. That is why mummers living in Pernik return to their villages of origin to enact the rituals rather than establish mumming traditions in Pernik. The national awakening in Bulgaria occurred in a still thoroughly rural society, so the romantic reinvention of folk traditions as a generic national heritage was not foundational or even possible (cf. Hobsbawm and Ranger 1983).

Michael Herzfeld (2003) has explored how the quintessentially local quality of folklore comes to serve primarily nationalist agendas and identities in Greece, and Uli Linke (1990) has pointed out how it also provided a tool of state consolidation in Germany by offering administrators a way of knowing the population. Similar processes have occurred in Bulgaria, and Carol Silverman (1983) has provided a classic illustration of the national homogenization of folklore under socialism, but mumming never completely succumbed to these projects. The differences that distinguish village mumming traditions from one another are often the most important to participants. The latter emphasize these distinctions, and any imitation across villages is more likely to be considered theft, at least by the source, than fraternal sharing among co-nationals. For example, mummers from villages with deep traditions of using long-hair goatskin costumes were extremely irritated when other villages, especially those nearby, adopted this costume. But even when figures end up looking similar, practices remain radically distinct, and the imitators then stress the latter over any costume similarities. The exemplars are the adjacent villages of Lesichevo and Kalugerovo which now sport nearly identical mumming costumes but maintain completely different ritual activities.

The way that mumming is made national in festivals, through what might be called an agglutinative model of national folklore in which each village performs its particularity while the festival itself provides national unity, allows villages to retain their local distinctions and mumming's value in local identification. The festival's emphasis on authenticity and tradition abets this continuity as these objectives protect local practice. This protection is not complete since some practices or costumes that are recognized as authentic in other villages, especially in the same area, can be adopted without paying a price in authenticity—they are not judged as absolute "innovations" but rather as fusions of "related" and equally "authentic" traditions. Thus change and homogenization are taking place, but the process also rewards and encourages the maintenance of local particularity to some degree, and the uneven changes discussed in this book, such as the inclusion of Roma and women, create new differences. Of course, this agglutinative model also easily incorporates the variant practices of people currently outside the boarders of the Bulgarian state, such as those in Greece and Macedonia. In other words, it also works with the nationalistic agenda for a greater Bulgaria and this dimension has been gaining momentum.

Still, this means of national incorporation operates on a more generalized, often regional, basis rather than village by village, and the distinctions of mumming traditions according to the latter retain their contrary force as a counterweight to nationalist discourse. This is not to suggest that Bulgarians do not identify with the area of the country they come from, just that it does not eclipse more specific village identifications, especially for those still living in a village or those with close relatives in a natal village. Moreover, Bulgarian villagers have notoriously bad relations with residents of adjacent villages, usually attributed to historical disputes over pasturage, forests, water, and other resources, which fragment strong regional affiliations As a retired man in Varvara volunteered when asked about mumming traditions in the neighboring villages: "There is no such thing as brother villages in Bulgaria. Neighboring villages never get along." He then dismissed the two adjacent villages that have a history of mumming (another nearby village does not) as "weak," but he also admitted that residents from those villages commonly dismiss Varvara's elaborate performances and costumes as frivolous and untraditional, and thus actually inferior to their own anemic activities. Another factor that renders mumming an uncertain national emblem is that it is not found in every village or even in a majority of them. Unlike folk song, folk dress, and folk dance, which are omnipresent, even if varied across villages, mumming is not found across the breadth of the nation.

To borrow Nancy Churchill's (2006:3) assessment of carnival in Puebla, Mexico, mumming "expresses and reinforces a deep sense of belonging in both space and time." In Bulgaria that space/time is commonly a village. Mumming both reflects and maintains the primacy of village identity. This identity and its recognized distinctiveness make the inclusion of non-ethnic co-villagers possible, indeed necessary to a degree, albeit in a marginal and discriminatory way. This relationship is based on village affiliation and is thus more expansive than that based on close proximity or neighborliness (cf. Bougarel 1996), although more limited in what might be expected. The importance of village identification, and the notion of community it requires and reproduces, is behind the purported "Bulgarian ethnic model," and its associated "weak nationalism" (Todorova 2009). As I have elaborated elsewhere (Creed 2002), the notion of community evident in villages, in both relations between ethnic groups and within them, produces a rather muted nationalism when imagined or projected onto the state. Mumming enthusiasm both reflects that identification and sustains it against the currents of homogenizing nationalism. Gypsies are not Bulgarian, but unlike the nationalistic racial exclusions documented elsewhere in Europe (Brown 2004; Gilroy 1987; Stolcke 1995), the presence of, and interaction with, Gypsies is an essential part of *being* Bulgarian. This close association increasingly serves as a means of racial/ethnic Europeanization by highlighting Bulgarians' whiteness and continental connections in contrast to the more explicitly nonwhite, non-European Gypsies.

The increasing popularity of nationalist sentiment evident in the political success of the nationalistic coalition Ataka (Attack) in the 2005 parliamentary election signals a shift. This "ragtag coalition of radical nationalist parties . . . ended up winning 21 seats [out of 240] despite having been little more than a blip on the radars of most political pundits" (Ganev 2006:75). This development was provoked by numerous factors, especially political frustration. After trying various political options over fifteen years of democracy during which nationalist parties garnered minimal support, the latter eventually emerged as the only remaining untried option. The attraction was abetted by Western multicultural models imported and implemented in Bulgarian society and polity that focused attention on minorities. This attention, which was heightened by the EU accession process, was desperately needed, but the way it was done bypassed and undermined extant types of inclusion demonstrated in mumming, which actually damaged social relations between ethnic groups.

Moreover, the timing was deadly. The focus on ethnic minorities in the wake of the wholesale collapse of the countryside was an affront to rural ethnic Bulgarians. As I have described elsewhere (Creed 2010), the devastation experienced by Bulgarian villagers between 1992 and 2002 was traumatic. Villagers watching a way of life disintegrate and seeing no political concern for their plight viewed the EU's and NGOs' concern for minority rights as an additional assault. Ethnic Bulgarian villagers saw themselves as victims, and the greater attention to the plight of the Roma or Turks in this national disaster seemed odd, even wrongheaded, as the desperate rural circumstances required general redress if the situation for rural Roma and Turks was to be improved. In fairness, the EU anticipated help for rural ethnic Bulgarians in the form of subsidies after accession, but minority rights were a *precondition*. Skeptical villagers tended to focus on current priorities, and the perceived concern only for the Roma was a nationalist provocation.

A generational dynamic also gradually made an exclusionary nationalist model more compatible with Bulgarian experience. Since urbanization
in Bulgaria was a predominantly postwar phenomenon, most urbanites in
the socialist era had rural roots. During fieldwork in the 1980s I rarely met
an adult city resident in Bulgaria who did not have a close relative living in
a village. In 2006 this was no longer the case. The country as a whole has
moved another generation away from the kind of local identification evident
in mumming. The lack of a deep experiential connection to a local/village
identity has made these individuals more susceptible to the dominant nationalist identity now gaining political resonance and, in the process, redefining
the meaning of mumming.

The more recent massive migration from rural areas that began after 1989
(a release of suppressed movement during socialism, exacerbated by the economic decimation mentioned previously) has amplified the separation, for
although these more recent migrants have an experiential village identity of
inclusion, they also associate this with the rural context and are aware of the
increasing distance between these images and those of the urbanites they
join. In short, they recognize (and articulate) that their notions of community are no longer apropos in the city among longtime urban residents.

This decoupling has been abetted by economic difficulties in the village.
I have argued elsewhere for the importance of occupational identity under
socialism (Creed 1998). While one's occupation was touted by villagers to
escape the derogatory image of the backward peasant, these occupations,
whether in the collective farm or local industry, were still identified with the
village to a significant degree. Unemployment has thus further eroded the
status of village identities even for those still living there. In short, this identification is a victim of the decimation of the countryside. Studies of nationalism have highlighted the history of places in shaping the particular nature
of nationalism and national identification (Ballinger 2003; Brown 2003), and
studies of race have likewise shown the difference that place makes in one's
racial identification (Brown 2004; Khan 2004). I suggest that a type of place—
rural and ethnically diverse—can also have an impact on how one experiences ethno-national identity or, perhaps more accurate, the consequences of
that identity in everyday life and politics.

Still, nationalism in Bulgaria had its origin and development as an anti-
colonial struggle against the Ottoman Empire and remains closely defined
vis-à-vis Turkey. Turks, not Gypsies, are the iconic national other (indeed,
Roma do not even have a political homeland), and this has authorized and

sustained the incorporation of Roma into local imaginings of the nationalist community. Turkish Bulgarians do not "enjoy" the same ambivalence. Their otherness, rooted in this history of colonial domination, is reinforced by close association with another nation-state (Turkey) and greater geographical segregation (most live in predominantly Turkish settlements and regions). Turks are also recognized as having had a major influence on national culture. Bulgarians relive this influence every day in the mundane acts of speaking and eating. To push Neuburger's (2004) felicitous phrasing to the psychological, they are truly "the orient within." This connection explains why Turks are often evaluated more positively than Roma by ethnic Bulgarians—it is self-validating. This same connection, however, makes their local inclusion less useful for, and perhaps a threat to, marking Bulgarians as European. The ambivalent inclusion of Gypsies, more generically despised, is, ironically, more helpful and less fraught.

Consequently I found no evidence of Turks participating in mumming activities as either performers or hosts[9] (although mummers in the village of Bachkovo reported visiting the houses of several Pomaks). In addition, explicitly Turkish figures in mumming, usually Ottoman soldiers who perform historical events associated with the Bulgarian liberation struggle, exhibited no evidence of the ambiguity that qualified Gypsy-like characters. The images that might possibly reference Turkish inclusion in mumming are those that radically distinguish them from Bulgarians, including Islamic references and clothing such as shalvari and fezzes. Even here they are rarely identified directly with Turks but rather with Arapi, other potential victims of the Turks.

The Turkish exclusion also helps us see the limits to Romani inclusion, as ethnic Bulgarians commonly distinguish between "Bulgarian" and "Turkish" Gypsies, and offer their begrudging inclusion more fully to the former. This distinction, which divides the Bulgarian population of Roma nearly in half,[10] is sometimes rendered as "Christian" versus "Muslim" or, to make the valuation explicit, "good" versus "bad." While religion and language might be the foci here, the essential difference is assimilation. The "good"/"Christian"/ "Bulgarian" Gypsies are those that are most like ethnic Bulgarians. This might be evident by their participation in mumming rituals, and certainly only this category of Roma would be visited by ethnic Bulgarian mumming troupes. So the pervasive image of "the Gypsy other" exists along with "the other Gypsies." The latter makes it possible for ethnic Bulgarians to embrace their Gypsy village co-residents without completely threatening their own national identity. The existence of Turkish Gypsies also helps explain why public opinion surveys show that many more ethnic Bulgarians admit to negative attitudes toward Gypsies than toward Turks despite the ambivalent inclusion of the former in local villages—collectively Gypsies suffer a double stigma as both Gypsies and possibly Turks/Muslims. Still, location/village residence is the trump card, as Turkish Gypsies within a village are also often accorded a begrudging recognition, albeit less enthusiastically and reliably than their Bulgarian counterparts. Gypsies are more derided as a group but more likely to be incorporated conceptually within local communities, whereas Turks are somewhat more benignly evaluated as a group and yet less componential to notions of local community.

If as Fonseca (1996:113) insists, the Roma of Bulgaria are, along with those in the former Czechoslovakia, the most deracinated in Eastern Europe, then perhaps this also facilitates assimilation and helps explain the extent of inclusion suggested here at the village level. If so, then it is itself the product of an earlier cultural dispossession of Roma (see Silverman 1986). One could make the same argument about Bulgarian Jews and the absence, until recently, of rabid anti-Semitism. This fact is detectable historically in the country's much touted refusal to deport Jews during its alliance with Germany in World War II (Chary 1972; Todorov 2001). Since that time the Jews remaining in the country have thoroughly assimilated (see Bohlman 2000), preventing a new national anti-Semitism. A fresh wave of anti-Semitism in the early twenty-first century can be traced to increasing exposure to publications about the global Jewish conspiracy that flooded the market following the end of socialist censorship. Like the new nationalism with which it is often combined, the global Jewish conspiracy is an attractive explanatory device after more than a decade of unexplainable political and economic frustration for a population with historical reasons to entertain conspiracy theories.

Complications

National and ethnic identity in Bulgaria is not uniform even across the same ethno-national population. Moreover, it is intertwined with other important identity vectors, including occupation, and especially with locally defined village-based identities. Differences in the latter refract national ideas differently. In many villages there is a local identity that includes Roma because of their residence in a place where conflict and tension actually constitute community. For many years this image of community has been projected/imagined onto the state level to soften an alternative exclusionary image of the nation. At the same time, and increasingly, a more exclusive national identity is coming back to the village from above which might or might not meet friction with this local identity depending on local circumstances. Mumming articulates this tension. In ethnically homogeneous villages there is less friction, which may have sustained some of the most derogatory imagery of ethnic others. Even here, however, the inclusion of Gypsy images can be interpreted as a reflection of national inclusion, albeit deflected by derision. In other villages a nationalistic identity is in daily tension with a village identity that includes "good Gypsies," and this is often reflected in mumming in less derogatory Gypsy representations, the replacement of Gypsies by more ambiguous characters, and perhaps the participation of Roma themselves. Still, the same person who feels obliged to acknowledge village Roma, and perhaps involve them in mumming, may have no compunction about disparaging Gypsies generically in other contexts.

Another complication emerges in the case of rituals maintained primarily by former villagers who return for the event. These individuals may not have lived in the village for decades and might even be second-generation urbanites who never lived there at all. In this case ritual participation is still very much about a local identification in the sense of origin or "roots" but not in the more intimate sense of a lived experience, and thus it does not reflect the same intense interaction with all villagers. Even though local affiliation remains strong, when not lived daily the ambivalent inclusion of Roma eventually erodes and allows for a more categorical racist intent (and interpretation) that works more easily with nationalistic exclusion. The villages most dependent on the return of urban residents to stage mumming events are also likely to be the most depopulated, which, of course, correlates with poverty, the lack of Roma in the village, and more derogatory images of Gypsies.

For these migrants and others, the locally experienced notions of inclusion suggested in this chapter are being replaced by a homogenized general Western idea of ethnic tolerance/multiculturalism. These ideas are not "bad," but in order to be effective in this context they require creating the homogeneous pervasive racism that knows little nuance against which they were originally formulated. Whether such a simplistic homogeneous racism existed in the West is another question, but my Bulgarian experience leads me to conclude that it was not the model that existed in many villages and towns in 1989. I even believe that the relations of ambivalent inclusion were somewhat reciprocal, as I witnessed Romani ritual events, such as weddings and soldier sendoffs, in which ethnic Bulgarians were sometimes incorporated as guests but more often congregated on the margins to observe the festivities much as Roma do in mumming. These avenues of village inclusion could have been used as the beginning point to challenge ethnic and racial essentializations, but they were missed and squandered.

Globalization has defined racism significantly around the experiences of the African diaspora primarily in the developed West. This has provided the Roma a useful and inspirational model in the Civil Rights movement (Emmons 2006), but it has also allowed many in Bulgaria and elsewhere to deny their continuing racism against Roma, as racism itself has been nearly monopolized by the African diaspora (see Olomoof 2006). As one of Alaina Lemon's Russian informants put it: "Racism is something you have in America" (Lemon 2000:63). Roma's embrace of the appellation "black" is partially an effort to break through this limitation and highlight the parallels. This use of "black" mirrors its political signification in Liverpool, where Jacqueline Brown (2004) found that the term always referenced political activism as distinct from an apolitical "African."

Once while having dinner with a Bulgarian family, the grandfather interrupted the conversation at the table insisting that we all look at what "those Gypsies" were doing. I could not figure out what Gypsies he was referring to until his son curtly told him: "never mind those Negroes." I only then realized that he had been referring to Africans on a television documentary as Gypsies. Years later, in the village of Kamen, I was talking to a mummer while he donned his costume. Like costumes elsewhere, it was too complicated to manage alone. Upon growing impatient waiting for fellow mummers who were supposed to come by to help, he called the boy next door to assist. The boy, perhaps ten years old, was a Rom, and it was apparent from their conversation that the boy was often called upon to help (what he received in exchange was not clear, but the boy did come over promptly and enthusiastically). In a most uncomfortable exchange in front of the young man, the mummer proceeded to refer to him as a "Negro" and kept trying to describe Roma by repeating the statement "they're like your Negroes." This exchange may be interpreted in multiple ways. He may have been trying to tap into what he assumed was my white American racism toward blacks to validate his own anti-Gypsy racism, as well as the use of his neighbor as an apparent servant. He might also have been commenting on the discrimination that Roma face in Bulgaria. My own impression from his delivery was that it included some of both but primarily the former. I was too embarrassed for the boy to encourage the conversation, so I do not have additional comments to support this conclusion.

Ethnic Bulgarians became increasingly aware of the derogatory interpretation of mumming images, especially black face, over the period of my research, as evinced by an increasing incidence of unprovoked explanations. In the 1980s and early 1990s ethnic Bulgarians never felt compelled to defend their use of black face, but by the late 1990s ethnic Bulgarians at mumming events commonly assured me, without any question on my part, that it was not an imitation of black or dark skin but rather "just a disguise" (not unlike some of my arguments above). When I asked why black was used rather than some other color, the standard response was that soot/ash was readily available and free. A few said that it was symbolically important because it came from the fire that inaugurated the mumming event. Their rationalizations do not displace the racist interpretation, but they do show a new awareness of that interpretation.

One can certainly not fault the Roma or their political advocates for following the model of a powerful Civil Rights movement. Unfortunate, however, is the way that this strategy authorizes and validates a Western expertise, first by implying that American or European racial politics was a complete success and then suggesting a wholesale replication of those models. The latter may not be bad, although some elements, especially the notion of multiculturalism, have been questioned (Hale 2002), but employing them does contribute to a paternalistic approach of how "we" can help the Roma. The model is not completely inappropriate, as the deep, extreme racism toward Roma in Bulgaria and its socioeconomic consequences parallel the suffering of African Americans in many ways. But focusing on the similarities may deflect attention from differences, especially the overarching fact that Bulgarian racism is partly a defensive posture driven by ethnic Bulgarians' sense of national inferiority rather than confident racial superiority. This recognition could have alerted attention to the different relations of racism evident in mumming which could have inspired alternative strategies of redress. The success of imported models may require the replication of the relations the model was designed to redress, which may actually reformulate existing relations into more antagonistic ones.

In an argument that links nicely with my critique of civil society as a civilizing initiative, Sullivan (2006:157) claims that "discrimination and violence against the Roma in Europe can be seen as increasing precisely because of the 'civilizing' influence of the Western world upon Central Europe." Her focus is on the impact of development and modernization paradigms which require central Europeans to dissociate themselves from anything "wild" and non-Western, qualities they associate with the Roma, even as they are also required to make progress on human rights. Hayden's (2002) analysis of Bosnia suggests that the positive tolerance imagined and desired by Westerners is actually incompatible with the democracy they valorize/enforce (see also Hayden 2007; Creed 1990). Vassilev suggests the opposite: that the continuing and worsening plight of the Roma is a result "of the incomplete and shallow democratization of post-Communist Bulgaria" (Vassilev 2004:41) discussed in chapter 3. Although these models are not necessarily compatible, they all point to disappointments and contradictions in the evolution of ethnic relations after 1989 which may be a result of poor appreciation of the nature of prior ethnic relations, at least in the village context.

This failure is abetted by the need or desire to find solutions on a state level. This requires a homogenization of relations in order to apply a single solution. As clearly demonstrated in this chapter, the idea of an ambivalent inclusion of Roma by ethnic Bulgarians was not only limited predominantly to rural and small town locations; its character varied significantly according to a number of particular local characteristics. As James Scott (1998) has noted, such variation is anathema to any state project: it simply cannot be considered in devising a generic answer to a generic "ethnic problem." Uniform solutions, especially to the degree that they come with desperately needed resources, may end up creating the contexts that they need to work, namely, the imagined generic context that inspired them even if it was not operative beforehand.

I do not claim that the relations I detected in mumming between Roma and ethnic Bulgarians were ideal or even deserved preservation. As I have tried to make clear throughout this chapter, the inclusion I found was ambivalent at best and never threatened a foundational racism which desperately needed to be challenged. I am only imagining what might have been possible in this effort had these relations been recognized by politicians or activists at both the national and international levels, and then used as the basis to expand or redefine inclusion. The evidence was there. Even the Helsinki Watch Report from 1991 that indicted Bulgaria for the treatment of Roma included several contrary comments by Roma noting the positive elements of Bulgarian-Roma relations (Helsinki Watch 1991:29, 40, 50). These comments parallel the relations I have explicated in mumming. On these

bases, one could have imagined new or alternative models for improving ethnic relations or, perhaps more accurate, for improving the situation of Roma
without necessarily worsening relations. Instead, like other elements of cultural wealth lost in the transition, they were eradicated by solutions that assumed a categorical opposition and eventually helped promote nationalism
to a real political force.

MODERNITY IN DRAG

The issues refracted through mumming in the preceding chapters share a connection: all are elements of a Euro-American vision of modernity. Sexual equality, democracy, civic engagement, and minority rights are commonly (mis)understood as uniquely modern, Western accomplishments. Such glorious achievements seemingly provide a self-validation of the modern project, whatever downside it might also entail. In short, these ideals are presented as the contemporary "ends" of modernization, justifying the tried and true (read Western) "means" of getting there. Because the means are the most important elements of democratic capitalism (that is, mechanisms such as elections and free markets), this is a rather effective formula in establishing Western-style political economies; the latter then survive any subsequent failure to deliver the goods, since disappointing results can be blamed on free will and the invisible hand. Alternative means to the same desirable goals challenge the assumed superiority and/or exclusivity of the Western models shored up by the teleology of their positive outcomes. That modernity has also produced or inspired some despicable outcomes, from Nazism to Stalinism, requires redemption in relation to indisputable or universal ideals and projects.

As noted earlier, the possible alternative means to these goals evident in mumming went unnoticed by theorists of postsocialism partly because mumming itself seems so premodern. Indeed it is ancient, and its continued practice bespeaks an incomplete modernization that never fully supplanted preexisting ways of being and living—not a likely location for modern ideas.

The ancient association, however, makes mumming useful for the quintessential modern project of nationalism, which is always justified as primordial. Thus mumming's modern role is to represent the premodern. The characterization of mumming as premodern undercuts any consideration of cultural resources that might be compatible with other goals or components of modernity. Of course, appearances notwithstanding, Bulgarian mumming is thoroughly modern in many ways. A reexamination of these modern components provides a final vindication of the lessons offered in the previous chapters.

One could argue that modernity was both the subject and product of the earliest social theory, and it has remained, in some form, the focus of social analysis ever since. Over the last several years, appropriately coinciding with another fin de siècle, modernity has been taken up anew by anthropologists attempting to understand the cultural paradoxes of globalization, specifically the proliferation of cultural differences in the face of increasing interconnections. As James Ferguson (2002) notes, earlier models explained the practices of colonized peoples who adopted Western goods and ideas in distinctive ways as either a misunderstanding of Western culture (ignorance), a parody of Western culture (resistance), or the adaptation of Western materials to indigenous cultural objectives (continuity). Dissatisfied with these options in the face of an ever growing diversity of outcomes, anthropologists and others have tried to break away from the dichotomous opposition underlying earlier analyses by making modernity plural and qualifying it with a plethora of adjectives, including "alternative," "vernacular," "multiple," "parallel," "critical," and simply "other" to capture a more ambiguous relationship in which people engage with Western modernity, without being subsumed by it (see, e.g., Gaonkar 2001; Knauft 2002a). Through global interactions people are redefining what it means to be "modern," even as they aspire to elements of a Western paragon.

The idea of multiple modernities provides anthropologists with a means to plot the complexity of contemporary cultural politics without the limitations inherent in earlier notions of hybridity and creolization, which inadvertently suggest pristine starting points, equitable interactions, or positive outcomes (Khan 2001, 2007). The concept of an alternative modernity, however, can still homogenize and efface the diversity of motives that animate local practice. In Bulgaria the experience with dynamics commonly associated with modernity has been quite different from one village to another. Even in a single locale different people may engage in the same activity with different interpretations and divergent objectives. To be analytically useful, then, alternative modernities must always be recognized as fractured: an uneasy coalescence of different motivations and interpretations, including antimodern ones—a paradox that Bruce Knauft (2002b) captures with the notion of the "oxymodern." The variety of terms offered in the effort to qualify modernities is, in part, diagnostic of this underlying limitation—no single qualification can adequately convey all the caveats or requirements essential to its productive utilization.

Nevertheless, the engagement with modernity is a useful way to foreground the different motivations and agendas that underlie mumming practice. Some people are trying to resist modern/Western intrusions by filling space and time with traditional practices; others are trying to influence and nuance the practices of Western modernity just as they domesticated state socialism (Creed 1998). Still others are just satirizing these modern forms in full knowledge that there is no option, and others are actually using mumming as an instrument of Westernization and modernization. Villagers frustrated by one of these agendas may switch to another without any evident change in their ritual practice or their degree of ritual commitment. This complexity is perhaps captured best by what Jonathan Shannon (2006:66–68), in his examination of music in Syria, calls "improvising modernity." As we have seen, however, the improvisations can come around to a very Western-looking paradigm. Mummers attempt to sustain mumming to convey a distinctive message, but they employ strategies that end up sabotaging the message or, at best, adding new ones to it more compatible with those they were originally attempting to counter, diluting mumming's corrective or distinctive content. Their continuing dedication to the rituals, now reconfigured in subtle ways, invests them in the very social and cultural reconfigurations they were previously resisting. In this unintended way, alternative modernities are often stripped of their alterity. Alternatives appear, multiply, and disappear over time, and so understanding the dynamics of modernity requires a temporal sensitivity.

Bulgaria's postsocialist experience with modernity is shaped by the rather explicit, rigid, and pervasive images of socialist modernity that preceded it. A Western capitalist image of modernity is hegemonic in Bulgaria, installed first by the IMF and then by the EU, but villagers still engage with this objective through their past experiences. Between 1989 and 2005 most Bulgarian villagers experienced a major decline in their economic well-being and quality of life. Ill-conceived "transition" programs destroyed much of the ag-

ricultural infrastructure and threw villagers "back" upon subsistence cultivation (see Creed 1995). Other sectors of the society rebounded more quickly,
but rural areas remained less touched by postsocialist improvements longer
and villagers understandably lost hope, their desperation dismissed as socialist nostalgia (Creed 2010). Many rural residents, especially younger ones, de-
camped for urban locales or foreign destinations.

In the context of such insecurity and disappointment, mumming became
a mechanism for asserting the resilience of rural residents and the value of
village life—an intention that is patently obvious in mummers' commentary.
Yet this attitude is not simply an expression of neo-traditionalism. To the
contrary, participants and believers use sophisticated analytic frameworks to
defend the appropriateness of mumming activities and beliefs in the current
political and economic context. They explain mumming as an apt metaphor
for the experience of rural postsocialism—a system where unreason reigns
and every economic initiative is more of a gamble than a calculated venture.
In their experience, the shift Westward made life more Byzantine, market
principles produced patently irrational programs, and democracy generated
rather unenlightened political stalemates. Mumming is the perfect response
to this difficulty and uncertainty. It is not a return to magic but an assessment
of the felicitous affinity between ineffective magical practices and postsocialism. The visceral experience of mumming as somewhat chaotic and unregu-
lated only adds to its affective correlation with the postsocialist condition.
Villagers have found new meaning in mumming not because they are backward but because they are thoughtful, expressive beings and see in mumming
an image of their inexplicable and unredeemable predicament. For many, it
is precisely because they have a modern secular interpretation of mumming
as old-fashioned, unrestrained, and even superstitious that it resonates so
beautifully with their contemporary lives! For these mummers, the appeal
to tradition is not so much a rejection of modern options as an indictment of
the current system's failure to deliver the modern spoils they were implicitly
promised.

But motivations are fractured, and in a few villages my queries provoked
arguments between the majority of villagers who saw things in this way and a
few who insisted on the supernatural efficacy of mumming for promoting or
insuring fertility or abundance. Even the latter, though, explained their belief
in quasi-social, scientific terms. When I pressed one in 2002 about why more
people expressed belief now than had done so just a few years earlier, he gave
an analytical explanation: "since 1989 people have embraced various political

and religious ideas and actions to help them through the changes and none of them have worked, so why not mumming?" Indeed, nearly every "believer" I queried attempted to explain or justify their beliefs sociologically rather than in religious or supernatural terms. Mummers' use of "enlightened" sociological discourse to explain their own "superstitious" beliefs encapsulates the manipulation of modernity accomplished in mumming.

The geographical variation evident in mumming's resurgence supports this interpretation. My field research revealed uneven revitalization even within a single region of the country. The most devastated and marginalized villages actually evinced a decline in mumming activity and interest. This verifies the modern link since, by definition, an alternative modernity requires, and is in dialogue with, a hegemonic form. Areas of the greatest devastation do not even have the meager resources or resident personnel necessary to continue the practice. Thus mumming emerges as a viable resource for those villagers who are engaged with the promises of modernity, such as those who live closer to urban centers or have some other advantage such as mining options in the vicinity. The most extensively de-developed regions are not even in the conversation with modernity upon which alternatives and counter discourses are premised, and mumming in these places is dying out rather than reviving, much to the distress of older participants. Put simply, mumming is strengthening not in the most "traditional" or "backward" villages but in those that are more articulated with modernizing forces and prospects, limited as they may be.

Villagers often complained about being "behind" the rest of Europe and expressed desires for a "normal life," which clearly convey acceptance of a generic Western version of modernity that we might thus call a dominant or hegemonic or normative modernity. Gauging by the longtime popularity of the Bulgarian author Aleko Konstantinov's writings, which satirize Bulgarian backwardness vis-à-vis Western Europe and the United States, this has been the case for much of the twentieth century (Neuburger 2006; Todorova 1997). Alternatives to the normative, however, emerge in relation to specific activities. Using mumming as a window to modernity requires looking at specific arenas of lived experience reflected or represented in mumming that are conceptually linked to modernity, rather than engaging the notion as a whole, precisely because the notion is so monopolized by Western models. I have highlighted several connections, including gender, sexuality, democracy, civil society, community, nation, and ethnicity. The allusion to belief requires at least a nod to one final issue: religion.

The analysis of religion, always complex, becomes even more complicated when examined in relation to modernity in a postsocialist context. The
tainted socialist era was defined to such an extent by atheism and antireligious
sentiment that the secular quality of Western modernity sits uncomfortably
with subsequent "progress." To delegitimize socialism is to support religion,
but iconic images of modernity are secular, raising the question of how mod-
ernizers manage this conundrum. The relations between religion, secularism,
and modernity have been nicely historicized by Talal Asad (1993, 2003), who
suggests that the very category of religion was produced by the Western Enlightenment and shaped by a Christian emphasis on belief over practice that,
in another self-validating circularity of modernity, becomes a hallmark of
much vaulted secularism.

Mumming provides a fecund context for thinking about these associations. Its apparent survival of repressions by the Orthodox Church might invite assumptions about committed "pagan" believers, but it can also be read
as evidence of a precocious secularism that rendered the sanctions of the
Orthodox Church unthreatening. This is especially compelling given what
seems like a rather long history of disbelief in mumming's supernatural efficacy on the part of mummers themselves. Indeed, it is hard to document
the historical role of belief in these processes, as no one I spoke with had
vivid memories of pervasive supernatural belief on the part of mummers
they had known or heard about. Rather, they expressed a general recognition
that people had believed at some time in the distant past, an assumption replicated without much substantiation by folklore scholars. That is why I characterize contemporary expression of such belief as a response to the impacts
of postsocialism, as this belief was never expressed in the last years of socialism (1980s) or the first decade of transition (1990s), which was otherwise rife
with expressions of previously prohibited opinions and sentiment. New expressions of belief in mumming's supernatural roles were only evident after
villagers had experienced several years of transition difficulties.

The discovery that mumming vouched limited supernatural belief probably underlay Communist Party leaders' change of heart on mumming prohibitions; once they fully appreciated that continued practice did not actually reflect backward superstitious beliefs anathema to socialist modernism,
mumming's obvious utility for nationalist consolidation became attractive
(cf. Kligman 1988:259). The current refusal by the majority of observers to acknowledge mummers as an embodiment of evil, or even to acknowledge that
this was the idea at an earlier time, is evidence of the ritual's long alignment

with a modernist worldview. This view makes mumming more compatible with Christian belief, but we do not end up with a hybrid or syncretic form; instead, Christian imagery is incorporated as parody. The priest figure partners with the mummers to drive away evil (understood simply as modern bad luck or fate) and to invite abundance (good luck), but both are granted about equal chance of having an impact. Their equivalence reinforces the powerlessness of both. The parallel is challenging to Christian and non-Christian beliefs, suggesting nonreligious motives as the driving force behind mumming. It all sounds quite secularly modern.

Nonetheless the process is still connected to the spiritual in the sense that it must be done, and the reason it must be done often comes from the mummer's "soul." Enacting the ritual satisfies or completes the soul. So despite being rather thoroughly disenchanted in affect, mumming retains a spiritual dimension predicated on practice rather than belief, suggesting another dimension of modern alterity. This also clearly separates mumming from other enjoyable activities such as sport. Mummers did not talk about their unbridled passion for soccer as "spiritual" in the way that they often characterized their connection to mumming, although musicians do talk about music in similar ways (Buchanan 2006; Rice 1996). Nor did they talk about their "religious" activities (i.e., those related to Christianity) in this way, saying instead that such actions as church attendance and lighting candles "should" or were "expected" to be done without the same kind of spiritual compulsion. The sense of obligation around elaborate and demanding mortuary practices was significantly greater than other religious activities, but, notably, many people I observed performing these rites denied believing in an afterlife. In a sense, the practices without any strong underlying belief, or perhaps more separable from belief because less dependent upon the church, were the ones that people felt most compelled to perform.

The ambivalent relationship to the church is illustrated in the role of the mumming priest. Many villages have no such figure, and participants in some of these locations even opined that priests were inauthentic or frivolous innovations. No one complained that such figures were sacrilegious or even disrespectful to the church, although in one case the mumming group I accompanied was met by a Protestant convert who tried to give us religious tracts instead of treats, certainly implying a critical stance. The priest figure is more central to New Year's practices than to pre-spring events, although he appears in many of the latter as well. In the former, the priest accompanies the bridal party while the costumed mummers with bells often circulate at a distance, a bit removed from the bridal group, sometimes only entering the yard after the bridal party has departed. Combined with the anticlerical elements of the priest's persona, one message of this separation is that the priest is human, that he is part of well-known human actions and limitations, and that his helpfulness does not extend beyond confirming predictable human choices such as sanctifying marriage.

Once the priest and other human figures depart, villagers have to take charge of their own fate and deal directly with the forces beyond human knowledge or control represented by the elaborately costumed mummers. One cannot rely solely on intermediaries like priests, and one must do all within one's power or ability to affect one's own household's destiny. Put this way, mumming represents a strong message of individual responsibility, quite comparable to modern Western notions. But this message of individualism is wrapped in a strongly communal ritual, bespeaking again a more complex relationship between individual, family, and society than common images of modernity accommodate. It also suggests an understanding of the limits of human agency. Villagers offer what they have—food, drink, and money—to reward these forces but without any certainty that this will be sufficient.

In this context the costume of the mummers takes on new significance. Mummers are often masked and always wildly dressed, and though components of the costume may be linked symbolically to pre-Christian beliefs, the eclectic combinations may also represent a generic unknown that cannot be categorized, reflecting the fact that villagers do not know exactly what they are dealing with when it comes to their agrarian or economic fortunes. Mummers do not represent a premodern belief in supernatural power but simply a modern recognition that some of the actual determinants of family fortunes are not explicit or recognizable, and thus beyond individual control. This is an enlightened recognition that what you do not know *can* hurt you and that without full knowledge you are not able to act responsibly. This all seems a much more reasonable way of thinking than the false sense of agency often associated with modern Western notions of individual responsibility. Here is another element that may account for current refusals to interpret mummers as embodied evil: it is not that villagers do not appreciate mummers' personification of capricious factors but, rather, that they understand that in representing evil or bad luck mummers are ultimately part of a benign and simply symbolic project—a quite "modern" appreciation.

Still, the interpretation of the financial transactions of mumming shifts dramatically if the mummers are not believed to actually embody evil. What

Figure 21. Food given to survakari in Batanovtsi in 2006 is collected in a baby carriage, while the proffered brandy is poured into a single plastic jug.

might be understood as a reciprocal sharing of nature's bounty with the non-human forces disturbed or violated by agricultural activity becomes, instead, a quasi-commercial exchange in which ritual specialists (mummers) are paid for their work (bringing luck). This different interpretation produces a stronger parallel with the priest's role as professional religious specialist and may account for the priest's involvement or greater integration with costumed mummers. Both mummers and priest may also be interpreted as extortionists, as some villagers opined.

The role of money brings to the fore a collection of other relations to modernity, notably the general shift from in-kind gifts to cash offerings. While offerings of food and drink are universal elements in mumming, the significance of gifts of produce varies greatly across the country. In some locations these gifts are extensive, requiring designated mummers to push carts to transport the goods. These range from discarded baby carriages in Batanovtsi (see figure 21) to sturdy handcarts otherwise used to transport materials between house and field in Turiya. In Lesnovo a donkey is required to haul the goods. In some places particular products, such as eggs, must be provided. All such offerings, however, are expected in addition to cash, not as a substitute, and cash is the main objective. Some older villagers complained about the increasing expectation for money since 1989. During the late socialist period money was a standard expectation, but it was more accessible for most villagers and there were fewer attractive alternatives for its disposal. So complaints about the increasing expectation for money in the twenty-first century reflect its greater shortage rather than its previous absence from mumming. Reflecting its cultural centrality, mumming provides a vehicle for complaining about the radical shift in the role of money since 1989, even though money's role is not so different. Indeed, in all my mumming experiences I never witnessed an exchange in which the amount of money was an issue. Mummers take whatever is offered graciously and understand that their fellow villagers do not have a lot to spare.

A more substantive change in the economics of mumming is its increasing commercialization and relationship to class formation. In some villages, as economic prospects improved, villagers' reception of mummers became an acceptable (because communal) venue for demonstrating status through elaborate offerings of food as well as money. In the socialist and early postsocialist eras such variations commonly reflected villagers' differential engagement with mumming, but the varied levels of investment are increasingly exposing villagers' different economic fortunes. Similarly village businesses have become a primary target for mumming visits, with mummers often spending more time at these locations than at any village household. In a few cases villagers who have done very well economically have sponsored the mumming groups in more significant ways, such as providing funds for new costumes as well as for travel to festivals both in the country and abroad. These efforts revitalize mumming and mute the shock of class formation, without significant redistribution.

The limits to such redistribution have inspired some mummers to entrepreneurial efforts of their own. In numerous villages where I observed mumming events, village activists were trying to market the events to tourists.

My presence and fascination with the rituals provided inadvertent support for their enterprise, and I was sometimes asked to help locate more potential consumers like myself. In one village organizers asked me to pay a substantial sum for observing and documenting the events, and foreign tourists who showed up a few days later for the major ritual finale were also hit up for contributions. Given the language barriers these requests were hardly subtle, leaving the tourists uneasy about what was actually being requested, and so it is no surprise that many simply refused to pay and left. None of the Bulgarian visitors to the event was approached. In every village I visited during mumming events I was expected to contribute to the collection, as is anyone who might be around during the rituals. I always gave generously, calibrated according to the time I had spent with the group, but in some villages in the last year of my research, before I could even volunteer my contribution, a participant subtly informed me that a significant contribution was in order. At other times I was closely interrogated about my intentions and was fairly certain that only my noncommercial objectives, confirmed by my occupation as an educator, excused me from more explicit payment demands.

Where commercial attempts were not already under way I was often asked my opinion about the economic feasibility of this strategy. My experiences in villages that had attempted commercialization led me to offer rather pessimistic assessments. The timing of the rituals in winter, the rather remote locations, and the lack of other accommodations or attractions undercut prospects in areas without other significant tourist attractions. One experience in particular left me with a strong negative impression regarding mumming and tourism. At a village I was visiting near Pernik a tour bus arrived at the village square for the mumming finale. It parked nearby and the foreign tourists watched events through the bus windows, emerging into the frigid cold just for a few minutes to snap pictures. The bus took off after only a short time (and this was a stunning display and performance with expert musicians and magnificent masks). Villagers, who had been forewarned of the tour's visit, had prepared a spread of local food specialties and wine for the tourists, set up in a traditional folk manner in the village chitalishte, all in a special effort to impress the tourism company with the hope of perhaps establishing a regular commercial arrangement. Villagers were crushed when the tour guide informed them that the group did not have time to sample the proffered food and ambiance. The whole event was extremely demoralizing, as were most other efforts to commercialize village mumming that I witnessed.

Recognizing the local limitations to these efforts, some mummers took their show on the road and traveled to more popular tourist areas such as the Black Sea coast during the summer and ski resorts in the winter. There they would target locations popular with tourists, such as restaurants, and try to get the owners to pay them to perform for the customers, or just solicit tips from the patrons. This is generally profitable only for mummers in villages near these locations, as the costs of travel otherwise consume any proceeds.

The idea to commercialize village mumming was inspired by some national successes in tourism generally, including rural tourism, and the high-profile success of the Pernik municipality in attracting tourists to its mumming festival. The latter achievement owes a great deal to the socialist government that initiated these collective celebrations and provided state support to underwrite them, elevating them to international events that mummers from all over the country wanted to attend. Since the withdrawal of state support, the Pernik municipality has continued its event, securing sponsors from national and international foundations as well as private enterprises. It has increased its international profile, inviting and accommodating more carnival and mumming groups from other countries and joining the European Federation of Carnival Cities. The municipality has also commercialized the events significantly, sometimes requiring tourists to pay for permits to photograph or film the events. These permits also grant privileged access to a special viewing stand on the square. The significant number of tourists attending the event provides customers for a souvenir market in mumming paraphernalia spread out on tables along the edges of the town square. International exposure at this event has generated invitations for village mumming groups to attend folk festivals in Europe and Asia, situating mumming within a European and even global modern folk movement.

In towns other than Pernik these festivals have been taken over, or initiated, by new commercial enterprises, such as a winery in the town of Yambol, as part of public relations and advertising efforts. In Yambol the ancient patina of mumming is used to convey the image of an ancient tradition in viticulture, which in fact is fairly recent. The winery owns vineyards in villages with mumming traditions, and these mumming groups feature prominently in both the sponsored festival and the winery advertising. When I was there in 2002 the winery owner was making inquiries about registering the town with the European Federation of Carnival Cities, and although his expressed motives were strictly civic rather than commercial, clearly the winery's link to mumming locally could be a means for commercial exposure if these particular mumming groups garnered international attention. This new role of mumming in marketing is an explicitly modern one.

Another modern dimension of contemporary mumming is its role in (re) connecting mummers to places they have left behind. As noted numerous times, in many locations the vitality of mumming depends strongly on its role as a form of homecoming or reunion for the masses of villagers who have left the village for urban residence and occupations. Income from these jobs can underwrite village mumming activities, especially in villages so decimated by these processes that there is little hope of recouping expenses from the offerings villagers provide. In many cases, however, only the festival performance actually serves to bring together villagers from many nearby towns. Former villagers show up for the festival and perhaps some practices for the performance, but they do not necessarily participate in the village ritual, which can be quite anemic. Others do, however, and, importantly, some young men who have grown up in the city return to their parents' village to participate in the ritual. Mumming's survival and perpetuation in these contexts is a product of modern processes set off originally by socialist modernization and driven heavily by capitalist processes since 1989.

These quintessentially "modern" dimensions of mumming help reproduce the ritual, but they also erode or weaken its distinctive cultural content as they replicate the form. This is compounded by the fact that any residual distinctive content is missed by actors with preconceived ideas of what modernity looks like and how to produce it. Both these processes undermine a culturally grounded modernity in Bulgaria comparable to what evolved in the history of Western modernity. Within Western Europe different countries and even localities produced quite modern elements, including institutionalized political parties, from culturally specific building blocks, such as social clubs and confraternities that organized festival celebrations not unlike mumming. This luxuriant cultural grounding is a hallmark of Western modernity and perhaps a basis of its successful expansion. To gauge from anthropological recognition and documentation of qualified modernities in other parts of the world, the process seems to have developed with at least some degree of cultural sensitivity in places outside Europe as well (Piot 1999; Shannon 2006). As the chroniclers of these variations themselves note, however, casting these outcomes as alternatives or variations can inadvertently validate a Euro-American model as iconic. Any deviations from that model by people outside these modern heartlands can only ever be alternatively modern, an implicit confirmation that modernity in any unqualified sense remains the monopoly of Euro-Americans. This reminds us that permutations of modernity are stratified into dominant and subordinate forms, but it misses the fact that some places, like postsocialist Bulgaria, are denied any permutation at all.

Efforts to avoid the implicit authorization of Western modernity emphasize that modernity was a joint product of Europe and its colonies (Shannon 2006:62–63) or propose "provincializing" Europe in order to allow the stories of non-Western people to stand on their own (Chakrabarty 2000; Rofel 1999). While these efforts remain sensitive to the exclusions and constitutions of difference that produced a unified sense of Euro-American modernity, in the current moment the provincialization project can easily deflect attention from the history of enforced standardization that produced a single Euro-American modernity, a point David Nugent (2008: 55–56) makes specifically in regard to democracy. It misses the degree to which "new" members of Europe, including Bulgaria, are culturally provincialized by their incorporation into Europe. The requirements established for EU membership forced Bulgaria and other countries to simply replicate models that had evolved as culturally specific institutions elsewhere. Not surprisingly the results were often a poor imitation of Western models, and the inexact replication was then used to deny the country the same rights and respect accorded Western EU members. Bulgaria and other new EU members were left waiting for currency integration as well as numerous other benefits of EU membership.

The associated lack of respect was given graphic public display in January 2009 with the unveiling of the sculpture *Entropa* in the atrium of the European Council building in Brussels. The large installation, commissioned from Czech artist David Černý to mark the Czech Republic's turn in the rotating EU Council Presidency, was a sort of mosaic with maps of EU countries held together by a plastic grid resembling that which connects the pieces of a modeling kit before they are broken apart in order to be assembled (explicitly and self-consciously modernist). Each map was constructed and embellished to convey a national stereotype, and though none of them was flattering, only Bulgaria's was rendered graphically premodern and abject: the map of the country was constructed from a collection of different-sized squat (a.k.a., "Turkish") toilets. Although many political leaders registered complaints about the representation of their countries, only the Bulgarian map was considered offensive enough to require redress, and a week after the un-veiling it was covered in black cloth (inadvertently producing a different mes-sage of disdain).

The lessons learned from mumming in Bulgaria demand that we attend to the conditions that shape the possibility or probability of a culturally grounded modernity versus those that mitigate against it, producing instead moder-nities that eviscerate cultural practices or remake them into mere shadows of what they were. In Bulgaria the latter outcome was a product of "nesting" orientalisms (Bakić-Hayden 1995) and "balkanism" (Todorova 1997), com-bined with cold war dichotomies that overlapped the oriental/occidental one for a double dose of derision. The stereotypes of communism—that it eviscer-ated local culture, replacing it with a drab socialist uniformity, which was it-self a complete failure at delivering the goals of modernity—would seem to leave Bulgaria with little to offer the ongoing evolution of modernity and sug-gest that anything it did have to offer would be too alien to be useful or even adaptable (as opposed to the potential offerings of Poland or the Czech Re-public). Bulgaria shares these conditions with other postsocialist countries in the Balkans, but it is distinguished by its closer proximity to "the Orient" and its reputation as an unusually orthodox communist country throughout the cold war.

We must remember that the original (and singular) alternative moder-nity was socialism (Donham 1999; Shannon 2006:64). Thus the very idea of multiple and alternative modernities is a postsocialist product, and it is no coincidence that publications promoting the notion began to flourish a few years after 1989. The collapse of the socialist option both opened up a space for new alternatives and forced social theorists to find them in order to stave off the purported "end of history" (Fukuyama 1992). But it also foreclosed recognizing any of those options in the former heart of socialism where Bul-garia resides.

The alternatives evident in mumming were denied and ignored by oth-ers, while the effort on the part of mummers to sustain them ended up re-making mumming in ways more in keeping with Euro-American norms. The resulting profile of mumming allows participants to culturally engage a Eu-ropean modernity and aspire to realize it more closely through such efforts as membership in European carnival organizations, travel abroad, and com-mercialization. In these ways mumming is made thoroughly modern but at the cost of its potential alterity. It is now just modernity in premodern drag. Moreover, even its premodern disguise is vulnerable, as traditional masks are replaced by innovative designs like those in Varvara or by new commercially produced "carnival" masks, while elaborate folk bridal attire is supplanted by the generic white wedding gown among transvestite brides in Kalugerovo. But for now the premodern is still predominant and herein lies hope—drag always includes a disruptive potential—a refusal to allow the normal to go unchallenged or to sit without commentary. A modernity in drag is still a modernity in question, protecting a space for reconsideration.

INTRODUCTION

1. For a more extended comparison of postcolonialism and postsocialism, see Chari and Verdery 2009.

1. A MUMMING SEASON

1. The word is not the literal Bulgarian translation of New Year, which is *nova godina*, but it is always associated with the event. *Surva, surva godina,* is a more traditional form of happy New Year compared to *chestita nova godina*, and the verb *survachkam* is to wish someone a happy, healthy New Year by hitting him or her with a decorated branch from a cornel tree, called a *survachka*.

2. The word for other dances is *tants* and the verb form is *tantsuvam,* which is more equivalent to English usage and is probably borrowed from the French. There is no verb form for *horo,* and, importantly, Bulgarians do not use *tantsuvam horo* but rather *igraya horo,* which means "to play," and mumming rituals are also sometimes referred to as *igri* (games). I believe this usage rather than an assumption of simple play is what is implied in this term, although horo were the games for young people at one time, and mumming is certainly fun. The term *igraya* is also used for "prance" as with horses, which, of course, is not unlike the actions of some mummers.

3. Orthodox Easter is calculated in the manner it was calculated under the Julian calendar, so it falls on a different date than the Easter of Western Christendom whose method of calculation was shifted with the adoption of the Gregorian calendar.

4. The term "Arap" is Turkish for Arab, but Bulgarians use "*Arab*" for Arab and Bulgarian-English dictionaries translate "Arap" as "darkie." I do not do so because of the implications of darkie in English and because the Bulgarian term is not related to other color terms, suggesting greater historical significance. "Arap" is also sometimes used in colloquial Turkish to refer to blacks. Perhaps an Ottoman usage combining these referents, such as for dark-skinned Arab conscripts from other parts of the empire, was adopted by Bulgarians. According to Donna Buchanan (personal communication), Bulgarian ballads are full of references to Arapi, who are distinct from Turks and Roma, and always dark or black but often connected with the Ottoman military in some way.

5. This element also appears in early-winter events (see figure 4), and in some villages this camel-like figure and its entourage constitute a separate and distinct ritual known as *dzhamala*. The term, however, is also used in some villages (e.g., Kalugerovo) for mumming rites without a camel figure.

6. "Chalga" is a genre of Bulgarian music drawing on local folk traditions blended with Arabic, Turkish, Greek, and Romani influences. Although popular in dance clubs and pubs, it is considered tawdry by many and criticized for its foreign elements and trivial lyrics (Buchanan 1996, 2006; Silverman 1996).

7. See also Deema Kaneff (2004) and Carol Silverman (1983) for important analyses of folklore's central political role in socialist Bulgaria.

8. Of course, the Party's subsequent reversal and embrace of the rituals rendered the link between contemporary practice and past resistance suspect, and indeed several informants admitted that the rituals were not performed in their village during the years they were officially prohibited but rather were revived once the prohibition was lifted.

9. Such expressions replicate those recorded from Bulgarian musicians who repeatedly point to the soul and heart as the real sources of musical expression (Buchanan 2006; Rice 1994).

10. The different timing may also reflect the historical shift in the marking of the New Year, which was likely linked to the spring equinox in the distant past. When the beginning of the year was shifted to January, some mumming groups may have shifted their events to the new date while others kept the timing and eventually changed the justification to Lent. Even so, the relative attractiveness of these different options could still be explained by the different ecologies noted here.

2. GENDER AND SEXUALITY

1. In the Strandzha region the central mumming figure is traditionally expected to be married (Raichevski and Fol 1993), but in most villages I visited, villagers reported a defunct tradition of preferential bachelor participation.

2. Eleshnitsa is unique in performing their mumming activities on Easter.

3. The Brezhani mines were still operating when I was there in 2002 although not at socialist-era levels. Conversations with Brezhani mummers at the Pernik festival in 2006, however, revealed that they had since been shut down, leaving only the dangerous option of looting scrap metal from the shafts.

4. I later realized that this suggestion was not as absurd as it first seemed. In my travels around different villages, the mayor of one village where no mumming activity had occurred for several years offered to put on an exemplary demonstration for me if I promised to return around the time of the rituals. I declined, citing a conflicting obligation.

5. Although not expressed, or even experienced, as such by participants, I believe the elements are explicit enough for my suggestions to escape the criticism that they simply reflect a Western gaze "that conflates, via fear, any male/male contact with the homoerotic" (Amico 2007:41). If a cigar is sometimes just a cigar, I think it is rather obvious in these descriptions that this is *not* one of those times.

6. In keeping with this interpretation, borrowing is more common by younger boys, who are still outside a sexual calculus, and by relatives, for whom kin connections and incest prohibitions obviate sexual implications. But such considerations may not be the only ones limiting the sharing of bells. Given their value, bells, whether purchased or inherited, are status symbols. To wear someone else's bells, unless that person is a relative with the same family fortunes, could suggest pretentious deception. Overall, however, wealth displays are not paramount in the mumming experience, and I do not want to push any of these observations too far, as there is significant loaning of bells and it figures in my analysis in the next chapter.

7. In the case of Romanian miners this insecurity leads to new antagonistic interpretations of the sexual banter between miners (Kideckel 2008:174).

8. These deployments preclude recognition of the social construction of gender, which would otherwise seem to be a logical conclusion of the gender

continuum model. The outcome in much of the West, then, has not been a wholesale acceptance of social constructionism but rather some halfway recognition that pits men in a competitive struggle to acquire more of a variable, but still essential, manhood.

3. CIVIL SOCIETY AND DEMOCRACY

1. See also Sydel Silverman (1975) on how Italian notions of *civilta* include political activity and imply the qualities of urban life.

2. Notably the bells, which are more durable and valuable (sometimes extremely so depending on their age or size), are not usually stored at such locations but kept instead in the homes and stables of individual mummers.

3. On a short comparative research trip to Philadelphia, for example, I discovered the existence of "mumming widows": the lonely wives of mummers who spend all their free time with their mumming buddies in both civic and recreational pursuits.

4. A Sofia newspaper article on the devidzhi finale in Lesnovo in 2004 reported several elements of political critique. A priest figure carried a placard with disturbing village statistics for the previous year: 300 deaths and only 3 births; men dressed in camouflage and gasmasks paraded as soldiers destined for Iraq; and a donkey cart carried the message: "The Prime Minister promised to take us forward in 800 days, but he has set us back 800 years" (Kostov 2004:3). This coverage included two large color photographs on the front page of the issue.

4. AUTONOMY AND COMMUNITY

1. Some of these invocations rhyme in Bulgarian, which accounts for the contorted wording.

2. One could also read this as a meta-ritual incorporation of mumming rites into the martenitsi tradition, and indeed it could be both.

3. This chapter and the next elaborate on two different elements of an earlier argument (Creed 2004). Here I focus on social relations between ethnic Bulgarians, taking ethnicity out of the picture and focusing specifically on the atomization thesis (see also Creed 2008). Chapter 5 looks at how relations between ethnic groups are affected by the expectations for social relations exposed here.

4. Ironically, at the same time, the decline in such family networks is blamed for every social malady in the United States—apparently the family is valuable only in a very narrowly defined range.

5. ETHNICITY AND NATIONALISM

1. The parallels to Christian Lenten traditions on Ash Wednesday are too obvious to ignore, even if coincidental.

2. Notably this response is essentially identical to that written by an African American in a letter to the *Philadelphia Evening Bulletin* regarding the debate over black face in the Philadelphia mummers' parade (Welch 1970: 137–138).

3. These comments replicate the sentiment of Bulgarian Rom Mitko Tonchev as conveyed to Fonseca: "'It didn't use to be like this. We didn't use to *know* we were Gypsies. Everyone had jobs. Now we are not free in ourselves'" (Fonseca 1996:124; emphasis in the original).

4. Tim Pilbrow (2003) argues that the criticism of "Bulgarian work" is a means of self-validation rather than national condemnation. By invoking the phrase, individual Bulgarians elevate themselves as arbiters of quality and distinguish themselves from the inferiority around them. I acknowledge this possibility, but because it operates in this way only for the individual, it still affirms the inferiority commonly associated with the term on the national scale.

5. They used the diminutive form of the noun "Gypsy," which could indicate size and age or endearment. Here, as in many uses of the diminutive form in Bulgarian, I believe it actually incorporates both meanings. For that reason, as well as to convey the uncertainty and ambiguity, I have translated the two utterances of the term differently, even though the same word was used both times.

6. This man was both a mumming enthusiast and full-time shepherd, so his expressed motivation for collecting bells was twofold.

7. The word "pure" is one translation of the Bulgarian term "*chist*," more commonly translated as "clean." Although "pure" seems more appropriate in this context, the notion of "clean," with its obvious opposition to the stereotype of "dirty" Gypsies and its conceptual link to ethnic cleansing, should not be ignored

8. While ethnic Bulgarian children from another town might have been vulnerable to the same dismissal, they would likely have been given the benefit of the doubt of having a village connection, whereas Roma were suspect by default.

9. This despite the fact that Turks are also negatively stereotyped as overly prolific in childbearing and thus, like Gypsies, a potential source for conta-

gious fertility. The refusal to tap this possible contribution in contrast to the symbolic embrace of Gypsy fecundity is suggestive.

10. I have delayed giving population statistics for Roma, as the numbers are so uncertain. Official census numbers from 2001 put the Romani population at nearly 371,000, slightly less than 5 percent of the population, making it the second largest minority after Turks. Romani advocacy groups, however, insist that there is a high incidence of Roma reporting themselves as Bulgarian or Turkish in the census in order to escape the Gypsy stigma and that the real number is anywhere between 500,000 and 1,000,000 (see Vassilev 2004:42).

WORKS CITED

Åberg, Martin. 2000. "Putnam's Social Captial Theory Goes East: A Case Study of Western Ukraine and L'viv." *Europe-Asia Studies* 52 (2): 295–317.

Altman, Dennis. 2001. *Global Sex*. Chicago: University of Chicago Press.

Amico, Stephen. 2007. "Blue Notes: Gay Men and Popular Music in Contemporary Urban Russia." Ph.D. diss., City University of New York.

Anderson, Benedict. 1991 [1983]. *Imagined Communities: Reflections on the Origin and Spread of Nationalism*. Rev. ed. New York: Verso.

Arens, William. 1975. "The Great American Football Ritual." *Natural History* 84:72–80.

Argyrou, Vassos. 1996. *Tradition and Modernity in the Mediterranean: The Wedding as Symbolic Struggle*. New York: Cambridge University Press.

Asad, Talal. 1993. *Genealogies of Religion: Disciplines and Reasons of Power in Christianity and Islam*. Baltimore, Md.: Johns Hopkins University Press.

———. 2003. *Formations of the Secular: Christianity, Islam, Modernity*. Stanford, Calif.: Stanford University Press.

Badone, Ellen, ed. 1990. *Religious Orthodoxy and Popular Faith in European Society*. Princeton, N.J.: Princeton University Press.

Bakhtin, Mikhail. 1984. *Rabelais and His World*. Trans. Hélène Iswolsky. Bloomington: Indiana University Press.

Bakić-Hayden, Milica. 1995. "Nesting Orientalisms: The Case of Former Yugoslavia." *Slavic Review* 54 (4): 917–931.

Ballinger, Pamela. 2003. *History in Exile: Memory and Identity at the Borders of the Balkans*. Princeton, N.J.: Princeton University Press.

Banfield, Edward. 1958. *The Moral Basis of a Backward Society*. Glencoe, Ill.: Free Press.

Bell, Peter. 1984. *Peasants in Socialist Transition: Life in a Collectivized Hungarian Village*. Berkeley: University of California Press.

Benovska-Săbkova, Milena. 1998. "The Signs of Protest: January 1–February 2, 1997." *Ethnologia Bulgarica* 1:67–77.

Berdahl, Daphne. 1999. *Where the World Ended: Re-Unification and Identity in the German Borderland*. Berkeley: University of California Press.

Binns, Christopher A. P. 1979. "The Changing Face of Power: Revolution and Accommodation in the Development of the Soviet Ceremonial System: Part I." *Man* 14:585–606.

———. 1980. "The Changing Face of Power: Revolution and Accommodation in the Development of the Soviet Ceremonial System: Part II." *Man* 15:170–187.

Blim, Michael. 2000. "Capitalisms in Late Modernity." *Annual Review of Anthropology* 29:25–38.

Bohlman, Philip V. 2000. "To Hear the Voices Still Heard: On Synagogue Restoration in Eastern Europe." In *Altering States: Ethnographies of Transition in Eastern Europe and the Former Soviet Union,* ed. Daphne Berdahl, Matti Bunzl, and Martha Lampland, 40–69. Ann Arbor: University of Michigan Press.

Boissevain, Jeremy, ed. 1992. *Revitalizing European Rituals.* London: Routledge.

Bokova, Irena. 2000. "Gradsko nasledstvo i folklorna kultura. Industrialniyat grad i 'vuzstanovenata' traditsiya—po primera na gr. Pernik." *Bulgarski Folkor* 26 (4): 45–60.

Borneman, John, and Nick Fowler. 1997. "Europeanization." *Annual Review of Anthropology* 26: 487–514.

Botusharov, Lyuben. 2000. "Hem muzh, hem zhena—'predi' i 'sled tova.' Refleksii na tipa tsivilizatsiya vurhu traditsionnata kultura." *Bulgarski Folkor* 26 (4): 31–32.

Bougarel, Xavier. 1996. *Bosnie: Anatomie d'un conflict.* Paris: Éditions La Découverte.

Boym, Svetlana. 1994. *Common Places: Mythologies of Everyday Life in Russia.* Cambridge, Mass.: Harvard University Press.

Brandes, Stanley. 1981. "Like Wounded Stags: Male Sexual Ideology in an Andalusian Town." In *Sexual Meanings: The Cultural Construction of Gender and Sexuality,* ed. Sherry B. Ortner and Harriet Whitehead, 216–239. New York: Cambridge University Press.

———. 2006. *Skulls to the Living, Bread to the Dead: Celebrations of Death in Mexico and Beyond.* Malden, Mass.: Blackwell.

Bringa, Tone. 1995. *Being Muslim the Bosnian Way: Identity and Community in a Central Bosnian Village.* Princeton, N.J.: Princeton University Press.

Brown, Jacqueline Nassy. 2004. *Dropping Anchor, Setting Sail: Geographies of Race in Black Liverpool.* Princeton, N.J.: Princeton University Press.

Brown, Keith. 2003. *The Past in Question: Modern Macedonia and the Uncertainties of Nation.* Princeton, N.J.: Princeton University Press.

Brubaker, Rogers. 2002. "Ethnicity Without Groups." *European Journal of Sociology* 43 (2): 163–189.

Buchanan, Donna A. 1996. "Wedding Musicians, Political Transition, and National Consciousness in Bulgaria." In *Retuning Culture: Musical Changes in Central and Eastern Europe,* ed. Mark Slobin, 200–230. Durham, N.C.: Duke University Press.

———. 1997. "Bulgaria's Magical *Mystère* Tour: Postmodernism, World Music Marketing, and Political Change in Eastern Europe." *Ethnomusicology* 41 (1): 131–158.

———. 2002. "Soccer, Popular Music, and National Consciousness in Post–State-Socialist Bulgaria." *British Journal of Ethnomusicology* 11 (2): 1–27.

———. 2006. *Performing Democracy: Bulgarian Music and Musicians in Transition.* Chicago: University of Chicago Press.

Burawoy, Michael, and Katherine Verdery, eds. 1999. *Uncertain Transition: Ethnographies of Change in the Postsocialist World.* Lanham, Md.: Rowman and Littlefield.

Butler, Judith. 1990. *Gender Trouble: Feminism and the Subversion of Identity*. New York: Routledge.

Cancian, Frank. 1992. *The Decline of Community in Zinacantan*. Stanford, Calif.: Stanford University Press.

Cellarius, Barbara A. 2004. *In the Land of Orpheus: Rural Livelihoods and Nature Conservation in Postsocialist Bulgaria*. Madison: University of Wisconsin Press.

Chakrabarty, Dipesh. 2000. *Provincializing Europe: Postcolonial Thought and Historical Difference*. Princeton, N.J.: Princeton University Press.

Chari, Sharad, and Katherine Verdery. 2009. "Thinking between the Posts: Postcolonialism, Postsocialism, and Ethnography after the Cold War." *Comparative Studies in Society and History* 51 (1): 6–34.

Chary, Frederick B. 1972. *The Bulgarian Jews and the Final Solution, 1940–1944*. Pittsburgh: University of Pittsburgh Press.

Churchill, Nancy. 2006. "Dignifying Carnival: The Politics of Heritage Recognition in Puebla, Mexico." *International Journal of Cultural Property* 13 (1): 1–24.

Cohen, Abner. 1993. *Masquerade Politics: Explorations in the Structure of Urban Cultural Movements*. Berkeley: University of California Press.

Cohen, Jean, and Andrew Arato. 1992. *Civil Society and Political Theory*. Cambridge, Mass.: MIT Press.

Cole, John. 1976. "Familial Dynamics in a Romanian Worker Village." *Dialectical Anthropology* 1:251–266.

Connell, R. W. 1987. *Gender and Power: Society, the Person, and Sexual Politics*. Stanford, Calif.: Stanford University Press.

———. 1995. *Masculinities: Knowledge, Power and Social Change*. Berkeley: University of California Press.

Cowan, Jane K. 1992. "Japanese Ladies and Mexican Hats: Contested Symbols and the Politics of Tradition in a Northern Greek Carnival Celebration." In *Revitalizing European Ritual*, ed. Jeremy Boissevain, 173–197. New York: Routledge.

Creed, Gerald W. 1991. "Civil Society and the Spirit of Capitalism: A Bulgarian Critique." Paper presented at the Annual Meeting of the American Anthropological Association, Chicago, Ill., November 20–24.

———. 1993. "Rural-Urban Oppositions in the Bulgarian Political Transition." *Südosteuropa* 42: 369–382.

———. 1995. "The Politics of Agriculture: Identity and Socialist Sentiment in Bulgaria." *Slavic Review* 54 (4): 843–868.

———. 1998. *Domesticating Revolution: From Socialist Reform to Ambivalent Transition in a Bulgarian Village*. University Park: Pennsylvania State University Press.

———. 2002a. "Economic Crisis and Ritual Decline in Eastern Europe." In *Postsocialism: Ideals, Ideologies, and Practices in Eurasia*, ed. C. M. Hann, 57–73. London: Routledge.

———. 2002b. "(Consumer) Paradise Lost: Capitalist Disenchantment in Rural Bulgaria." *Anthropology of East Europe Review* 20 (2): 119–126.

———. 2006. "Community as Modern Pastoral." In *The Seductions of Community: Oppressions,*

Emancipations, Quandaries, ed. Gerald W. Creed, 23–48. Santa Fe, N.M.: School of American Research Press.

———. 2008. "Conflitto e collettività nelle mascherate Bulgare." *SM Annali di San Michele* 21: 153–184.

———. 2010. "Strange Bedfellows: Socialist Nostalgia and Neoliberalism in Bulgaria." In *Post-Communist Nostalgia,* ed. Maria Todorova and Zsuzsa Gille, 29–45. New York: Berghahn.

Creed, Gerald W., and Barbara Ching. 1997. "Recognizing Rusticity: Identity and the Power of Place." In *Knowing Your Place: Rural Identity and Cultural Hierarchy,* ed. Barbara Ching and Gerald W. Creed, 1–38. New York: Routledge.

Creed, Gerald W., and Janine R. Wedel. 1997. "Second Thoughts from the Second World: Interpreting Aid in Post-Communist Eastern Europe." *Human Organization* 56 (3): 253–264.

Crowley, John. 1996. *Carnival, Canboulay, and Calypso: Traditions in the Making.* New York: Cambridge University Press.

Danforth, Loring M. 1982. *The Death Rituals of Rural Greece.* Photography by Alexander Tsiaras. Princeton, N.J.: Princeton University Press.

Demetriou, Demetrakis Z. 2001. "Connell's Concept of Hegemonic Masculinity: A Critique." *Theory and Society* 30 (3): 337–361.

Denich, Bette S. 1974. "Sex and Power in the Balkans." In *Woman, Culture, and Society,* ed. Michelle Zimbalist Rosaldo and Louise Lamphere, 243–262. Stanford, Calif.: Stanford University Press.

Dimova, Rozita. 2006. "Modern Masculinities: Ethnicity, Education, and Gender in Macedonia." *Nationalities Papers* 34 (3): 305–320.

Dirks, Nicholas. 1997. "The Policing of Tradition: Colonialism and Anthropology in Southern India." *Comparative Studies in Society and History* 39 (1): 182–212.

Dundes, Alan. 1978. "Into the Endzone for a Touchdown: A Psychoanalytic Consideration of American Football." *Western Folklore* 37 (2): 75–88.

Elias, Norbert. 1978. *The Civilizing Process,* Vol. 1, *The History of Manners.* Trans. Edmund Jephcott. Oxford: Blackwell.

Emmons, Caroline. 2006. "The Next Civil Rights Movement? A Comparison of Roma and African American Freedom Struggles." Paper presented at the Annual Convention of the International Studies Association, San Diego, Calif., March 22–25. Available at http://www.allacademic.com/meta/p98183_index.html (accessed September 12, 2009).

Enloe, Cynthia. 2000. *Maneuvers: The International Politics of Militarizing Women's Lives.* Berkeley: University of California Press.

Fol, Valeria. 2004. "Mask and Masquerade: From Mysterious Initiation to Carnival in Bulgaria." In *¡Carnaval!* ed. Barbara Mauldin, 45–62. Seattle: University of Washington Press.

Fonseca, Isabel. 1996. *Bury Me Standing: The Gypsies and Their Journey.* New York: Vintage.

Frazer, James George. 1920. *The Golden Bough: A Study in Magic and Religion.* Vol. 2, pt. 5. London: Macmillan.

Fukuyama, Francis. 1992. *The End of History and the Last Man.* New York: Free Press.

Gal, Susan. 1991. "Bartok's Funeral: Representations of Europe in Hungarian Political Rhetoric." *American Ethnologist* 18 (3): 440–458.

Gal, Susan, and Gail Kligman. 2000a. *The Politics of Gender after Socialism: A Comparative and Historical Essay*. Princeton, N.J.: Princeton University Press.

———, eds. 2000b. *Reproducing Gender: Politics, Publics, and Everyday Life after Socialism*. Princeton, N.J.: Princeton University Press.

Ganev, Venelin I. 2006. "Ballots, Bribes, and State Building in Bulgaria." *Journal of Democracy* 17 (1): 75–89.

———. 2007. *Preying on the State: The Transformation of Bulgaria after 1989*. Ithaca, N.Y.: Cornell University Press.

Gaonkar, Dilip Parameshwar, ed. 2001. *Alternative Modernities*. Durham, N.C.: Duke University Press.

Geertz, Clifford. 1973. *The Interpretation of Cultures: Selected Essays*. New York: Basic Books.

Genchev, Stoyan. 1988. *The Wedding*. Trans. Marguerite Alexieva. Sofia: Septemvri.

Ghodsee, Kristen. 2005. *The Red Riviera: Gender, Tourism, and Postsocialism on the Black Sea*. Durham, N.C.: Duke University Press.

———. 2007. "Men, Mines, and Mosques: Gender and Islamic Revivalism on the Edge of Europe." School of Social Science Occasional Paper 28. Princeton, N.J.: Institute for Advanced Study.

———. 2010. *Muslim Lives in Eastern Europe: Gender, Ethnicity, and the Transformation of Islam in Postsocialist Bulgaria*. Princeton, N.J.: Princeton University Press.

Gilmore, David D. 1998. *Carnival and Culture: Sex, Symbol, and Status in Spain*. New Haven, Conn.: Yale University Press.

Gilroy, Paul. 1987. *"There Ain't No Black in the Union Jack": The Cultural Politics of Race and Nation*. London: Hutchinson.

Glasius, Marlies, David Lewis, and Hakan Seckinelgin, eds. 2004. *Exploring Civil Society: Political and Cultural Contexts*. London: Routledge.

Glassie, Henry H. 1975. *All Silver and No Brass: An Irish Christmas Mumming*. Bloomington: Indiana University Press.

Gluckman, Max. 1963. *Order and Rebellion in Tribal Africa*. London: Cohen and West.

Goody, Jack. 1998. *Food and Love: A Cultural History of East and West*. New York: Cambridge University Press.

Gutmann, Matthew C. 1997. "Trafficking in Men: The Anthropology of Masculinity." *Annual Review of Anthropology* 26:385–409.

Hale, Charles R. 2002. "Does Multiculturalism Menace? Governance, Cultural Rights, and the Politics of Identity in Guatemala." *Journal of Latin American Studies* 34 (3): 485–524.

Halpern, Joel Martin. 1958. *A Serbian Village*. New York: Columbia University Press.

Halpert, Herbert. 1969. "A Typology of Mumming." In *Christmas Mumming in Newfoundland*, ed. Herbert Halpert and G. M. Story, 34–61. Toronto: University of Toronto Press.

Hammel, Eugene. 1968. *Alternative Social Structures and Ritual Relations in the Balkans*. Englewood Cliffs, N.J.: Prentice Hall.

Hammoudi, Abdellah. 1993. *The Victim and Its Masks: An Essay on Sacrifice and Masquerade in the Maghreb*. Trans. Paula Wissing. Chicago: University of Chicago Press.

Handelman, Don. 1990. *Models and Mirrors: Towards an Anthropology of Public Events*. New York: Cambridge University Press

Hann, C. M. 1985. *A Village without Solidarity: Polish Peasants in Years of Crisis*. New Haven, Conn.: Yale University Press.

———. 2003. "Civil Society: The Sickness, Not the Cure?" *Social Evolution and History* 2 (2): 34–54.

———. 2004. "In the Church of Civil Society." In *Exploring Civil Society: Political and Cultural Contexts*, ed. Marlies Glasius, David Lewis, and Hakan Seckinelgin, 44–50. New York: Routledge.

———. 2006. *"Not the Horse We Wanted": Postsocialism, Neoliberalism, and Eurasia*. Munich: Lit Verlag.

Hann, C. M., and Elizabeth Dunn, eds. 1996. *Civil Society: Challenging Western Models*. New York: Routledge.

Harding, Susan Friend. 2000. *The Book of Jerry Falwell: Fundamentalist Language and Politics*. Princeton, N.J.: Princeton University Press.

Harvey, David. 2003. *The New Imperialism*. New York: Oxford University Press.

Hayden, Robert M. 2002. "Antagonistic Tolerance: Competitive Sharing of Religious Sites in South Asia and the Balkans." *Current Anthropology* 43 (2): 205–231.

———. 2007. "Moral Vision and Impaired Insight: The Imagining of Other People's Communities in Bosnia." *Current Anthropology* 48 (1): 105–131.

Hearn, Jonathan S. 1997. "Scottish Nationalism and the Civil Society Concept: Should Auld Acquaintance Be Forgot?" *PoLAR: Political and Legal Anthropology Review* 20 (1): 32–39.

Helsinki Watch. 1991. *Destroying Ethnic Identity: The Gypsies of Bulgaria*. New York: Helsinki Watch.

Herzfeld, Michael. 1982. *Ours Once More: Folklore, Ideology, and the Making of Modern Greece*. Austin: University of Texas Press.

———. 1985. *The Poetics of Manhood: Contest and Identity in a Cretan Mountain Village*. Princeton, N.J.: Princeton University Press.

———. 2003. "Localism and the Logic of Nationalistic Folklore: Cretan Reflections." *Comparative Studies in Society and History* 45 (2): 281–310.

Hobsbawm, Eric, and Terence Ranger, eds. 1983. *The Invention of Tradition*. New York: Cambridge University Press.

Holmgren, Beth. 1995. "Bug Inspectors and Beauty Queens: The Problems of Translating Feminism into Russian." In *Postcommunism and the Body Politic*, ed. Ellen E. Berry, 15–31. New York: New York University Press.

Honey, Larisa. 2006. "Transforming Selves and Society: Women, Spiritual Health, and Pluralism in Post-Soviet Moscow (Russia)." Ph.D. diss., City University of New York.

Humphrey, Caroline. 1983. *Karl Marx Collective: Economy, Society, and Religion in a Siberian Collective Farm*. New York: Cambridge University Press.

———. 1991. "'Icebergs,' Barter, and the Mafia in Provincial Russia." *Anthropology Today* 7 (2): 8–13.

Iankova, Elena A. 2002. *Eastern European Capitalism in the Making*. New York: Cambridge University Press.

Ivanova, Radost. 1984. *Bulgarskata folklorna svatba*. Sofia: Izdatelstvo na bulgarskata akademiya na naukite.

Jansen, Stef. 2008. "Misplaced Masculinities: Status Loss and the Location of Gendered Subjectivities amongst Non-'Transnational' Bosnia Refugees." *Anthropological Theory* 8 (2): 181–200.

Johnson, Mark. 1998. "Global Desirings and Translocal Loves: Transgendering and Same-Sex Sexualities in the Southern Philippines." *American Ethnologist* 25 (4): 695–711.

Joseph, Miranda. 2001. *Against the Romance of Community*. Minneapolis: University of Minnesota Press.

Kaneff, Deema. 2004. *Who Owns the Past? The Politics of Time in a "Model" Bulgarian Village*. New York: Berghahn.

Kaplan, Robert D. 1998. "Hoods Against Democrats." *Atlantic Monthly* 282 (6): 32–37.

Kebalo, Martha. n.d. "Women in Central Ukraine: Personal Narratives of Leadership and Community Activism in Cherkasy Oblast." Unpublished manuscript.

Kenedi, János. 1982. *Do It Yourself: Hungary's Hidden Economy*. London: Pluto.

Kennedy, Michael D. 2002. *Cultural Formations of Postcommunism: Emancipation, Transition, Nation, and War*. Minneapolis: University of Minnesota Press.

Kertzer, David. 1991. "The Role of Ritual in State-Formation." In *Religious Regimes and State-Formation: Perspectives from European Ethnography*, ed. Eric R. Wolf, 85–103. Albany: State University of New York Press.

Khan, Aisha. 2001. "Journey to the Center of the Earth: The Caribbean as Master Symbol." *Cultural Anthropology* 16 (3): 271–302.

———. 2004. *Callaloo Nation: Metaphors of Race and Religious Identity among South Asians in Trinidad*. Durham, N.C.: Duke University Press.

———. 2007. "Good to Think? Creolization, Optimism, and Agency." *Current Anthropology* 48 (5): 653–673.

Kideckel, David A. 1983. "Secular Ritual and Social Change: A Romanian Example." *Anthropological Quarterly* 56 (2): 69–75.

———. 1993. *The Solitude of Collectivism: Romanian Villagers to the Revolution and Beyond*. Ithaca, N.Y.: Cornell University Press.

———. 2008. *Getting by in Postsocialist Romania: Labor, the Body, and Working-Class Culture*. Bloomington: Indiana University Press.

Kimmel, Michael. 2007. "Global Masculinities: Restoration and Resistence." *Gender Policy Review*. Available at http://gender-policy.tripod.com/journal/id1.html (accessed December 3, 2007).

King, Charles. 2001. "Potemkin Democracy: Four Myths about Post-Soviet Georgia." *National Interest* 64 (summer): 93–104.

Kinser, Samuel. 1990. *Carnival American Style: Mardi Gras at New Orleans and Mobile*. Chicago: University of Chicago Press.

Kligman, Gail. 1981. *Căluș: Symbolic Transformation in Romanian Ritual*. Chicago: University of Chicago Press.

———. 1988. *The Wedding of the Dead: Ritual, Poetics, and Popular Culture in Transylvania*. Berkeley: University of California Press.

———. 1998. *The Politics of Duplicity: Controlling Reproduction in Ceausescu's Romania*. Berkeley: University of California Press.

Knauft, Bruce M., ed. 2002a. *Critically Modern: Alternatives, Alterities, Anthropologies.* Bloomington: Indiana University Press.

———. 2002b. "Trials of the Oxymodern: Public Practice at Nomad Station." In *Critically Modern: Alternatives, Alterities, Anthropologies,* ed. Bruce M. Knauft, 105–143. Bloomington: Indiana University Press.

Konrád, György, and Ivan Szelényi. 1979. *The Intellectuals on the Road to Class Power.* Trans. Andrew Arato and Richard Allen. New York: Harcourt Brace Jovanovich.

Konstantinov, Yulian. 1996. "Patterns of Reinterpretation: Trader-Tourism in the Balkans (Bulgaria) as a Picaresque Metaphorical Enactment of Post-Totalitarianism." *American Ethnologist* 23 (4): 762–782.

Konstantinov, Yulian, Gideon M. Kressel, and Trond Thuen. 1998. "Outclassed by Former Outcasts: Petty Trading in Varna." *American Ethnologist* 25 (4): 729–745.

Kornai, Janos. 1992. *The Socialist System: The Political Economy of Communism.* Princeton, N.J.: Princeton University Press.

Kostov, Krasen. 2004. "Kukeri izprashtat trima v Kerbala." *Sofiyanets* 4 (2): 1, 3.

Kozhuharova-Zhivkova, Veska. 2000. "Sotsiologicheska interpretatsiya na smyanata na maskite." *Bulgarski Folklor* 26 (4): 33–38.

Kraev, Georg. 1996. *Bulgarski Maskaradni Igri.* Sofia: Alissa.

Krustanova, Kipriyana. 1986. *Traditsii na trudova vzaimopomosht v Bulgarskoto selo.* Sofia: Izdatelstvo na Bulgarskata Akademiya na Naukite.

La Barre, Weston. 1962. *They Shall Take Up Serpents: Psychology of the Southern Snake-Handling Cult.* Minneapolis: University of Minnesota Press.

Lampland, Martha. 1975. *The Object of Labor: Commodification in Socialist Hungary.* Chicago: University of Chicago Press.

Lane, Christel. 1981. *The Rites of Rulers: Ritual in Industrial Society—the Soviet Case.* New York: Cambridge University Press.

Le Roy Ladurie, Emmanuel. 1979. *Carnival in Romans.* Trans. Mary Feeney. New York: Braziller.

Ledeneva, Alena V. 1998. *Russia's Economy of Favours: Blat, Networking, and Informal Exchange.* New York: Cambridge University Press.

Lemon, Alaina. 1995. "'What Are They Writing about Us Blacks?' Roma and Race in Russia." *Anthropology of East Europe Review* 13 (2).

———. 2000. *Between Two Fires: Gypsy Performance and Romani Memory from Pushkin to Postsocialism.* Durham, N.C.: Duke University Press.

Lewis, I. M. 1971. *Ecstatic Religion: An Anthropological Study of Spirit Possession and Shamanism.* Harmondsworth: Penguin.

Linke, Uli. 1990. "Folklore, Anthropology, and the Government of Social Life." *Comparative Studies in Society and History* 32 (1): 117–148.

Mach, Zdzislaw. 1992. "Continuity and Change in Political Ritual: May Day in Poland." In *Revitalizing European Rituals,* ed. Jeremy Boissevain, 43–61. London: Routledge.

Mandel, Ruth. 2002. "Seeding Civil Society." In *Postsocialism: Ideals, Ideologies, and Practices in Eurasia,* ed. C. M. Hann, 279–296. New York: Routledge.

MacDermott, Mercia. 1998. *Bulgarian Folk Customs*. Philadelphia: Jessica Kingsley.

Manova, Tsvetana. 2002. "Survakarite s maski i bez maski." Paper presented at the conference Svetut: Pogled izzad maskata, Pernik, Bulgaria, January 18.

Markova, Eugenia, and Barry Reilly. 2007. "Bulgarian Migrant Remittances and Legal Status: Some Micro-level Evidence from Madrid." *South-Eastern Europe Journal of Economics* 1:55–69.

Markowitz, Fran. 1993. *A Community in Spite of Itself: Soviet Jewish Emigres in New York*. Washington, D.C.: Smithsonian Institution Press.

Massad, Joseph A. 2007. *Desiring Arabs*. Chicago: University of Chicago Press.

Mauldin, Barbara. 2004. "Introduction: Carnival in Europe and the Americas." In *¡Carnaval!* ed. Barbara Mauldin, 3–18. Seattle: University of Washington Press.

McKeehan, I. V. 2000. "A Multilevel City Health Profile of Moscow." *Social Science and Medicine* 51 (9): 1295–1312.

Meurs, Mieke. 2001. *The Evolution of Agrarian Institutions: A Comparative Study of Post-Socialist Hungary and Bulgaria*. Ann Arbor: University of Michigan Press.

Milićević, Aleksandra Sasha. 2006. "Joining the War: Masculinity, Nationalism and War Participation in the Balkan War of Succession, 1991–1995." *Nationalities Papers* 34 (3): 265–287.

Minnich, Robert Gary. 1979. *The Homemade World of Zagaj*. Occasional Paper 18. Bergen: Sosial-antropologisk institutt Universit i Bergen.

Mosely, Philip E. 1940. "The Peasant Family: The Zadruga or Communal Joint Family in the Balkans and Its Recent Evolution." In *The Cultural Approach to History*, ed. Caroline Ware, 95–108. New York: Columbia University Press.

Mosse, George L. 1996. *The Image of Man: The Creation of Modern Masculinity*. New York: Oxford University Press.

Munn, Jamie. 2006. "Gendered Realities of Life in Post-Conflict Kosovo: Addressing the Hegemonic Man." *Nationalities Papers* 34 (3): 265–288.

Nagel, Joane. 1998. "Masculinity and Nationalism: Gender and Sexuality in the Making of Nations." *Ethnic and Racial Studies* 21 (2): 242–269.

Neuburger, Mary. 2004. *The Orient Within: Muslim Minorities and the Negotiation of Nationhood in Modern Bulgaria*. Ithaca, N.Y.: Cornell University Press.

———. 2006. "To Chicago and Back: Aleko Konstantinov, Rose Oil, and the Smell of Modernity." *Slavic Review* 65 (3): 427–445.

Noyes, Dorothy. 1995. "Group." *Journal of American Folklore* 108 (430): 449–478.

Nuggent, David. 2008. "Democracy Otherwise: Struggles over Popular Rule in the Northern Peruvian Andes." In *Democracy: Anthropological Approaches,* ed. Julia Paley, 21–62. Santa Fe: School for Advanced Research Press.

Olomoofe, Larry. 2006. "Why Are You Working for the ERRC?" *Roma Rights Quarterly*. Available at http://www.errc.org/cikk.php?cikk=2466 (accessed March 22, 2008).

Ortner, Sherry B. 1996. *Making Gender: The Politics and Erotics of Culture*. Boston: Beacon.

Paley, Julia, ed. 2008. *Democracy: Anthropological Approaches*. Santa Fe, N.M.: School for Advanced Research Press

Papataxiarchis, Evthymios. 1991. "Friends of the Heart: Male Commensal Solidarity, Gender, and

Kinship in Aegean Greece." In *Contested Identities: Gender and Kinship in Modern Greece,* ed. Peter Loizos and Evthymios Papataxiarchis, 156–179. Princeton, N.J.: Princeton University Press.

Phillips, Sarah D. 2008. *Women's Social Activism in the New Ukraine: Development and the Politics of Differentiation.* Bloomington: Indiana University Press.

Pilbrow, Timothy. 2003. "European or Bulgarian: Irony and the Definition of National Identity." Paper presented at the Seventh Joint North American–Bulgarian Studies Conference, Columbus Ohio, October 9–12.

Piot, Charles. 1999. *Remotely Global: Village Modernity in West Africa.* Chicago: University of Chicago Press.

Platz, Stephanie. 2000. "The Shape of National Time: Daily Life, History, and Identity during Armenia's Transition to Independence, 1991–1994." In *Altering States: Ethnographies of Transition in Eastern Europe and the Former Soviet Union,* ed. Daphne Berdahl, Matti Bunzl, and Martha Lampland, 114–138. Ann Arbor: University of Michigan Press.

Putnam, Robert D., with Robert Leonardi and Raffaella Y. Nanetti. 1993. *Making Democracy Work: Civic Traditions in Modern Italy.* Princeton, N.J.: Princeton University Press.

Raichevski, Stoyan, and Valeriya Fol. 1993. *Kukerut bez maska.* Sofia: Universitetsko izdatelstvo "Sv. Kliment Ohridski."

Regalado, Mariana. 2004. "Entroido in Laza, Spain: A Continuing Rural Carnival Tradition." In *¡Carnaval!* ed. Barbara Mauldin, 21–43. Seattle: University of Washington Press.

Rev, Istvan. 1987. "The Advantages of Being Atomized: How Hungarian Peasants Coped with Collectivization." *Dissent* 34:335–350.

Rice, Timothy. 1994. *May It Fill Your Soul: Experiencing Bulgarian Music.* Chicago: University of Chicago Press.

Ries, Nancy. 1997. *Russian Talk: Culture and Conversation during Perestroika.* Ithaca, N.Y.: Cornell University Press.

Rofel, Lisa. 1999. *Other Modernities: Gendered Yearnings in China after Socialism.* Berkeley: University of California Press.

Rogers, Douglas. 2005. "Introductory Essay: The Anthropology of Religion after Socialism." *Religion, State, and Society* 33 (1): 5–18.

Rogin, Michael. 1996. *Blackface, White Noise: Jewish Immigrants in the Hollywood Melting Pot.* Berkeley: University of California Press

Rose, Richard. 1995. "Russia as an Hour-Glass Society: A Constitution without Citizens." *East European Constitutional Review* 4 (3): 34–42.

———. 1999. "Living in an Antimodern Society." *East European Constitutional Review* 8 (1/2): 68–75.

———. 2000. "How Much Does Social Capital Add to Individual Health? A Survey Study of Russians." *Social Science and Medicine* 51 (9): 1421–1435.

Roseberry, William. 1991. "Potatoes, Sacks, and Enclosures in Early Modern England." In *Golden Ages, Dark Ages: Imagining the Past in Anthropology and History,* ed. William Roseberry and Jay O'Brian, 19–47. Berkeley: University of California Press.

Roth, Klaus. 1990. "Socialist Life-cycle Rituals in Bulgaria." *Anthropology Today* 6 (5): 8–10.

Said, Edward W. 1978. *Orientalism.* New York: Pantheon Books.

Sampson, Steven L. 1996. "The Social Life of Projects: Importing Civil Society to Albania." In *Civil Society: Challenging Western Models,* ed. C. M. Hann and Elizabeth Dunn, 121–142. New York: Routledge.

———. 2002. "Beyond Transition: Rethinking Elite Configurations in the Balkans." In *Postsocialism: Ideals, Ideologies and Practices in Eurasia,* ed. C. M. Hann, 297–316. New York: Routledge.

Sanders, Irwin. 1949. *Balkan Village.* Lexington: University of Kentucky Press.

Santino, Jack, ed. 1994. *Halloween and Other Festivals of Death and Life.* Knoxville: University of Tennessee Press.

Schäuble, Michaela. 2007. "Future Nostalgia: Some Reflections on Conceptualising Suffering and Hope in Post-War Rural Dalmatia." Paper presented at the workshop "Towards an Anthropology of Hope? Comparative Post-Yugoslav Ethnographies," University of Manchester, November 9–11.

Schrand, Thomas. 2002. "Socialism in One Gender: Masculine Values in the Stalin Revolution." In *Russian Masculinities in History and Culture,* ed. Barbara Evans Clements, Rebecca Friedman, and Dan Healey, 194–209. New York: Palgrave.

Schneider, Jane. 1990. "Spirits and the Spirit of Capitalism." In *Religious Orthodoxy and Popular Faith in European Society,* ed. Ellen Badone, 24–54. Princeton, N.J.: Princeton University Press.

Scott, James C. 1998. *Seeing Like a State: How Certain Schemes to Improve the Human Condition Have Failed.* New Haven, Conn.: Yale University Press.

Seremetakis, C. Nadia. 1991. *The Last Word: Women, Death, and Divination in Inner Mani.* Chicago: University of Chicago Press.

Shannon, Jonathan Holt. 2006. *Among the Jasmine Trees: Music and Modernity in Contemporary Syria.* Middletown, Conn.: Wesleyan University Press.

Shreeves, Rosamund. 2002. "Broadening the Concept of Privatization: Gender and Development in Rural Kazakhstan." In *Markets and Moralities: Ethnographies of Postsocialism,* ed. Ruth Mandel and Caroline Humphrey, 211–235. New York: Berg.

Sider, Gerald M. 1986. *Culture and Class in Anthropology and History: A Newfoundland Illustration.* New York: Cambridge University Press.

Sik, Endre. 1988. "Reciprocal Exchange of Labour in Hungary." In *On Work: Historical, Comparative and Theoretical Approaches,* ed. R. E. Pahl, 527–547. New York: Basil Blackwell.

Silverman, Carol. n.d. "The Contemporary Bulgarian Village Wedding." Unpublished manuscript.

———. 1983. "The Politics of Folklore in Bulgaria." *Anthropological Quarterly* 56 (2): 55–61.

———. 1986. "Bulgarian Gypsies: Adaptation in a Socialist Context." *Nomadic Peoples* 21/22 (December): 51–62.

———. 1995. "Persecution and Politicization: Roma (Gypsies) of Eastern Europe." *Cultural Survival* 19 (2): 43–49.

———. 1996. "Music and Marginality: Roma (Gypsies) of Bulgaria and Macedonia." In *Retuning Culture: Musical Changes in Central and Eastern Europe,* ed. Mark Slobin, 231–253. Durham, N.C.: Duke University Press.

Silverman, Sydel. 1975. *The Three Bells of Civilization: The Life of an Italian Hill Town.* New York: Columbia University Press.

Silverstein, Paul. n.d. "Masquerade Politics: Race, Islam, and the Scales of Amazigh Activism in Southeastern Morocco." Unpublished manuscript.

Simic, Marina. 2007. "Exit to Europe: Music and Identity Politics in Serbia." Paper presented at the workshop "Towards an Anthropology of Hope? Comparative Post-Yugoslav Ethnographies," University of Manchester, November 9–11.

Skovierová, Zita. 1988. "Contemporary Neighbourly Relations and Their Traditional Expression in Slovakia." *Ethnologia Slavica* 20:49–61.

Spivak, Gayatri Chakravorty. 1988. "Subaltern Studies: Deconstructing Historiography." In *Selected Subaltern Studies*, ed. Ranajit Guha and Gayatri Chakravorty Spivak, 3–32. Oxford: Oxford University Press.

Stahl, Henri H. 1980. *Traditional Romanian Village Communities: The Transition from the Communal to the Capitalist Mode of Production in the Danube Region.* Trans. Daniel Chirot and Holley Coulter Chirot. New York: Cambridge University Press.

Stallybrass, Peter, and Allon White. 1986. *The Politics and Poetics of Transgression.* Ithaca, N.Y.: Cornell University Press.

Stamenova, Zhivka. 1982. *Kukeri i survakari.* Sofia: Durzhavno Izdatelstvo "Septemvri."

Stark, David. 1996. "Recombinant Property in East European Capitalism." *American Journal of Sociology* 101:993–1027.

Steinberg, Mark D., and Catherine Wanner, eds. 2009. *Religion, Morality, and Community in Post-Soviet Societies.* Bloomington: Indiana University Press.

Stewart, Michael. 1997. *The Time of the Gypsies.* Boulder, Colo.: Westview.

Stolcke, Verena. 1995. "Talking Culture: New Boundaries, New Rhetorics of Exclusion in Europe." *Current Anthropology* 36 (1): 1–24.

Sullivan, Shannon. 2006. *Revealing Whiteness: The Unconscious Habits of Racial Privilege.* Bloomington: Indiana University Press.

Supek, Olga. 1982. "A Hundred Years of Bread and Wine: The Culture, History, and Economy of a Croatian Village." Ph.D. diss., University of Michigan.

Tausz, Katalin. 1990. "The Case of Eastern Europe: Why Community Development Still Has Yet to Find a Role in Hungary." *Community Development Journal* 25 (4): 300–306.

Taylor, Mary N. 2008. "The Politics of Culture: Folk Critique and the Transformation of the State in Hungary." Ph.D. diss., City University of New York.

Terzieff, Juliette. 2006. "Bulgaria Pushed to Clean Up Women's Workplace." *Womens ENews,* May 5, 2006. Available at http://www.hartford-hwp.com/archives/62/401.html (accessed December 2, 2007).

Todorov, Tzvetan, ed. 2001. *The Fragility of Goodness: Why Bulgaria's Jews Survived the Holocaust.* Trans. Arthur Denner. Princeton, N.J.: Princeton University Press.

Todorova, Maria. 1995. "Bulgarian Historical Writing on the Ottoman Empire." *New Perspectives on Turkey* 12:97–118.

———. 1996. "The Ottoman Legacy in the Balkans." In *Imperial Legacy: The Ottoman Impact on the Balkans and the Middle East,* ed. L. Carl Brown, 45–77. New York: Columbia University Press.

———. 1997. *Imagining the Balkans*. New York: Oxford University Press.

———. 2009. *Bones of Contention: The Living Archives of Vasil Levski and the Making of Bulgaria's National Hero*. Budapest: Central European University Press.

Vassilev, Rossen. 2004. "The Roma of Bulgaria: A Pariah Minority." *Global Review of Ethnopolitics* 3 (2): 40–51.

———. 2005. "Bulgaria's Demographic Crisis: Underlying Causes and Some Short-Term Implications." *Southeast European Politics* 6 (1): 14–27.

Verdery, Katherine. 1991. *National Ideology under Socialism: Identity and Cultural Politics in Ceauşescu's Romania*. Los Angeles: University of California Press.

———. 1999. *The Political Lives of Dead Bodies: Reburial and Postsocialist Change*. New York: Columbia University Press.

———. 2003. *The Vanishing Hectare: Property and Value in Postsocialist Transylvania*. Ithaca, N.Y.: Cornell University Press.

Wedel, Janine R. 1986. *The Private Poland*. New York: Facts on File.

———. 1992. "Introduction." In *The Unplanned Society: Poland During and After Communism*, ed. Janine R. Wedel, 1–20. New York: Columbia University Press.

Welch, Charles E. 1970. *Oh! Dem Golden Slippers*. New York: Thomas Nelson.

West, Barbara A. 2002. *The Danger Is Everywhere! The Insecurity of Transition in Postsocialist Hungary*. Prospect Heights, Ill.: Waveland.

West, Harry, and Todd Sanders, eds. 2003. *Transparency and Conspiracy: Ethnographies of Suspicion in the New World Order*. Durham, N.C.: Duke University Press.

White, Anne. 1990. *De-Stalinization and the House of Culture: Declining State Control over Leisure in the USSR, Poland, and Hungary, 1953–89*. London: Routledge.

Williams, Brackette F., ed. 1996. *Women Out of Place: The Gender of Agency and the Race of Nationality*. New York: Routledge.

Worobec, Christine D. 1991. *Peasant Russia: Family and Community in the Post-emancipation Period*. Princeton, N.J.: Princeton University Press.

Zborowski, Mark, and Elizabeth Herzog. 1952. *Life Is with People: The Jewish Little-Town of Eastern Europe*. New York: International Universities Press.

Zhelyazkova, Antonina. 2001. "The Bulgarian Ethnic Model." *East European Constitutional Review* 10 (4). Available at http://www1.law.nyu.edu/eecr/vol10num4/focus/zhelyazkova.html (accessed February 25, 2009).

Zivkovic, Marko. 2006. "Introduction: Ex-Yugoslav Masculinities under Female Gaze, or Why Men Skin Cats, Beat up Gays, and Go to War." *Nationalities Papers* 34 (3): 256–263.

Italicized page numbers indicate illustrations.

NEW ANTHROPOLOGIES OF EUROPE

DAPHNE BERDAHL, MATTI BUNZL, AND MICHAEL HERZFELD,
FOUNDING EDITORS

GERALD W. CREED

is Professor of Anthropology at Hunter College and the City University of New York Graduate Center, where he is Executive Officer of the Anthropology Program. He is author of *Domesticating Revolution: From Socialist Reform to Ambivalent Transition in a Bulgarian Village*; editor of *The Seductions of Community: Emancipations, Oppressions, Quandaries*; and co-editor of *Knowing Your Place: Rural Identity and Cultural Hierarchy*.